Helion & Company Limited
Unit 8 Amherst Business Centre
Budbrooke Road
Warwick
CV34 5WE
England
Tel. 01926 499 619
Email: info@helion.co.uk
Website: www.helion.co.uk
Twitter: @helionbooks
Visit our blog https://helionbooks.wordpress.com/

Typeset by Oliver Barstow, Milan, Italy
Cover design by Paul Hewitt, Battlefield Design (www.battlefield-design.co.uk)

ISBN 978-1-804515-79-2

British Library Cataloguing-in-Publication Data
A catalogue record for this book is available from the British Library

We always welcome receiving book proposals from prospective authors.

CONTENTS

Note: In order to simplify the use of this book, all names, locations and geographic designations are as provided in *The Times World Atlas*, or other traditionally accepted major sources of reference, as of the time of described events.

ABBREVIATIONS AND ACRONYMS

ARH	active radar homing (missile guidance system)
ATGM	anti-tank guided missile
BMP	*Boyevaya Mashina Pyekhoty* (infantry combat vehicle)
Bort	two-digit side number on Russian and Ukrainian military aircraft and helicopters
BTG	*batalonnaja takticheskaja gruppa* (battalion tactical group) (Russia and Ukraine)
BTR	*bronyetransportyor* (armoured personnel carrier)
CAA	Combined Arms Army (Russia)
COMINT	communications intelligence
ECM	electronic countermeasures
ELINT	electronic intelligence
EO	electro-optical (missile guidance system)
FSB	*Federalnaya Sluzhba Bezopasnosti* (Federal Security Service) (Russia)
GenStab	*Generalnyi shtab* (General Staff) (Russia and Ukraine)
GRU	*Glavnoye Razvedyatelnoye Upravleniye* (Main Intelligence Directorate) (Russia)
GTA	Guards Tank Army
IADS	integrated air defence system
IAP	international airport
INS	inertial navigation system (missile guidance system)
IR	infrared
LOC	Line of Control
MANPAD(S)	man-portable air defence (system)
MOD	Ministry of Defence
NATO	North Atlantic Treaty Organisation
OSK	Объединённое стратегическое командование (Strategic Operational Command) (Russia)
PGM	precision guided missile (or munition)
PMC	private military company (group) or private military contractor (individual)
POL	petrol, oil, lubricants
PRH	passive radar homing (missile guidance system)
PSZSU	*Povitriyani syly Zbroiynyh syl Ukrayini* (Air Force of the Armed Forces of Ukraine)
SARH	semi-active radar homing (missile guidance system)
SBU	*Sluzhba Bezpeky Ukrayiny* (Ukraine Security Service)
SEAD	suppression of enemy air defences
SSO	*Syly spetsialnykh operatsii* (Special Operations Forces) (Ukraine)
TEL	transporter erecter launcher
TELAR	transporter erecter launcher and radar
UAV	Unmanned Aerial Vehicle
UCAV	Unmanned Combat Aerial Vehicle
USSR	Union of Soviet Socialist Republics
VDV	*Vozdushno-desantnye voyska* (airborne troops) (Russia)
VKS	*Vozdushno-kosmicheskiye sily* (Aerospace Forces) (Russia)
VSRF	*Vooruzhonnije Síly Rossíyskoj Federátsii* (Armed Forces of the Russian Federation)
ZSU	*Zbroiynyh syl Ukrayiny* (Armed Forces of Ukraine)

INTRODUCTION

Continuing the coverage of the air war over Ukraine since the start of the Russian all-out invasion of that country, Volume 7 in this mini-series focuses on various battlefields during the period from mid-March until late June 2022. While its total content might be slightly less than that about the period from late February to early March of the same year, the amount of high-quality information that is publicly available remains immense. Combined with constant updates and frequent cross-examination this enables a very good picture of the timeline of the ground war and, because most of the air war is closely related to developments on the ground, also of the aerial warfare. Eventually, this is what dictated the construction of this volume: while the Russian missile offensives on targets deeper inside Ukraine were largely conducted without direct relation to the developments on the front lines, most of the tactical aviation of both parties was conducting interdiction strikes and close air support for ground forces. Because of this, the primary focus in this volume is not only on the Russian missile offensives (and the first Ukrainian attempts to strike back in a similar fashion), but upon air warfare within the scope of the Russian offensives in north-eastern and eastern Ukraine during March, April, May, and June 2022. We intend to return to operations in south-eastern and southern Ukraine during the same period and then continue with the first two Ukrainian counteroffensives in a later volume.

While working on this book we could not avoid the conclusion that there are still a lot of cases where both the officially and unofficially released information from the two sides is far from at least roughly aligning; there are lots of operations dependent on developments considered top secret by both sides, and it is going to take much longer to independently verify every single detail. Even more so, the reasoning and requirements for specific operations are likely to remain hidden for decades longer. Nevertheless, it is now possible to put together data sets presenting not only general trends but including plenty of hard and independently confirmed figures.

As in Volume 6, while preparing this volume, we have intentionally left out the discussion of the socioeconomic and geostrategic background and context and have almost entirely focused on combat operations. Nevertheless, we have taken care to provide additional, contextual formation in the form of 'boxes'.

1
SECOND RUSSIAN MISSILE OFFENSIVE

At 05.00hrs on 24 February 2022, on order from President Vladimir Vladimirovich Putin, the Armed Forces of the Russian Federation (VSRF) launched an all-out invasion of Ukraine. According to claims by the Russian Ministry of Defence, within the first 48 hours of that operation, the Russian Aerospace Forces (VKS) targeted more than 100 objects related to Ukrainian air defences, including 19 air defence radar systems and 39 other radar stations. According to the same source, within the same period of time, ballistic and cruise missiles fired by other branches of the VSRF targeted another 60–70 military facilities. Aim points included the majority of Ukrainian command and control nodes, air bases, many of the major bases of the ground forces and the navy, as the initial onslaught aimed to knock out the capability of the Air Force of the Armed Forces of Ukraine (PSZSU) to defend the nation's airspace. Although the missile onslaught was combined with a major cyberattack on the strategic communication facilities of the Armed Forces of Ukraine (ZSU), and exactly like the government in Kyiv, the majority of the PSZSU – which included not only flying units, but also ground-based air defences, and exercised control over the major air defence systems of the ground forces – survived. Arguably, the majority of combat aircraft and helicopters were dispersed on forward operating bases (FOBs), and most operational transport aircraft evacuated from the country. However, all too many of the ground-based air defence units were either not alerted at all, or were only alerted much too late, and thus suffered extensive losses in equipment and personnel. Consequently, the PSZSU played a relatively minor role in spoiling the Russian invasion – or what can be described as 'Putin's Plan A' – which expected to quickly topple the government in Kyiv and rapidly secure several major urban centres around the country. Once Putin realised that his original plot had failed, he changed his strategy to what can be described as his 'Plan B': an attempt to isolate both Kyiv and the major concentration of ZSU forces still deployed along the so-called Line of Control (LOC) – the cease-fire-line from 2015 – in Donbas. Correspondingly, the General Staff of the Armed Forces of the Russian Federation (*GenStab*) in Moscow aimed to support its operations through deploying ballistic and cruise missiles against a new set of targets, including not only air bases, but also ammunition depots and supply centres, with the aim of keeping Ukraine under pressure while disabling its capability to defend. For the PSZSU, this resulted in a sort of paradox: the force's ground-based air defences were redeployed to protect their own ground forces, in turn finding themselves ill-positioned to counter the Russian missile offensive.

A still from a video released by the Russian Ministry of Defence on 28 March 2022, showing the launch of two Kalibr cruise missiles from a Buyan-M-class corvette 'against a Ukrainian arms depot outside Rovno'. According to the same source, these were two out of eight 3M54 missiles launched by warships of the Black Sea Fleet at the same target that night. (Russian Ministry of Defence)

Table 1: Principal Air-Launched Guided Missiles in service with the VKS, 2022		
Russian designation	**ASCC/NATO reporting name**	**Notes**
		Air-to-Ground
Kh-22/32	AS-4 Kitchen	tactical anti-ship missile (range: 600km/320nm) deployed for ground attack; ARH; Kh-32 was an upgraded land-attack variant with INS guidance and lighter warhead to stretch the range (range: 1,000km/540nm); deployed by Tu-22M-3s only
Kh-25	AS-12 Kegler	tactical PGM (range: 10–60km/5–32nm); PRH (Kh-25P); deployed by Su-24 & Su-34
Kh-29	AS-14 Kedge	tactical PGM (range: 10–30km/5–16nm); laser (Kh-29L) or Electro-Optical (Kh-29T) guidance; deployed by Su-24 & Su-34
Kh-31	AS-17 Krypton	tactical PGM (range: 7–110km/4–60nm); PRH (Kh-31A), PRH or IR (Kh-31P); deployed by Su-30, Su-34, Su-35
Kh-35	AS-20 Kayak	tactical PGM and/or anti-ship missile (range: 130km/70nm); INS, ARH and IR; deployed by Su-34
Kh-58	AS-11 Kilter	tactical PGM (range: 120–200km/65–107nm); PRH; deployed by Su-24 and Su-34
Kh-59	AS-13 Kingbolt	tactical PGM (range: 115km/62nm); EO (Kh-59T) or laser (Kh-59L); deployed by Su-24 and Su-34
Kh-59	AS-18 Kazoo	tactical PGM (range: 200–290km/107–156nm); EO; deployed by Su-24 and Su-34
Kh-101	AS-23 Kodiak	cruise missile (range: 3,000km/1,600nm); INS/GPS/GLONASS and EO-SMG; deployed by Tu-95MS and Tu-160
Kh-555	AS-15 Kent	cruise missile (range: 3,000km/1,600nm); INS/GPS/GLONASS and TCM; deployed by Tu-95MS and Tu-160
		Air-to-Air
R-33	AA-9 Amos	long-range (range 160km/85nm); SARH (R-33) or ARH (R-33S)
R-37	AA-13 Axehead	long-range (range: 208km/112nm), ARH
R-40	AA-6 Acrid	medium-range (range: 50–80km/27–43nm); SARH on R-40RD and IR on R-40TD
R-60	AA-8 Aphid	short-range (range: 8km/5nm); IR
R-73/R-74	AA-11 Archer	short-range (range: 20km/11nm – 30km/16nm); IR
R-77/R-77-1	AA-12 Adder	medium-range (range: 80km/43nm); ARH

Virazh-Plansheet

As described in Volume 6, the integrated air defence system (IADS) of Ukraine as of early 2022 was the third largest in Europe. Code-named Virazh-Plansheet, at its core were four radio-technical brigades and five communication regiments deployed to cover the borders and the complete airspace of the country. The former group of units was equipped with a mix of old and new equipment, mainly consisting of early warning and surveillance radar systems as detailed below.

Developed by KP NVC Iskra in Zaporizhzhya in the 1980s, the 35D6 was one of the best radars to emerge in the final years of the Soviet Union. This trailer-mounted three-dimensional system (towed by KrAZ-6322 or KrAZ-6446 trucks) was originally developed to support the S-300 surface-to-air missile (SAM) system, had a maximum detection range of 360km and was capable of simultaneously tracking up to 300 targets. Of interest is that since 2014, the Ukrainians not only introduced to service their own 36D6M-1 variant, but that Iskra significantly upgraded older 35D6s through the installation of advanced processors and a much better cooling system: the latter was not only of importance in significantly increasing the service life of their klystrons (high-power microwave vacuum tubes used as amplifiers for high radio frequencies, and as such the cores of radar systems), but also through significantly improving the system's performance. Their maximum detection range was reported at around 360km.

Like the 35D6M, the 79K6 Pelikan came into being in the late 1980s, designed by Iskra in Zaporizhzhya. Indeed, its development was incomplete by the time Ukraine gained its independence, and the work was resumed only in 2006. Trailer-mounted, the Pelikan was to serve as a surveillance radar for SAM systems and took about 30 minutes to deploy from the time it stopped moving. It offered a maximum detection range of up to 400km. Striving to field a more advanced and quicker-to-deploy system for export, Iskra then designed the 80K6M Phoenix, which entered service in 2021: this was a truck-mounted, S band radar that excelled with its low pulse power, phase-modulated intrapulse modulation that provided it with a maximum range of around 400km, excellent range resolution, and extremely quick deployment time (5–6 minutes). Initially, the Phoenix was meant to replace the old 9S18M1 Kupol-M1 early warning system of the Ukrainian Buk M1 SAMs, but since the Russian all-out invasion, the three or four Phoenixes that became available were frequently deployed in conjunction with other SAM systems.

Since 2012, the PSZSU received a total of six 1L13-3 Nebo-SV radars overhauled and upgraded by Aerotekhnika-MLT. Designed in the second half of the 1980s, these were trailer-mounted and had a maximum detection range of around 275km. In addition to modern radars like the 35D6M/36D6M-1, 79K6/80K6M, or Nebo-SV, the PSZSU also operated a large number of older systems. The main examples of these were about a dozen old P-14 Lena (stationary) and P-14 Van (road-mobile) systems. Well-known in the West under their ASCC/NATO reporting name 'Tall King', the P-14 was a surveillance radar with a classic, large spiderweb-like antenna (spanning around 32 metres, and 11 metres tall), with a maximum detection range of around 300km. The complete equipment of a single station included no fewer than six units (two semi-trailers with equipment, two semi-trainers with antenna-mast device, and two trailers with diesel generators for power supply), and a semi-trailer with a cabin and two displays: as such, they were troublesome to relocate and in 2022 quickly proved highly-vulnerable to Russian

The 35D6M-1 represented a Ukrainian modification of the radar designed in the late 1980s originally developed to support the work of S-300 SAM systems. About a dozen were in operation in 2022. (Iskra)

attacks. Since 2011, about 70 percent of available systems had been upgraded to the variant designated 5N84A Defence-14: this introduced a modular design of support equipment, an increased number of working frequencies and improved immunity to noise jamming, and the capability to automatically track targets. Because the 5N84A could only provide the azimuth and range of the target (i.e. was a 2D system), each was accompanied by modernised PRV-13 or PRV-17 height-finding radars.

Even more important than the P-14 was the large number (about 30) of old but overhauled and upgraded P-18MA (made by Aerotekhnika-MLT) and P-18MU Malkhit (made by Ukrspetstechnika) radars. Since 2007 and 2012, respectively, they received digital processors and flat screen displays, and had all of their equipment compressed into two trucks (one for the antenna and the other for the equipment and power generator, compared to two trucks and two trailers of the original P-18). The P-18MUs had a maximum detection range of 400km and could simultaneously track up to 256 targets.

As of the early 2000s, the PSZSU was still operating some 50 old P-19 radars from the 1970s. In 2007, the service introduced the upgraded Aerotekhnika-MLT P-19MA radar, which included advanced processors and displays, had automatic target tracking capability, and a maximum detection range of about 300km. In 2012, Ukrspetstechnika followed with the P-19MU, which added the capability to track targets with low radar cross-section.

Overall, as of 2022, some 70 radar stations of the PSZSU were deployed and operational, of which at least 40 included 35D6Ms and 36D6M-1s. As far as can be assessed, at least 50 of these survived the first four days of war intact.[1]

As well as a large number of early warning/surveillance radars, the PSZSU operated advanced electronic support measures (ESM) systems. The most common of these was the Kolchuga, developed by the Rostov military institute of the GRU and Topaz of Donetsk in the late 1980s. Consisting of three truck-mounted stations, a single Kolchuga was a passive system capable of direct-line detection of aerial targets, through triangulating their electronic emissions, out to a range of 600–800km. Ukraine is known to have inherited 18 Kolchugas from the USSR and eight additional upgraded Kolchuga-M systems are known to have been delivered by 2001. Because Kyiv lost control over the manufacturer in 2014, it transferred further research and development to Iskra and relaunched production, resulting in a few additional upgraded systems, starting in 2021. It remains unknown how many of these had become operational by February of the following year.

An 80K6M Phoenix radar of the PSZSU deployed for operation. Only three or four were operational in 2022. (Iskra)

Arguably, before the invasion, this radar network provided the Ukrainians with a good view over all of their own airspace, and into most of western and south-western Russia, but only a very poor picture over the Black Sea. Thanks to the station forward-deployed at Mariupol airport, they had a relatively good view over the Sea of Azov, but – as described in Volume 6 – this was knocked out by Russian missiles early on 24 February.

Above all, unlike that of the ZSU, the communication system supporting the Virazh-Plansheet system remained intact: therefore, the commander of the PSZSU, Colonel General Mykola Oleshchuk and his staff experienced far fewer problems in exercising command and control over the force. Where they did experience major problems was the fact that their service had no operational ability: it was structured, equipped and trained to provide air defence against aircraft and helicopters, primarily for the units deployed along the LOC. However, it was not structured, trained or equipped to counter simultaneous Russian invasions in the north, east, and south, and missile strikes against facilities of strategic importance all over the country, and its commanders were never trained to demonstrate initiative: to act on their own, quickly move to new positions and operate without detailed orders. The air force and the air defence force also lacked mobile headquarters: indeed, most of its command nodes were fixed in position, and often exercised command and control over units hundreds of kilometres away. While this made things easier in peace, it was to prove deadly during war – if for no other reason than because it made the task of targeting Ukrainian command nodes much easier for the Russians. Finally, before the war – other than in Donbas – ground-based air defence assets of the PSZSU did not regularly train to cooperate with ground forces within the area of responsibility of the Joint Headquarters: there was no communication system for this purpose, nor liaison teams assigned to the headquarters of the ZSU brigades. All of these lessons had to be learned in combat and paid for in blood first.

Air Combat

On 28 February, the Ministry of Defence in Moscow reported the destruction of 1,150 military targets in Ukraine and declared the VKS to be 'in possession of total aerial superiority'. Both claims were significantly exaggerated, but gauging by similar reporting about the Russian operations in Syria, it can be deduced that each 'destroyed' target actually meant one target that had been attacked – whether by aircraft or by missiles – while 'total aerial superiority' was true for most, but by no means all, of the airspace over the areas controlled by the Russian ground forces at the time. Indeed, only a few hours before the press conference in question was held, the Russians fired a number of ballistic missiles from the territory of Belarus at Lutsk Air Base (AB). These are known to have knocked out at least five stored Sukhoi Su-24 tactical bombers (including borts 06, 21, 25, and 93). Also hit were fuel depots and numerous stored aircraft at Bila Tserkva, Starokostyantyniv and Ivano-Frankivsk air bases. Finally, Zhytomyr Airport is known to have been hit by two 9K720 Iskander-M ballistic missiles fired from the Mozyr area, also in Belarus.

Later that morning, the VKS began deploying Sukhoi Su-30SMs and Sukhoi Su-34s to strike targets in north-western Ukraine. Always supported by Beriev A-50 airborne early warning and control aircraft, Ilyushin Il-20M airborne command posts, Mil Mi-8MTPRI helicopters equipped for electronic warfare, Sukhoi Su-24MP reconnaissance aircraft, and Sukhoi Su-30SM and Su-35 interceptors (usually each armed with up to four R-77-1 medium-range air-to-air- and two Kh-31P/PD anti-radiation missiles), the involved fighter-bombers operated in formations of between two and six aircraft. Early on, their pilots tended to deploy their anti-

A still from a video taken early during the war, showing a Su-35S taking-off. Of interest is the dual installation of R-77-1 medium-range air-to-air missiles in between the intakes. (Russian Ministry of Defence)

A Kh-31PD seen upon launch. The weapon was the primary anti-radiation missile of the VKS in 2022. (KTRV)

radiation weapons from high altitudes and as far as 200 kilometres away. It was only once the VKS figured out that this practice was not particularly effective that it attempted to hit some Ukrainian SAMs using Kh-29 and Kh-59 electro-optically guided PGMs.[2]

For their part, and thanks both to its Kolchugas and the fact that most Russian combat aircraft tended to operate at medium- or high altitudes before approaching the combat zone – and thus in full sight of the active Ukrainian radars – the PSZSU was usually able to detect and track the activity of Russian combat aircraft well in advance.[3] Then its operators would wait until the Russians entered the zones covered by surveillance radars – such as the P-18s, P-19s, Nebos, Pelikans, Phoenixes and 35D6M/36D6M-1 – before these activated and started tracking. Radar stations, visual observation posts, or civilians would then inform the local headquarters about incoming Russian aircraft, at which time the PSZSU would use its nation-wide command and control network to advise its flying units and selected SAM units about an approaching enemy. The first that attempted to engage were MiG-29s and Su-27s. The pilots were briefed to keep their operations simple: scramble, try to approach at low altitude, engage with R-27R/T or R-27ER/ET medium-range air-to-air missiles, and regardless of whether successful or not, disengage and return straight back to base. However, whenever airborne, Ukrainian pilots found their radars and communication systems severely jammed by Russian electronic countermeasures: reportedly the three Ilyushin Il-22PP electronic warfare aircraft and the Mil Mi-8MTPR-1 electronic warfare helicopters proved

A Su-34 loaded with a total of eight OFAB-250-270 bombs (all installed on MDBZ multiple ejector racks under the intakes) rolling for take-off into a strike on north-western Ukraine in early March 2022. (Russian Ministry of Defence)

Another Su-34 taking-off from a base in Belarus, loaded with a total of eight FAB-250M-62 free-fall bombs, in early March 2022. (Russian Ministry of Defence)

highly effective in this regard. A few of the Ukrainian pilots pressed on, regardless of the odds, sometimes keeping their radars turned off and instead operating using data from their radar warning receivers while attempting to reach the range of their R-27T and R-27ET infrared-homing, medium-range air-to-air missiles – which required no radar support to be fired. Therefore, air combats were inevitable.

On 28 February, Su-27S Bort 11, piloted by Major Stepan Ivanovich Ciobanu of the 831st Brigade, was reported by the Ukrainians to have been shot down by Russian interceptors over the Kropyvnytskyi area. While it is possible that Ciobanu was another victim of Su-35s of the Baranovichi-based 23rd Fighter Aviation Regiment, the official explanation for his death as published by the PSZSU made no sense at all. Accordingly, Ciobanu 'distracted enemy aircraft over Kropyvnytskyi, was attacked by enemy missiles, as a result of which he received injuries incompatible with life… this allowed the remaining aircraft to take-off, take them out of under attack and redeploy to a reserve airfield'. However, positioned in Kyrovograd Oblast, in the geographic centre of Ukraine, Kropyvnytskyi was an area where no Russian combat aircraft are known to have ever operated during this war. This fact appears even more interesting considering that during the same night, Lieutenant Andrey Gerus, a MiG-29 pilot, claimed to have shot down a 'Russian Il-76' over Kropyvnytskyi, and was subsequently awarded the title 'Hero of Ukraine' for his feat. As in the case of all the claims for VKS transport aircraft made by Su-27 pilots of the PSZSU, no evidence for such an aerial victory has ever surfaced. Therefore, it is at least likely that Gerus actually made a mistake and blasted Ciobanu's Su-27S out of the skies. On the other hand, whether this affair was related to the loss of the Su-34 Bort 05 (registration RF-81259) – in which the weapons systems officer, Captain Vyacheslav Vyacheslavovich

A Su-24MR of the VKS, equipped with a Tangazh reconnaissance pod under the centreline, seen taxiing to the runway of a base in Belarus in early March 2022. The type was heavily involved in supporting air strikes on targets in north-western Ukraine and monitoring the rebuilding of the Ukrainian IADS. (Russian Ministry of Defence)

Maklagin (also a member of the headquarters of the 303rd Aviation Division) was killed on the same day – remains unknown.[4]

The quality of reports by the High Command of the Ukrainian air force became even more dubious on 2 March 2022, when – while simultaneously claiming that VKS interceptors were, generally 'remaining north of the border', inside Belarusian airspace – the same instance reported that a pair of its MiG-29s engaged a pair of Su-35s and claimed one, while another Russian fighter was then credited to its S-300s (after downing a PSZSU interceptor). Not only has no evidence for this clash has ever surfaced, but over the following days it transpired that in the early hours of 2 March, the Ukrainians did launch several air strikes on columns of the VSRF north-west of Kyiv; that these had top-cover from MiG-29s of the 40th Brigade; and that the PSZSU lost a total of three aircraft. The MiG-29S piloted by Major Oleksandr Brynzhala was shot down over the village of Rakovichi and its pilot killed – according to the Ukrainians: while combating 12 'instead' of the expected four Su-35s. Around 01.30hrs, the Russians intercepted an Su-24M of the 7th Brigade, crewed by Colonel Mykola Kovalenko and Captain Yevhen Kazimirov. The jet came under attack from Su-30SMs or Su-35s, was hit by at least one missile, and crashed between the settlements of Kamiany Brid, Bilka, and Dovbysh, killing the crew. As now usual, no corresponding Russian claims became known – primarily because the majority of those that were published by Moscow were all undated.[5]

The experience of Ukrainian MiG-29 and Su-27 pilots from the early days of the war showed that any unnecessary manoeuvring within the combat zone was essentially an invitation to be intercepted by Russian aircraft such as the Su-35. Accidentally, it was the statistics released by the 40th Brigade of the PSZSU on the evening of 2 March 2022 that illustrated this the best. Correspondingly, by that point in time its two squadrons of MiG-29s had flown a total of 25 combat sorties, shot down 20 enemy aircraft and helicopters and destroyed 37 ground vehicles. Flying 25 combat sorties in seven days of high-intensity war was very little for a brigade of two squadrons – especially considering the unit seems to have lost four aircraft and four pilots killed in action: such a rate of losses (one in every six missions) was simply unsustainable. Unsurprisingly, the task of serving as the first line of defence was subsequently assumed by ground-based air defences.

Rebuilding the Ukrainian IADS

The available Western reports about developments in Ukraine during March and April 2022, indicate that the PSZSU took three or four days – a week at most – to recover from the first shock and then 'sealed' the skies against Russian aircraft and helicopters over nearly all of the country. A closer examination of all the available claims and reports indicates a dramatically different situation.

Certainly enough, there were units operating ground-based air defence systems whose commanders acted on their own, and which took only hours after the opening Russian blow to recover and go into action. Generally, the pace of their recovery depended on a number of factors, including the availability and condition of equipment, military and political priorities, and the geographic area in question. Unsurprisingly considering the severity of the blows some units received at the start of the all-out invasion, many took at least 48 hours to recover and repair enough of their equipment to start dispersing away from their bases and go into action. For example, as of mid-2024, no reports are available about any ground-based air defence units of the PSZSU deployed along the Line of Control in Donbass suffering damage from Russian air strikes in the first few days of the war. Because of this, and because the VKS was preoccupied supporting multiple assault operations elsewhere, the ZSU units deployed along the LOC remained well-protected.[6]

That was a literal 'exception to the rule': elsewhere, the first coherent air defence system emerged in the area between Kyiv and Zhytomyr only towards the end of the first week of war. Arguably, this caused significant losses to the Russians (see Volume 6 for details) but this was still far from sealing that piece of the Ukrainian skies against the enemy. The next part of the Ukrainian IADS that recovered was the one responsible for the defence of Odesa and Mykolaiv: this significantly bolstered its effectiveness starting from 5 and 6 March. Additional elements of the Virazh-Plansheet IADS were meanwhile reactivated in western Ukraine, protecting Lviv, Starokostyantyniv, Zhytomyr and Vinnytsia. However, due to losses and general chaos, in other parts of the country – especially in the case of Kharkiv, Dnipro, and Kryvyi Rih – the PSZSU experienced immense problems just with finding enough units to recover local air defence zones, not to mention re-establishing its IADS. Indeed, as time was to show, and primarily due to the outright incompetence of several top commanders and the resulting poor training of

A Ukrainian pilot walking to his fully armed MiG-29 while a fuel depot hit by a Russian missile burns in the background. (Ukrainian Ministry of Defence)

subordinated units, in some cases the situation was not to experience a significant improvement even two years later.

Perhaps the steepest of learning curves was experienced by mobile ground-based air defence units deployed in the Izyum area: arguably, there it took the Ukrainians until the second half of March to build-up the first, small, though well-operating air defence zone. However, while facing overwhelming odds, the involved PSZSU units quickly learned to operate in the fashion of a guerrilla force – to disperse, hide, and wait for suitable opportunities – in turn converting this sector of the frontline into a particularly unpleasant one for the VKS. By May, the same was the true for the situation in the area between Severodonetsk and Kramatorsk. However, a deduction based on currently available information leaves little room for doubt: deeper behind the frontlines – and, combined with the lack of training in countering ballistic and cruise missiles – the force continued to experience immense problems and remained largely ineffective through the period covered in this volume.

Equipment

With a general overview of the PSZSU's integrated air defence systems being provided in Volume 6, it is sufficient here to summarise that as of late February 2022, the system comprised a total of about 60 battalions (or 'sites') equipped with radar-guided SAMs, including 35 S-300PM/PS/PTs, three S-300V1s, 15 Buk M1s, and nine S-125s.

Before the war, the PSZSU did train for the dispersion of its units, and this training paid some dividends – especially in regards of teaching ground crews of all the flying units, and the majority of SAM operators how to maintain their equipment under field conditions. However, it never trained to cooperate with ZSU units outside the area of responsibility of the Joint Headquarters in Donbas, nor had a reliable system of cooperation with ground forces: unsurprisingly, the latter had no clear picture about who was flying where and when, and the Ukrainian troops regularly opened fire at their own aircraft and helicopters. This resulted in dozens of

The launch of a 5V55 missile from a S-300PT SAM system of the PSZSU, one of the oldest variants of this family, originally developed for the Soviet air defence force. Also visible are missile containers (which act as launchers) of the 5P86 trailer. (Ukrainian Ministry of Defence)

'blue-on-blue' engagements, and that problem had not been entirely solved even as of 2024.[7]

Generally, once various parts of the Virazh-Plansheet had recovered, they operated in similar fashion to the manned interceptors of the PSZSU: rather than any kind of NATO-provided intelligence, as frequently claimed in the social media, Kolchugas remained the primary means of early warning and detection of all incoming Russian air strikes and many missile attacks. Units equipped with early warning/surveillance radars would then take over next in the chain, while SAM-equipped units were dispersed and usually operated under conditions of emission control (i.e. without emitting any kind of electromagnetic emissions). The latter would power up – and thus 'unmask' – their own radars only if informed that they were in a position that promised a successful engagement. Rather ironically, what happened next frequently depended on the geographic area and local level of experience, and the ability of the commanders in question to operate at their own discretion. Generally, units operating S-300s, and deployed in central- or western Ukraine were slow to learn to operate under emission control, or to frequently change their positions. On the contrary, especially units equipped with Buks and deployed closer to the frontline were quick to learn numerous related lessons. Finally, and just as in the case of flying operations by both the PSZSU and the VKS, and for exactly the same set of reasons (described in detail in Volume 6), so also the majority of operations of the Ukrainian ground-based air defences was closely related to the ground warfare.

Table 2: Principal SAM systems in Ukrainian Service, 2022

Russian designation	ASCC/NATO reporting name	Notes
S-125 Pechora 2D	SA-3 Goa	SARH/Command; operated by ZSU
2K22 Tunguska	SA-19 Grison	SARH/Command; operated by ZSU
9K33M3 Osa-AKM	SA-8B Gecko	SARH, operated by ZSU
9K35 Strela-10	SA-13 Gopher	IR homing; operated by ZSU
9K330 Tor	SA-15 Gauntlet	SARH; operated by ZSU
9K37M1 Buk M1	SA-11 Gadfly	SARH, operated by PSZSU
S-300PT/PS/PMU	SA-10B Grumble B	Command (PT), SAGG (PMU); operated by PSZSU
S-300V1	SA-12A/B Gladiator	GAI/SARH; operated by PSZSU

Strikes on Western Ukraine

The last big round of Russian strikes against targets in north-western Ukraine is known to have been initiated on 4 March 2022, by when the VSRF, the VKS and the Black Sea Fleet are known to have deployed more than 400 ballistic and cruise missiles against Ukraine. According to a release by the Ministry of Defence in Moscow from 5 March, by that point in time this resulted in hits on 61 different military facilities in Ukraine, including 22 depots, six ammunition and logistics warehouses and three radar stations. In particular, Starokostyantyniv AB was hit so often that the Russian Ministry of Defence declared that it had been 'disabled'. Additionally, on 4 March, two Su-34s of the VKS bombed the base of the 5th Slobozhan Brigade of the National Guard in Kharkiv, killing five troops, while Moscow also claimed to have shot down eight aircraft and two helicopters of the PSZSU, and destroyed an entire S-300 SAM system – all in a single day.[8]

At least one of the attacks in question – apparently the one in which at least two Su-34s bombed the Armour Works in Zhytomyr with free-fall bombs – provoked another clash with interceptors of the PSZSU, and around 08.00hrs on the morning of 5 March one of these was shot down in the Korosten area, about 80 kilometres north of Zhytomyr. This time, the Ukrainian pilot ejected safely from a jet that came down near the village of Tarasivka: the type in question remains unknown, but early on 7 March, the Russian MOD claimed the destruction of 'four Ukrainian Su-27s in an air battle over Zhytomyr Oblast'. Possibly related is the fact that a few days later, in the same area, the Ukrainians discovered the wreckage of Su-25SM Bort 10 (registration RF-91969), with the body of its pilot – Major Nikolay Prozorov from the 18th Assault Aviation Regiment – still in the cockpit. Moreover, around 21.00hrs on 5 March 2022, the crash of another Russian fighter-bomber – probably a Su-34 – was reported from the Kozhan-Gorodok area, 17 kilometres from Luninets AB in southern Belarus. The crew ejected successfully, but both the pilot and his weapons systems operator were then brought to a hospital in Minsk by a Mil Mi-8 helicopter, in 'moderately severe condition'.[9]

Wreckage of Su-34 Bort 05 (registration RF-81259), that crashed at Buzova airfield in Kyiv Oblast on 28 February 2022. The aircraft impacted the ground at a very high speed, and completely disintegrated. It remains unclear if it was assigned to the 2nd Composite Aviation Regiment or the 277th Bomber Aviation Regiment. (Ukrainian social media via TheMilitaryWatch)

A part of the aircraft skin from the forward left fuselage of Major Prozorov's Su-25, shot down in the Korosten area sometime between 5 and 9 March 2022. (Ukrainian social media via TheMilitaryWatch)

A still from a video showing the ascent of two Iskanders from the Mozyr area, in Belarus, early on 1 March 2022. (Belarussian social media)

Time Out

Despite Moscow's declaration of 'total aerial superiority', the Main Operations Directorate of the *GenStab* and OSK West continued targeting air bases in north-western Ukraine through the following week as well. On the night of 5 to 6 March, Tupolev Tu-95MS bombers are known to have released eight Kh-555 cruise missiles from stations over the Caspian Sea. Most of these hit Gavrishkova AB/Vinnytsia IAP: although the Ukrainians released no specific details, they did confirm 'lots of damage'.

Two days later, on 7 March 2022, Ozerne AB – the home-base of the 831st Tactical Aviation Brigade equipped with Su-27 interceptors – was hit heavily and at least three of its mounts (borts 26, 46, and 48) are known to have been damaged. Moreover, the Russians hit a 'petrol, oil, and lubricants' (POL) depot in Cherniyakiv (Zhytomyr Oblast) with Iskander ballistic missiles, setting it afire.[10]

Notably, according to currently available information, the latter was the last known Russian attack with ballistic missiles for nearly two weeks: whether because the VSRF's stocks of available Iskanders needed replenishing, or because the *GenStab* in Moscow wanted to review early experience (or for a combination of such and similar reasons), not one Iskander is known to have been fired again before 15 March 2022. What exactly the officers led by Lieutenant General Sergei Fedorovich Rudskoy – Director of the Main Operations Directorate of the *GenStab* – concluded, remains unknown. The Pentagon assessed that the Russians had deployed 380 ballistic and cruise missiles between 24 and 29 February, and that by 7 March this number had grown to more than 680.

What is certain is that during the next week the Russians continued their campaign in the form of long-range air strikes and strikes with cruise missiles, before resuming attacks with ballistic missiles, and that these operations developed in an unusual fashion: an endless series of incoherent efforts. Because of frequent refocusing on entirely different aiming points, regardless of the number of missiles deployed, and in stark contrast to similar campaigns conducted by the USA during two wars with Iraq in 1991 and 2003, it failed to produce decisive strategic effects. On the contrary, there was no fracture between the Ukrainian political and military leadership, or between those two and the Ukrainian public, while the command and control system of the ZSU (heavily hit by a cyberattack late on 23 February), rapidly recovered after the introduction of the StarLink satellite communication system. Regardless of how often hit in the first days of the war, and regardless of how slow, the recovery of the Ukrainian IADS also continued: at first in the Kyiv area, and then along the frontlines in the south and east, the Ukrainians returned to service an ever-larger number of S-300 and Buk M1 SAM systems in particular. Gradually, these began causing ever heavier losses to the VKS.

Finally, the planners of the Main Operations Directorate of the *GenStab* experienced much frustration due to their complete inability to track down and disrupt the flow of Ukrainian logistics, and especially the continuous flow of Western military aid from the borders with Poland and Romania. Certainly enough, the principal set of reasons for these failures was the same as those that plagued the planning and execution of the entire invasion. The main reason was the fact that the Ukrainians resisted far more fiercely than expected by Putin and his henchmen, and that the Federal Security Service (FSB), the Main Intelligence Directorate of the *GenStab* (GRU), VSRF and the VKS greatly underestimated the scale of strikes necessary to achieve the desired, paralysing effects. Another issue was the fact that the VKS was never meant, and thus neither equipped nor trained, to operate into the depth of enemy airspace: so

The Forpost UAV is the Russian version of the Israeli Aircraft Industries Searcher Mk. II. Russia acquired a total of 30 systems with three UAVs each. In 2019, Moscow also launched production of the Forpost-R, which can also be armed. (Russian Ministry of Defence)

much so that fewer than a handful of officers in the Main Operations Directorate of the *GenStab*, and in the headquarters of OSKs West and South, ever arrived at the idea of deploying it in that fashion.[11] Although the VKS was actually in possession of aerial supremacy not only over the parts of Ukraine controlled by ground forces, but also up to 50 kilometres beyond enemy lines, its fighter-bombers were rarely tasked with such operations. Moreover, even when these included the deployment of precision guided munitions (PGM) – like the Kh-29 and Kh-59 – they largely proved as ineffective as the strikes made with free-fall bombs. As such, they were no replacement for ballistic and cruise missiles. For all practical purposes, both the *GenStab* and commanders of OSKs West and South thus became hostages of the *GenStab*'s traditional illusions about there being no necessity to develop air power that could operate independently from the other branches of the armed forces.

That said, the overall efficiency of missile strikes could have been improved provided the intelligence services found a solution for their inability to obtain the necessary targeting intelligence in time. As mentioned above, most targeting information was obtained through so-called 'human intelligence' (HUMINT): not only was the flow and processing of this much too slow, but its quality regularly lay between 'dubious' and 'inadequate' – and this although, as subsequent developments were to show, the FSB and the GRU were in touch with numerous officers of the ZSU. This is why the GRU missed not only the fact that the ZSU began dispersing its stocks of artillery shells days before the war, but was also slow to adapt its targeting, in turn enabling the Ukrainians to keep their artillery brigades well supplied. Combined with the lack of long-range UAVs, it was also the reason why the Russians were regularly late in targeting combat aircraft of the PSZSU at their bases during the first days and weeks of the invasion.[12]

Long-Range Air Strikes

On 9 March 2022 – around the same time as the Russians might have conducted a heliborne assault in the Oyruch-Zalissya area, about 120–150km west of Kyiv (to widen the advance of their ground troops into this part of Ukraine, and thus better protect the flanks of the 35th Combined Arms Army that was still trying to advance south-west of the Ukrainian capital) – a pair of Su-34s of the VKS are known to have bombed targets in the Zhytomyr area. Apparently, their mission led to yet another air battle with interceptors of the PSZSU, in which MiG-29MU1 Bort 10 was shot down and its pilot, Major Yevhen Lisenko killed. Regardless of how limited, such successes appear to have emboldened the Ministry of Defence in Moscow to proudly announce, on 10 March 2022, that '90% of Ukrainian air bases' and the 'main body of the Ukrainian combat aviation' had been destroyed. As subsequent developments were to show, this was yet another overoptimistic assessment primarily meant for the domestic public.

Elsewhere, the VKS continued striking very varied targets. Early on 11 March 2022, three missiles hit the Dniprovsky Metallurgical Plant in Dnipro; two Su-34s bombed an unknown target in Korosten (north-west of Kyiv); while Lutsk AB and Ivano-Frankivsk AB were attacked by two cruise missiles each. That at least some of the Russian targeting intelligence was collected by means other than HUMINT became clear later the same day, when the Ukrainians shot down a Forpost reconnaissance UAV over Zhytomyr Oblast.[13]

Early on 12 March, the Russians then hit the Motor Works in Lutsk with cruise missiles, causing a major conflagration: by then, the number of ballistic and cruise missiles fired at Ukraine reportedly rose to 775. Furthermore, during the night of 12 to 13 March, the Russians targeted Vasilkiv AB with a total of eight cruise missiles, which cratered the runway, blew up the local ammunition depot, and caused a large fire in the POL depot. Late on 13 March, Tu-95 bombers of the VKS flew a major strike, reportedly releasing up to 30 Kh-555 missiles. About a dozen of these targeted the Military Academy of the Ground Forces and the International Peacekeeping and Security Centre in Camp Yavorov (Lviv Oblast, 18km from the border with Poland): a cross-examination of several reports in the Ukrainian media revealed that at least 35 ZSU troops and over 100 foreign volunteers undergoing training were killed, and at least 134 injured. Around the same time, Ivano-Frankivsk AB was hit by three Kh-555s again, while three other cruise missiles hit the city centre of Dnipro, killing 23 civilians. Finally, around 20.30hrs that evening,

The fireball caused by the Russian missile strike early on 14 March 2022 on the Lutsk Motor Plant that – amongst others – was undertaking overhauls and repairs to the RD-33 engines used by MiG-29s. (Ukrainian social media)

the 114th Brigade of the PSZSU lost a MiG-29S and its pilot, Major Stephan Tarabalka: the jet was shot down and the pilot killed in action over the village of Ivnytsia in Zhytomyr Oblast.[14]

It is possible that Tarabalka's MiG-29 was felled by Senior Lieutenant Ilya Perepelkin: according to the Russian MOD, this Su-35S pilot of the 23rd Fighter Aviation Regiment, was credited with intercepting 'two Ukrainian Su-27s', shooting down the enemy leader with one missile, then making a 180-degree turn and shooting down the other jet with two missiles. However, not only are no such losses of the PSZSU known during this period, but Moscow claimed that this air combat took place on 17 March 2022.[15]

First Kinzhal

The VSRF resumed deploying ballistic missiles against Ukraine on 14 March 2022, when separatists fired a single 9M79 Tochka-U missile with a cluster munition warhead at the centre of Donetsk in a false flag operation, reportedly killing 20 and injuring 28 people. A day later, Aviatorske AB/Dnipro IAP was hit by at least two 9M723 Iskander-Ms that damaged the runway and the main terminal. Then, early on 18 March, and with quite some fanfare, the Russian MOD announced the first combat deployment of the 9-S-7760 Kinzhal hypersonic missile (ASCC/NATO reporting name 'AS-24 Killjoy').[16]

For a number of reasons, the attack caused confusion both in Ukraine and the West: the video released by the Russians actually showed an attack on an unknown storage facility in eastern Ukraine, while Moscow claimed that the Kinzhal was deployed to strike an 'underground storage facility for missiles and ammunition' in Delyatin, in Ivano-Frankivsk Oblast. Although more than a handful of NATO's generals then expressed that they were deeply impressed by the weapon's performance, before long it turned out that it descended at a lower speed than expected – in turn increasing the confusion because many concluded that the Russians had actually deployed an older OTR-21 Tochka-U ballistic missile instead. Finally, while neither the West nor Ukraine commented about the aircraft used to deploy the Kinzhal in question, months later Moscow announced that 'the Su-34 aircraft used the Kinzhal missile for the first time', and 'the first crew that successfully accomplished such a task will receive state awards'. In some circles, this was misunderstood to mean that the first ever combat deployment of the Kinzhal in Ukraine – the one on 18 March 2022 – was undertaken from a Su-34.[17]

At least some of the excitement and confusion were no surprise: an air-launched version of the 9K720 Iskander, the 9-S-7760 Kinzhal (often wrongly reported as designated the 'Kh-47M2' by Ukrainian and Western media) entered 'experimental' service in late 2017. The first and only unit equipped with the system was worked up only from 2018, and thus relatively little was known about it, while the Russian propaganda machinery severely exaggerated its performance. As subsequent developments were to show, while the MOD in Moscow claimed its total range in excess of 2,000km (1,100nm), this figure actually included the MiG-31's combat radius without in-flight refuelling. Furthermore, because the missile was equipped with a solid-fuel engine which could not be turned off once fired, it could never reach, and even less so maintain the claimed speed of Mach 10 throughout its flight. Limited by its actual range and relatively low mass (approximately 1,000kg on launch), during the return to the atmosphere and thus the terminal flight stage, it slowed down to about Mach 3.7. Finally, the lack of a suitable steering system made any kind of sharp turns or rapid changes of direction impossible, which meant that its terminal fight route was predictable and made it easier to intercept than expected. That said, as of March 2022, the PSZSU possessed no weapon capable of accomplishing such a task: despite countless Russian and Western reports, even its S-300Vs were only sporadically successful in shooting down Iskanders and never claimed a single Kinzhal.

PRECISE VIOLATOR

The development of the Iskander complex was ordered by the Central Committee of the Communist Party of the USSR and the Council of Ministers of the USSR on 21 December 1988, with the aim of replacing both the OTR-23 Oka, which was banned by the Intermediate Nuclear Forces (INF) Treaty of 1987 (although the Oka had a range of less than 400km) and the older OTR-21 Tochka-U. The full-scale work was initiated in 1993 using the design of the OTR-23 at KB Mashinostroyeniya (KBM) in the town of Kolomna, by a design bureau led by Sergei Nepobedimy (also known as the Kolomna Machine Building Bureau). Initial progress was slow due to the collapse of the USSR, which also necessitated Nepobedimy and his team using various short-cut solutions. Primarily, they resized the airframe of the OTR-23 and equipped it with a new solid-fuel rocket motor. Following testing at Kapusting Yar test range in 2005, the system entered service with the 448th Rocket Brigade a year later. Meanwhile, the development of 9M728 cruise missile was completed which was, reportedly, a variant of the 3M54 Klub naval system: first flight-tested in 2007, this entered service in 2013, thus violating the INF Treaty which prohibited development and deployment of ground-launched cruise missiles with a range of more than 500km (in turn, this prompted the USA to withdraw from the treaty in 2019).

The centrepiece of each Iskander system were 9S552 and 9S920 processing stations mounted on KamAZ 43101 trucks, and equipped with R-168-100KA Aqueduct radio systems: by 2022, both were capable of processing real-time full-motion videos from UAVs such as the Forpost and Orlan-10, and could be connected to the Strelets automated tactical control system operated by GRU reconnaissance formations. The Strelets enabled selection of the target on a map, the transfer of the resulting coordinates to the missile, and its programming for engagement. The missile was then elevated from the horizontal to the vertical position and launched, with two missiles carried by the same transporter erector launcher (TEL) – manufactured by Titan-Barikady – being ready for action within less than a minute of each other. The firing order was issued either by a forward artillery spotter, the brigade or division commander, headquarters of the responsible OSK, or the National Defence Control Centre in Moscow. Moreover, the same TEL could carry two different variants of the missile and these were programmable to arrive at the target at the same time, thus complicating defence efforts. Finally, Iskanders could be combined with BM-30 Smerch 300mm multiple rocket launchers (maximum firing range 120km/65 nautical miles) to strike the same target.

Originally, each Iskander-equipped brigade comprised three battalions, each including four 9P78-1 TELs (each carrying two missiles), four 9T250 or 9T250E transporter-loader vehicles, the 9S552 command post vehicle, and the 9S920 information processing station. Correspondingly, a single brigade included 12 TELs and 24 ready-to-use missiles. However, in late 2019, the Kremlin authorised an expansion of all brigades through the addition of a fourth battalion: since 2021, instead of three battalions with 12 launchers, each brigade had four battalions with a total of 16 launchers, and thus the capability to deploy a salvo of 32 missiles at once.[18]

The 9K270 system had two principal types of missiles:

- Iskander-M: 9M723 or 9M723K1 quasi-ballistic missiles (capable of terminal phase manoeuvres), inertial and electro-optical guidance systems (of which the latter reportedly reduces the CEP to 5–10 metres), warheads weighing between 480 and 700kg (including cluster munitions), 9B999 decoys, solid-fuel rocket motor, and a range of around 500km if carrying a 700kg warhead.
- Iskander-K: 9M727, 9M728 (also known as R-500), and 9M729 cruise missiles (based on the 3M-14 family of sea-launched cruise missiles), with inertial navigation system supported by GPS/GLONASS, active radar homing and electro-optical guidance in the terminal flight phase, a warhead of 480kg, and range of 500km.[19]

Overall, the Iskander was designed for covert, quick, massive, and precise action: a single brigade equipped with the system was designed to be able to fire all of its 24 missiles (later 32) within one minute, and with significantly better precision than available before. Its purpose was to target particularly important, small-sized point targets or, if equipped with cluster munition warheads, area targets within the operational depth behind the frontline. Typical targets included command and communication

A 9P78-1 transporter erector launcher of the Iskander system, seen having its camouflaged removed and prepared for firing action. Early during the war, the VSRF deployed three of its rocket brigades equipped with Iskanders against Ukraine, including one in Belarus. Nevertheless, it did not deploy them as intensively as demanded by the VSRF's doctrine. (Russian Ministry of Defence)

nodes, missile systems, long-range artillery, and aircraft or helicopters at forward operating bases. The flight trajectory was not entirely ballistic: the missile would climb to slightly less than 50km high, then descend and accelerate up to speeds of Mach 7 while constantly changing its course, making turns of up to 20gs. Moreover, it had a partially controlled terminal flight phase, which is why Iskanders also became known as 'quasi-ballistic' missiles. In combat against Ukraine, the Russians initially tended to deploy one 9M723 or 9M723K1 missile per target: in May and June 2022, they introduced the practice of deploying two missiles against the same target, before returning to single-missile strikes, later on.[20]

As mentioned in Volume 6, the VSRF entered the war of 2022 with 13 Iskander brigades. While one additional brigade was subsequently redeployed to Belarus, two others were established in 2023 and 2024, one of which was deployed opposite Finland when it joined NATO. It is possible that one unit was actually equipped with North Korean-made NK-23 missiles acquired in 2023. For administrative purposes, all of the units in question – listed in Table 3 – were subordinated to the Rocket Troops and Artillery arm of the Russian ground forces. Operationally, they were subordinated to selected tank armies and combined armies, and thus the OSKs.

The wreckage of a cluster warhead from an Iskander missile found after an attack on Shpychkine railway station in March 2022. (National Police of Ukraine)

Table 3: VSRF Iskander Brigades 2011–2024

Unit	Base	Notes
630th Rocket Battalion	Kapustin Yar	activated 2005; research and development unit subordinated to the 60th Combat Employment Training Centre
1st Rocket Brigade	Molkino (Krasnodar)	activated November 2013; OSK South
12th Rocket Brigade	Mozdok (North Ossetia)	activated November 2015; OSK South
15th Rocket Brigade		activated December 2023; OSK East; former 41st Rocket Brigade; possibly re-equipped with KN-23 in 2023–2024
20th Rocket Brigade	Spassk Dalniy (Primorsky Krai)	activated March 2016; OSK East
26th Rocket Brigade	Luga (Leningrad)	activated October 2011; OSK West (6th CAA)
47th Rocket Brigade	Dyadkovskaya (Krasnodar)	activated January 2021; OSK South; CO Lieutenant Colonel Vitaly Bobyr
92nd Rocket Brigade	Totskoye (Orenburg)	activated November 2014; OSK Centre
103rd Rocket Brigade	Divisionnaya (Buryatia)	activated July 2015; OSK East
107th Rocket Brigade	Birobidjhan (Jewish)	activated June 2013; OSK East
112th Rocket Brigade	Shuya (Ivanovo)	activated July 2014; OSK West (1st GTA)
114th Rocket Brigade	Znamensk (Astrakhan)	activated
119th Rocket Brigade	Yelanskiy	activated November 2016; redeployed to Voronezh area April 2021; OSK South
152nd Rocket Brigade	Chernyakhovsk (Kalinigrad)	deployed October 2016; OSK North (XI AK)
448th Rocket Brigade	Kursk	activated November 2018; OSK Centre (20th CAA)
465th Rocket Brigade	Yuzhny (Osipovichy)	deployed February 2023; Belarus
??? Rocket Brigade	(Leningrad)	activated February 2024; OSK North[21]

The launch of an 9M728 missile of the Iskander-K complex, from a 9P78-1 transporter erector launcher (TEL).

FIRST AND ONLY: 44TH SPECIAL PURPOSE AVIATION REGIMENT

On 1 March 2018, the 712th Guards Fighter Aviation Regiment, based at Kansk AB (OSK Centre), was officially declared as the first unit operating 9-S-7760 Kinzhal hypersonic missiles. Indeed, by February 2019, its crews had reportedly performed more than 380 training sorties, of which at least 70 included in-flight refuelling from Ilyushin Il-78 tanker aircraft. In June 2021, a flight of MiG-31Ks from this regiment was demonstratively deployed to Hmeimim AB in Syria, where – according to the Russian MOD – they also flew their first combat sorties. However, this was merely an overture because, while preparing for the all-out invasion of Ukraine, the senior leadership of the Russian armed forces placed great emphasis on working up ever-more units equipped with overhauled, rebuilt, and modernised MiG-31 interceptors. By 2022, not only had all of the 110 MiG-31s still in service with the VKS been modified and returned to service, but so had 40 additional examples. This left only about 45 old MiG-31DZ airframes 'free' to be upgraded to carry the Kinzhal. Intended as a system for striking ground and naval targets, the MiG-31Ks did not 'fit' into an air defence unit like the 712th Regiment.

Correspondingly, effective from 1 December 2021, the MiG-31K fleet was reorganised into the 44th Special Purpose Aviation Regiment, home-based at Savasleika AB (Nizhny Novgorod). Assigned to the Long-Range Aviation, this unit was organised into three squadrons. The first of these was established and home-based at Akhtubinsk AB. The second was worked up at Savasleika AB, while the third – which was still working up as of 2023 – was home-based at Belaya AB.

The staff of the 44th Special Purpose Aviation Regiment was quite colourful. According to Ukrainian sources, the unit was initially commanded by Colonel Aleksey Filippovych Yamakydy (with colonels Denis Raufovych Akhmadeyev and Roman Sergeevich Semenyuk as deputies) and staffed by personnel drawn from the 4th Centre for Training of Aviation Personnel, the 929th State Flight Test Centre, the 52nd Heavy Bomber Aviation Regiment, and the 712th Guards Fighter Aviation Regiment. Originally assigned a total of 24 MiG-31s, including 11 MiG-31Ks, by 2023 the 44th was on the way to receiving its full nominal quota of 36 MiG-31Ks.[22]

Table 4: Known MiG-31Ks of the 44th Special Aviation Regiment, VKS, 2022–2024[23]

Bort	Registration	Notes
30 Blue	RF-92452	2nd Squadron (borts 30–39, Savasleyka)
31 Blue	RF-92332	
36 Blue	RF-92462	
37 Blue	RF-92463	
39 Blue	RF-33807	
43 Blue		3rd Squadron (borts 43–51, Belaya)
50 Blue		
51 Blue	RF-95194	
88 Red		1st Squadron (borts 88–99, Akhtubinsk)
89 Red	RF-95200	former 58 Red
90 Red	RF-95215	former 81 Blue
91 Red	RF-95216	former 82 Blue
92 Red	RF-95217	written off on 29 January 2022
93 Red	RF-92454	
94 Red		
95 Red		
96 Red	RF-92461	
97 Red	RF-92473	former 26 Red
98 Red	RF-92457	
99 Red	RF-95201	former 80 Blue

A still from a video showing a MiG-31K releasing a Kinzhal missile. (Russian Ministry of Defence)

MiG-31K Bort 36 (registration RF-92462) of the 44th Special Purpose Aviation Regiment, seen while taxiing to the runway, armed with a 9-S-7760 Kinzhal missile installed under the centreline, in early 2022. (Russian Ministry of Defence)

MiG-31K Bort 31 (registration RF-92332) moving from its parking spot, armed with a 9-S-7760 Kinzhal missile, during an exercise in Russia in early 2022. (Russian Ministry of Defence)

Switch to POL Facilities

The Russian missile offensive continued on 19 March, when Lviv was targeted by several Iskanders. Although at least one was shot down by Ukrainian S-300Vs, two or three others hit the maintenance facilities at the local air base, destroying two halls and setting their wreckage afire. At least as successful was a strike on the main base of the 79th Airborne Assault Brigade in Mykolaiv on that day, where up to 40 servicemen were killed. According to the Pentagon, these strikes brought the total number of ballistic and cruise missiles deployed against Ukraine since 24 February to more than 1,080.[24]

On 20 March the Russians fired a single Iskander-M at the Retroville shopping mall and sports facility in Kyiv, killing eight civilians, and then continued the practice of random targeting: a MiG-31K launched from Savasleyka AB deployed its Kinzhal to strike a POL dump, while Kalibr cruise missiles from warships in the Black Sea and from the Caspian Sea targeted the Nizhyn Mechanical Factory. Three days later, instead of Kalibr cruise missiles, the Russian Black Sea Fleet deployed six of its P-800 Oniks anti-ship missiles of the K-300P Bastion system (ASCC/NATO reporting name 'SS-C-5 Stooge') in land-attack mode, to blast a POL depot in Mykolaiv.

On 24 March, Russian warships launched six Kalibr cruise missiles against the Air Force Command Centre in Vinnytsia: while one is known to have been shot down by local air defences, the others caused – according to official Ukrainian reports – 'significant destruction of infrastructure'. Obviously, the majority of the PSZSU survived this blow: indeed, as described below, scattered around dozens of FOBs around the country, and although operating in bare-bones conditions, its ground personnel continued maintaining their aircraft, and pilots continued flying combat sorties: the claims by the Russian MOD to have destroyed '190 Ukrainian combat aircraft', published on 27 March, were just another wild exaggeration. Confirmation of this was delivered by the Russians themselves slightly over a day later: during the evening of 28 March, the Ukrainian air defences shot down two cruise missiles that were approaching Lviv, and two that were approaching Kyiv, but another pair of Russian weapons then demolished the POL depot of Starokostyantyniv AB. Finally, early on 29 March, two sea-launched Kalibr cruise missile destroyed the regional administration building in Mykolaiv, killing 37 civilians and wounding 34.

It was only around this point in time that, probably as a consequence of the meeting of the Security Council of the Russian Federation of 24 March (see below for details), the *GenStab* in Moscow scrambled to improve its long-range operations through establishing a dedicated targeting centre, the task of which was to coordinate all reconnaissance operations across Ukraine. The node in question began collecting all HUMINT, analysing it, and preparing a daily overview cross-referenced with geospatial intelligence supplied by the GRU. The resulting digests were then forwarded to the headquarters of OSKs West and South, which were tasked with deciding the methods of attack: cruise missiles launched by Tu-95 bombers of the VKS, warships of the Black Sea Fleet, or rocket brigades directly subordinated to either of the two OSKs. That said, the complete targeting cycle still took about 24 hours. Moreover, the digests contained too little contextual information to enable clear prioritisation, while – unlike the rocket brigades of the VSRF – warships of the Black Sea Fleet took their time to reach suitable firing positions. Finally, the Russians proved still unable to track down and target trains carrying supplies from western Ukraine to the Kyiv area, and a number of targets struck during the following period were military facilities obviously abandoned years ago.[25]

This was of particular importance because, although Ukraine had a well-developed network of highways, the principal means of transporting raw materials, agricultural products, and the heavy equipment and most supplies for the ZSU was its even bigger railway network maintained by the state-owned Ukrzaliznytsia corporation. Rather unsurprisingly, in early April 2022, the new Russian command node began advising the headquarters of OSK West and South to refocus their attention on railways, bridges and – even more so – POL facilities all over Ukraine. Late on 30 March, Su-34 fighter-bombers deployed Kh-59 missiles and brand-new UPAB-1500V electro-optically guided 1,525kg bombs (developed by the Tactical Missile Corporation, KTRV) to target forward POL storage facilities of the ZSU in Chuhiv and Lysychansk, while unidentified missiles – probably 3M54 Kalibrs – struck the POL dump in Novomoskovsk, outside Dnipro, and the Dnipropetrovsk Oil Extraction Plant, both in Dnipropetrovsk Oblast. During the following days, the Russians continued striking similar installations: on 1 April, Kh-555 cruise missiles demolished the huge Kremenchuk oil refinery; a day later, the fuel depot at Myhorod AB in Poltava Oblast was hit by at least two Kalibrs; and on 3 April, three missiles badly damaged Odesa's oil refinery and crude oil storage facilities, while others hit POL depots in Ternopil, Rivne, and Mykolaiv.[26]

A powerful detonation lights up the night sky over Mykolaiv, early on 6 April, as result of a Russian missile strike on a local POL facility. (Ukrainian social media)

The distinct shape of two BAZ-5921 TELs for the OTR-21 Tochka-U system is clearly visible in this video taken during their transfer along the road from Rechica to Gomel, in Belarus, early on 30 March 2022. (Belarusian Hajun Project/MotolkoHelp)

Smoke trails left by the launch of two 9M79 Tochka-U ballistic missiles fired by Russian-controlled separatist units from the Makiivka area early on 11 April 2022. (Russian social media)

Massacre in Kramatorsk

With the *GenStab*, OSK West and OSK South busy organising the withdrawal from northern-central and north-eastern Ukraine, and reshuffling VKS units from Belarus to air bases in Kursk and Belgorod oblasts (see following chapters for details), there followed another break of three days before the missile campaign was resumed. On 6 April, the Russian MOD reported 'strikes with high-precision air- and ground-based missiles' – the standard description for ballistic and cruise missile strikes – on POL facilities in Radekhiv (Lviv), Kozyatyn (Vinnytsia), Novomoskovsk (Dnipro), and Mykolaiv, and a 'concentration of military equipment' at the railway station of Novohrad-Volynskyi in Zhytomyr Oblast.

The offensive went on in what was for the Russians the now typical fashion: with barbarity. During the night of 7 to 8 April, Russian social media began warning civilians against evacuating from Slovyansk and Kramatorsk by railway. Indeed, around 10.10hrs on 8 April, the Russian MOD reported attacks on railway stations in Slovyansk, Pokrovsk, and Barvinkove with 'high-precision air-launched missiles'. Only 15 minutes later, the media affiliated with the self-declared People's Republic of Donetsk published videos showing the launch of ballistic missiles from the Shakhtarsk area and, at 10.30hrs, two 9M79s armed with cluster munition warheads hit the railway station at Kramatorsk while it was full of civilians in the process of evacuation (the wreckage of one of missiles, together with inscription 'ЗА ДЕТЕЙ ДОНБАССА – *za detey donbassa*/ for the children of Donbass – was subsequently found at the scene, which was a common Russian propaganda slogan). The result was a massacre: 63 civilians – including nine children – were killed and over 150 injured. Immediately after, Russian state media claimed successful attacks on a 'military transport target' in Kramatorsk, but the Russian MOD denied responsibility for the mass murder, declaring it did not deploy Tochka-U missiles. Indeed, it claimed 'yet another false flag' attack by the 19th Missile Brigade of the ZSU. However, the VSRF is not only known to have repeatedly deployed 9M79s for attacks on Ukraine since 24 February: the movement of a column including BAZ-5921/9P129 TELs and trucks carrying OTR-21s from Belarus to Ukraine was captured on several videos taken on 5, 18, and 30 March, and, subsequently, multiple firings of Tochka-U missiles from eastern Ukraine were recorded by the ZSU.[27]

COLD CASES

During the month of March 2022, and in addition to those mentioned elsewhere, MiG-29 units of the PSZSU suffered a number of losses, the circumstances of which remain unclear. While the loss of Major Oleksandr Brynzhala and his MiG-29 on the night of 1 to 2 March was probably related to operations by Ukrainian Su-24s and Su-25s against the Russian ground forces north-west of Kyiv, not only the circumstances but even the exact place of several other cases remain mysterious. For example, around 08.00hrs on 5 March 2022, in the Malyn area outside Korosten in Zhytomyr Oblast, the PSZSU lost an unknown fighter jet that, according to the local district court 'was fired upon'. The pilot ejected safely and was recovered. Who exactly fired at the aircraft in question was not mentioned with a single word even in the conclusion of the related official investigation.[28] With Malyn being about 85km west of Kyiv, on the western fringe of the then combat zone, it is as likely that the aircraft in question was fired upon by the Russians as by the Ukrainians.

While the Ministry of Defence in Moscow claimed one Ukrainian MiG-29 as destroyed in Zhytomyr Oblast on 6 March, and another a day later (though without specifying the geographic area), the next confirmed loss of that type occurred on 8 March 2022, when a MiG-29S of the 40th Brigade, piloted by Major Andriy Lyutashyn (Deputy Commander for Training of this unit), was shot down near Berezivka in the Bucha area, and the pilot killed. How and why remains unknown: none of the available official and unofficial contacts in Russia and Ukraine would say.

On 10 March, the MOD in Moscow claimed the destruction of yet another Ukrainian MiG-29, and this was probably related to the above-described loss of Major Lisenko. However, a day later the PSZSU command published an online report according to which Ukrainian MiG-29s and Su-27s 'fought 10 air battles in different directions against superior enemy forces, fired nine short- and medium-range air-to-air missiles, and returned without losses'. Although the report in question concluded with hope for 'good news', nothing has ever been published, nor has anybody ever found any kind of traces of such intensive air combats on that day.

On 14 April 2022, a French TV team captured a video showing the burned-out wreckage of a Ukrainian MiG-29 in an empty field. Published in early May, one of the related photographs eventually enabled the geolocation of the crash site to the Nova Basan area, in the south-eastern corner of Chernihiv Oblast. Examination of the camouflage pattern (unique to each individual Ukrainian MiG-29) on the right side of the right fin of the wreckage enabled the identification of the jet as Bort 15 White from the 40th Brigade, PSZSU. Only later on, it transpired that the aircraft in question was shot down on 15 March: gauging by the trail it left on the ground, it is possible that the pilot attempted a belly landing, but then ejected, it remains unclear how or why.

Finally, perhaps one of the most mysterious Ukrainian losses occurred on 23 March 2022, over the Tryhirya area of Zhytomyr Oblast: a village on the Terriv River, about 20 kilometres west of Zhytomyr. The jet in question was a MiG-29S from the 204th Brigade, piloted by Major Dmitry Chumachenko, who was killed. While some unofficial Ukrainian sources claimed Chumachenko went down 'in an unequal air battle', rather unusually, the fallen pilot was never as highly decorated as most of his colleagues killed in action over Zhytomyr and Kyiv oblasts during the same period. At least as unusual is that neither Kyiv nor Moscow ever issued any kind of commentary related to this loss – and that, while unofficial Ukrainian sources are tight-lipped about this case, at least one unofficial Russian contact went as far as to stress that 'there are cases where it's absolutely unsafe to investigate'.[29]

All of this is even more surprising considering that a few months later, the Ministry of Defence in Moscow officially announced that the top 'ace' of the 'special military operation' was Major Alan Georgievich Datiev. When Datiev was decorated with the prestigious Hero of the Russian Federation medal, this Su-35S pilot from the 23rd Fighter Aviation Regiment (the first unit to operate the Su-35S in 2017), was described as 'flying combat sorties from the first day of the 'special military operation'. Correspondingly, he is claimed to have 'shot down three Ukrainian fighters in a nocturnal air combat', then a Su-25 and two Mi-24s in the course of a single air combat, and that while flying a total of 250 sorties, during which he also was credited with destruction of 'five S-300 air defence systems'. According to the Ministry of Defence in Moscow, Datiev's total score included '12 enemy aircraft and helicopters': three Su-24s, three Su-25s, two Su-27s, a MiG-29, two Mi-24s, and a TB.2.[30]

A still from a video showing a Ukrainian MiG-29 releasing an R-27 medium-range air-to-air missile on 25 February 2022. (Ukrainian social media)

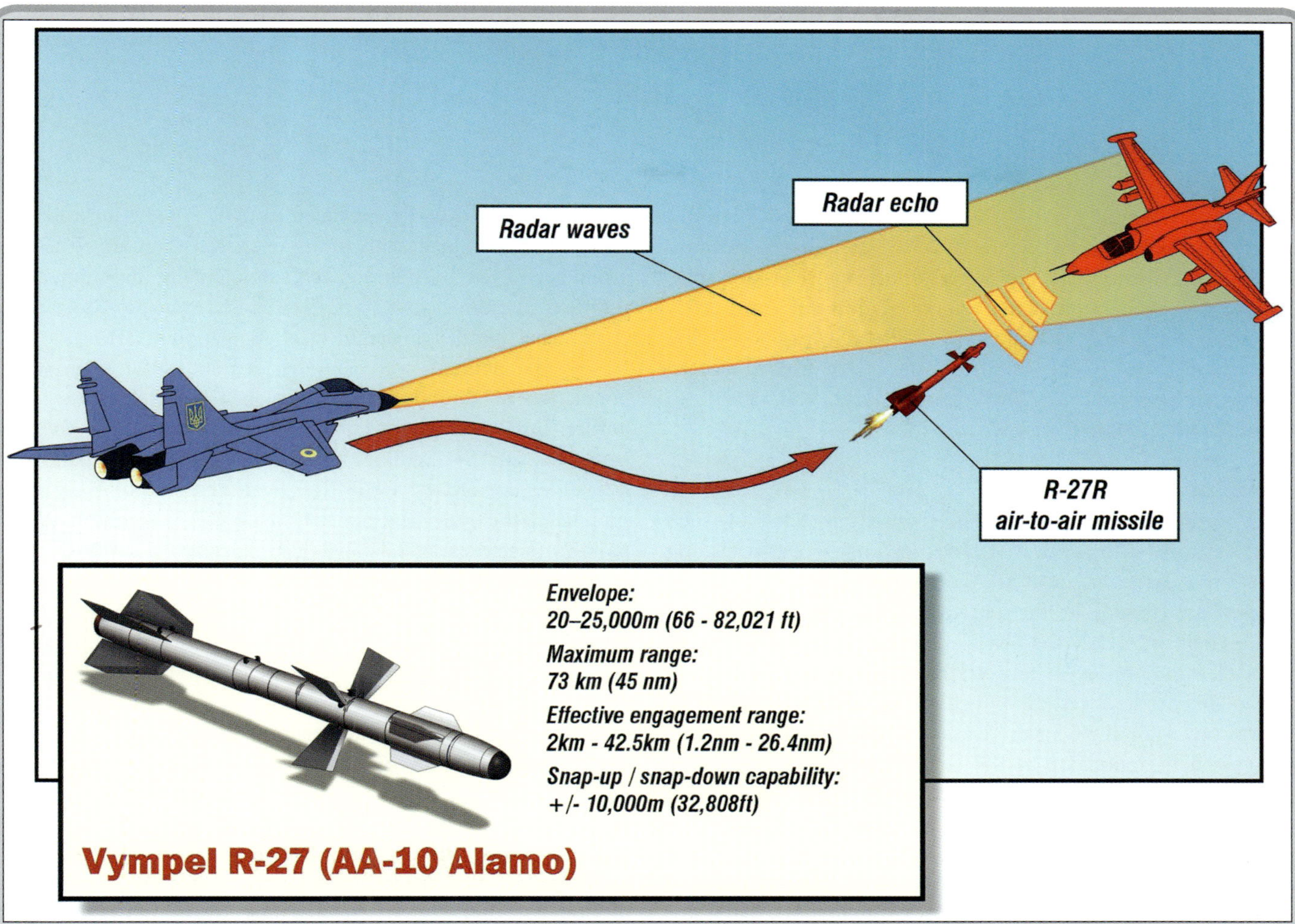

Radar waves
Radar echo
R-27R
air-to-air missile
Envelope:
20–25,000m (66 - 82,021 ft)
Maximum range:
73 km (45 nm)
Effective engagement range:
2km - 42.5km (1.2nm - 26.4nm)
Snap-up / snap-down capability:
+/- 10,000m (32,808ft)
Vympel R-27 (AA-10 Alamo)

The principal problem for Ukrainian MiG-29s and Su-27s in 2022 was their armament: their primary medium-range air-to-air missiles were the R-27R and R-27ER. Both required the launching aircraft to 'paint' the target for guidance. (Diagram by Anderson Subtil)

Helicopters
Aircraft
37 - 55km
(20 - 30nm)
Sukhoi Su-35
Vympel R-37M (AA-13 Axehead)

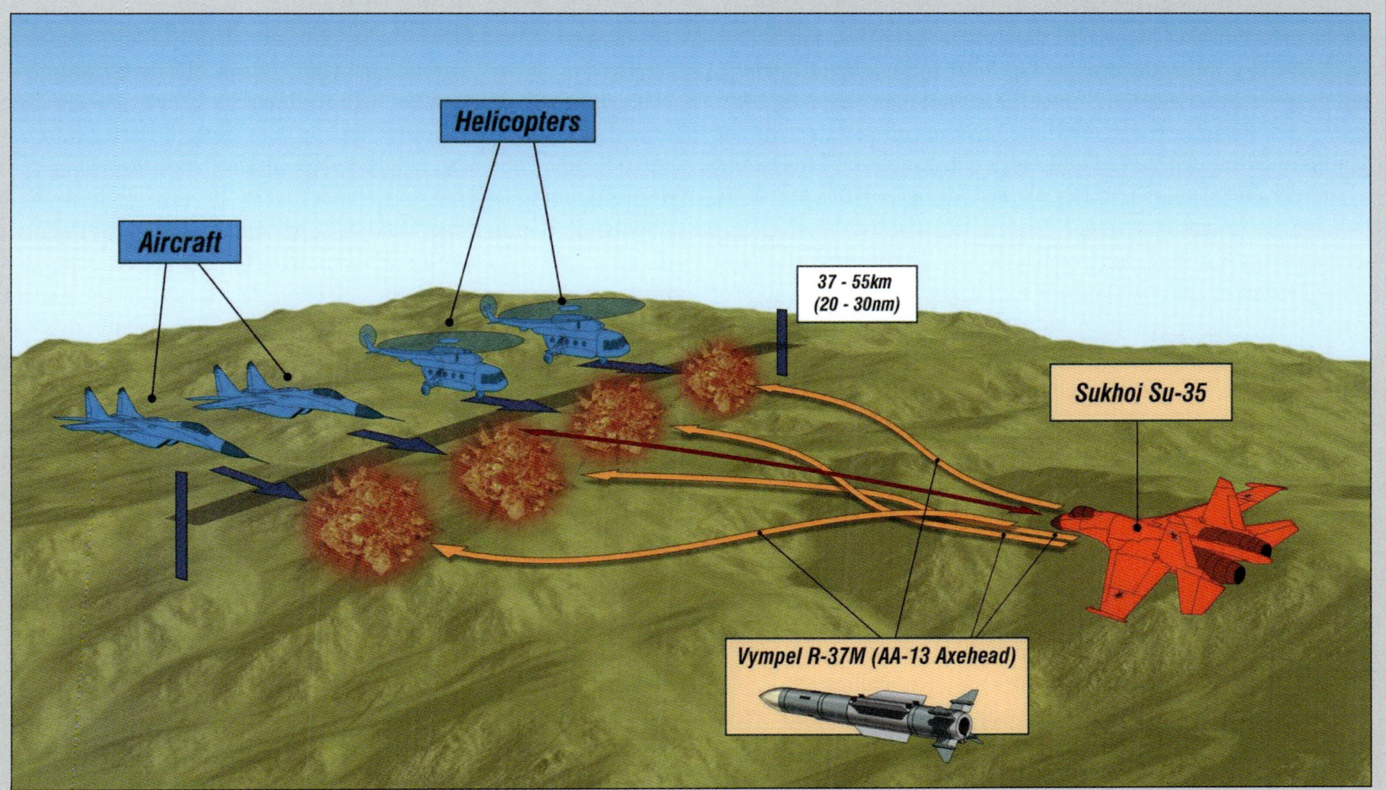

For comparison, thanks to availability of R-77-1 and R-37M active radar homing missiles, the Russian Su-35S was not only capable of simultaneously engaging multiple targets, but because they usually flew at high altitudes and high speeds, they could also do so from much longer ranges than low-flying Ukrainians armed with R-27s. (Diagram by Anderson Subtil)

2
IZYUM

Deeply overshadowed by the major battles for Kyiv, Chernihiv, Kharkiv, Mariupol, Kherson and Mykolaiv, the Russian advance into eastern Kharkiv Oblast, and the resulting capture of Kupyansk, Balakliya and Izyum, went almost unnoticed until early April 2022, when it threatened to drive into the rear of the ZSU positions along the northern sector of the so-called 'Line of Control' in eastern Ukraine: the area stretching from Slovyansk, via Kramatorsk, to Severodonetsk and Lysychansk.[1]

A Subplot[2]

While northern Ukraine was relatively well-protected by such natural obstacles as the Pripyat Marshes and huge forests stretching almost from Ratne in the north-west all the way to Chernihiv, and southern Ukraine by the Dnipro and Buh rivers, in eastern Ukraine there were only the Siversky Donets and Oskil rivers, as well as a few minor lakes in between that could be used by the ZSU to create defence lines resting on natural obstacles. Even then, the area was much too huge for the Ukrainian armed forces – which, as discussed in volumes 2 and 6, actually expected the Russian invasion to remain limited to Luhansk and Donetosk oblasts – to deploy enough active units to establish a continuous defence line right along the border. This in turn meant that, once they found themselves facing an all-out onslaught, the Ukrainians were left without options but to 'trade time for space': to withdraw ahead of the advancing Russians, while repeatedly ambushing or hitting their flanks, buying time for the mobilisation of additional forces in the rear. The flexible command system established by General Valeriy Zaluzhny since he was appointed the Commander-in-Chief ZSU in July 2021, did grant wide authority to local commanders, enabling them to operate as they found suitable and thus often unpredictably: indeed, to cause major troubles for the Russian commanders unused to doing anything without specific orders from above. This is why the latter found themselves facing a wide range of massive problems.

Certainly enough, the reason for the Russian forces advancing into the part of Ukraine immediately east of Kharkiv was the same corrupt system of rule by Vladimir Putin that was also in charge of the invasion: nobody less than Putin, Shoygu, and Gerasimov had launched an invasion in late winter, at the time the frost was thawing, resulting in much of the landscape converting into a sea of mud – the so-called *rasputitsa*. The second issue was the fact that the VSRF was critically short of logistic vehicles: it was completely dependent on railways for supplying the advance. The number of good roads in this part of Ukraine was limited and the majority ran either east-west or north-west-south-east, perpendicular to the main direction of the Russian advance. Combined, this meant that the movement of its units was limited to easily predictable routes along the local road system, and the entire advance actually depended on the VSRF's capability to secure the railway network and marshalling yards.

Although widely mis-assessed as a 'supporting effort' in the West, the Russian invasion of eastern Kharkiv was not only directly related to the assault on the second largest city in Ukraine, but also to the invasion of northern Luhansk Oblast. Indeed, it offered the promise of an advance into the rear of ZSU units defending the LOC: the part of the Ukrainian armed forces assessed by the Main (Intelligence) Directorate of the General Staff of the Armed Forces of the Russian Federation (in Russian abbreviated to GRU), as the most likely to seriously resist. Finally, this prong of the invasion aimed to seize a number of relatively minor, but sentimentally important urban centres – all claimed as 'historically Russian', even 'pro-Russian', due to the behaviour of some of the local population in 2014.

The first of these was Kupyansk: an industrial town with a population of around 27,000, positioned relatively close to the border: this was a major railway and highway hub on the links between Izyum, Severodonetsk, Slovyansk, and eastern Kharkiv, and it included one of very few bridges over the Oskil River capable of supporting the movement of heavy vehicles. The second important point in this area was Balakliya (also Balakliia): a town of around 26,000 on the Balakliia River, on the northeast side of the Siverski Donets River: an important railroad junction, and the site of one of the biggest ammunition dumps in north-eastern Ukraine. Arguably, on 23 March 2017, much of the latter was blown up in a series of massive explosions suspected to have been instigated by Russian saboteurs. The detonation and resulting debris and fires might have killed only one person and wounded about 20, but they damaged more than 250 buildings and forced the evacuation of almost the entire population of Balakliya. Moreover, this catastrophe was followed by two additional, similar incidents: one on 3 May 2018, and another on 15 November 2019. Combined, they destroyed up to a third of the ZSU's stocks of artillery shells and surface-to-air missiles left since the times of the USSR.[3]

Situated in a valley of the Donets River in eastern Kharkiv Oblast, the third principal objective of this prong of the Russian invasion was the industrial town of Izyum: about 120km south-east of Kharkiv, it was yet another major hub of highway and railway connections, and – together with Kramatorsk – the crucial military base in this part of Ukraine. Finally, Sloviansk, a town of around 100,000 in the northern Donetsk Oblast, was the principal objective of this operation. Based on the fact that in 2014 the majority of its population opposed the Maidan movement in Kyiv, and the place then became the epicentre of separatism and had to be reconquered by the ZSU in a three-month-long battle, Sloviansk became a sort of obsession both for Putin and the *GenStab* in Moscow. Unsurprisingly considering this set of circumstances, the task of securing Kupyansk, Balakliya, Izyum, Slovyansk and Kramatorsk was assigned to an entire combined arms army (CAA), and – at least from the Russian point of view – was anything but a 'supporting effort'.[4]

Commanded by Lieutenant General Vladislav Nikolaevich Yershov, the 6th Combined Arms Army (6th CAA) was tasked not only with seizing Sloviansk, but also with completing the encirclement of Kharkiv around its eastern and southern side and reaching Dnipropetrovsk. Because all these aims required a large force, Yershov's headquarters not only went into action with almost all of the units usually assigned to his command, but significantly reinforced. Amongst others, the 6th CAA controlled the 95th Command and 132nd Signals brigades, two battalion tactical groups (BTGs) from each of its principal manoeuvre assets – the 25th and 138th Guards Motor-Rifle brigades – as well as the entire 9th Guards Artillery Brigade, the 26th Rocket Artillery Brigade, the 5th Anti-Aircraft Missile Brigade, and the 30th Engineering Regiment. Additionally, it received six BTGs of the 144th Guards Motor-Rifle

The detonation of the Balakliya depot on 23 March 2017 destroyed vast stocks of ammunition left over from Soviet times, dramatically reducing the reserves of the entire ZSU. (Ukrainian Ministry of Defence)

Division, the 22nd Spetsnaz Brigade of the GRU, and a small BTG of the GRU-controlled Redut Private Military Company (PMC). Finally, OSK West was to provide the 6th CAA with a sizeable portion of air support from the 6th Air and Air Defence Forces Army. Commanded by Lieutenant Colonel Oleg Maktovetsky, this included the 332nd Helicopter Aviation Regiment and the 105th Composite Aviation Division, comprising the 14th Fighter Aviation Regiment (Su-30s), 47th Composite Aviation Regiment (Su-34s), 159th Fighter Aviation Regiment (Su-35s), and 790th Fighter Aviation Regiment (Su-35s).

While it must be kept in mind that the original plan developed by Putin, Shoygu, and Gerasimov over-optimistically (if not irrationally) assessed that the Ukrainians would not only not resist, but actually side with invaders, and the VSRF was thus expected to, essentially, march around Kharkiv and then all the way to Dnipropetrovsk. There is no doubt that the tasks assigned to the 6th CAA were wildly overoptimistic. Certainly enough, as of early 2022, and except in the areas east of Sloviansk and Kramatorsk, the ZSU had very few active units deployed: initially, these included just the 92nd Mechanised Brigade (which defended Kharkiv and Chuhuiv), and the partially mobilised 113th Territorial Defence Brigade (working up in between Chuhiv and Izyum). Arguably, between them, and the 53rd Mechanised and the 57th Motorised brigades – both deployed in northern Luhansk – there was a huge gap, covered by the Border Guards and the police only. It was only in early March that about a squadron of operators from the Special Forces Command (*Syly spetsialnykh operatsii*, SSO), a company or two from the Territorial Defence, elements of the 81st Airborne Assault Brigade, and then the 25th Mechanised Brigade reached the Izyum area. Correspondingly, and as in north-eastern Ukraine, early during the campaign, the ZSU had few options but to try stemming the Russian onslaught through ambushes and mobile defence, while doing its best to avoid encirclement, before starting to construct a frontline along the Siversky Donets River.

For its part, the PSZSU had not even one ground-based air defence unit deployed east of Chuhiv AB: indeed, as described in Volume 6, right at the start of their invasion, the Russians mauled both the 164th Radio-Technical Brigade and the 302nd Anti-Aircraft Missile Regiment (equipped with S-300PT SAM systems), effectively knocking out the air defences of Kharkiv. Moreover, Chuhiv AB was heavily hit, and whatever was left of Ukrainian aircraft and unmanned aerial vehicles (UAVs) quickly evacuated. Therefore, except for the organic anti-aircraft defence elements of the 92nd Mechanised Brigade (equipped with Osa-AKMs), and the few man-portable air defence systems (MANPADS) of that brigade and the 113th Territorial Defence Brigade, in this area, the Ukrainian air defences were next to non-existent in the early days of the war.

Capture of Kupyansk

Led by infiltrated operatives of the 78th Special Reconnaissance Centre and the 22nd Spetsnaz Brigade of the GRU, the associated Redut PMC, and local sympathisers, the spearheads of the 6th CAA crossed the border into Ukraine at 04.55hrs on 24 February 2022. In a matter of hours, the Russians secured Vovchansk: from there, one BTG of the 138th Motor-Rifle Brigade rushed to seize Staryi Saltiv, while another travelled via Prykolotne and Velykyi Burluk to cross the Siversky Donets River at Pechenihy. As described in Volume 2, this Russian advance occurred so quickly that it cut off the II Battalion of the 92nd Mechanised Brigade, deployed north of Staryi Saltiv. While searching for a way back to Kharkiv, the Ukrainian unit then moved down the T2104 road – only to run into a BTG of Rosgvardia and completely demolish it in the process. While the II Battalion of the 92nd thus managed to return to Kharkiv, another battalion of this brigade managed to stop one BTG of the 138th Motor-Rifle Brigade short of the E40 highway east of Kharkiv, while a third prevented the southern prong of the Russian advance from seizing Chuhuiv and the nearby air base. With this, the plan for the 6th CAA to circumnavigate and thus encircle and isolate Kharkiv

Su-35S Bort 23 (registration RF-81763), from the 159th Fighter Aviation Regiment, in 2021. (Photo by Daniele Faccioli)

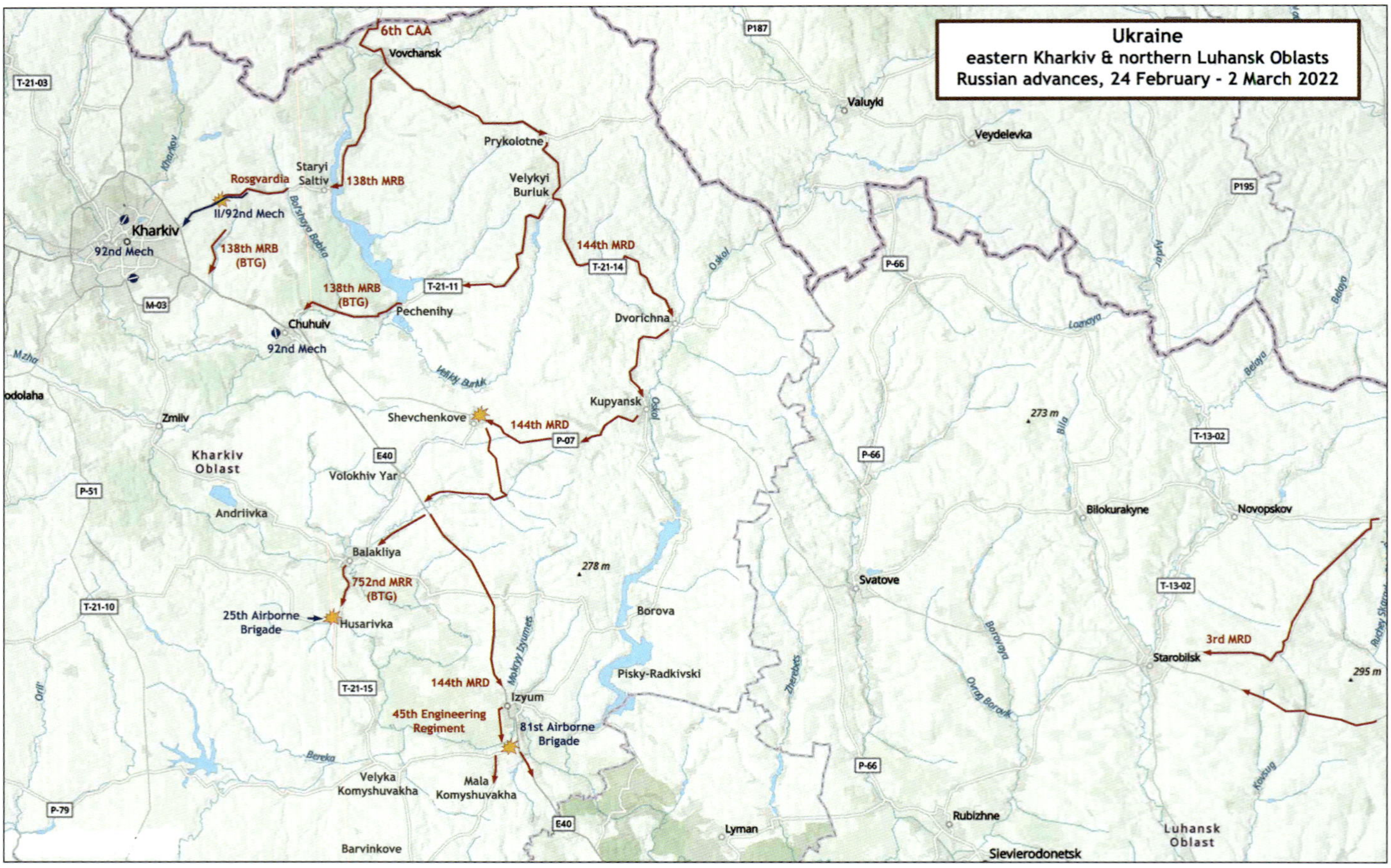

A map of eastern Kharkiv Oblast and northern Luhansk, reconstructing the advance of the 6th CAA from Vovchansk via Kupyansk and Balakliya to Izyum, 24 February – 2 March 2022. (Map by Tom Cooper)

around its eastern and southern sides, was completely ruined within the first 36 hours of the all-out invasion.[5]

However, east of the Siversky Donets River, Major General Vladimir Vitalyevich Sleptsov's 144th Motor-Rifle Division advanced much better. Moving via Dvorichna, its spearhead – a BTG of the 488th Motor-Rifle Regiment – approached Kupyansk on the afternoon of 24 February 2022. Although expected to be 'sympathetic', the local population proved largely anti-Russian: confused, but still keen not to turn the civilians against them, Yershov and Sleptsov then spent two days negotiating the surrender of the town. Finally, on 27 February, and after the Russians threatened to savage Kupyansk with their artillery, mayor Hennadiy Matsehora made a highly controversial decision to capitulate. With this critical traffic hub under their control, the Russians then rushed all available forces in the direction of Izyum. An attempt by a BTG from the 488th Motor-Rifle to seize Shevchenkove failed, but the unit then used secondary roads to find a way further south, and on 2 March 2022, spearheads of the 144th Motor-Rifle Division seized Balakliya. Once there, Yershov redirected the rest of Sleptsov's division to the south: after advancing down the M03, two days later his T-72s appeared on the northern approaches to Izyum. Thus began a bitter battle that was to last for almost a month.

Battle of Izyum

Regardless how well-motivated, how eager to oppose the invader, and how much this might have surprised the Russians, the Ukrainian defences of Izyum, early on, were weak. In addition to SSO operators and two companies of Territorial Defence, they included about a battalion of the 81st Airborne Assault Brigade. Additional reinforcements – including elements of the 3rd Tank and the 95th Airborne Assault brigades – were to arrive only days later. Therefore, the fate of Izyum initially mainly depended on what

A pre-war photograph of a Buk M1 TELAR. (Ukrainian MOD)

A still from a video showing a well-concealed Buk M1 TELAR of the PSZSU, launching a missile in the Izyum area on 30 March 2022. (ZSU)

the 92nd Mechanised was doing in the Chuhuiv area. There, on 6 or 7 March – as the 6th CAA was busy rushing additional troops towards Izyum – the Ukrainian brigade ambushed and mauled a BTG of the 138th Motor-Rifle Brigade. With his western flank thus being ripped open, and constantly troubled by mud, Yershov spent two days reorganising his troops 'instead' of continuing his push towards the south.

This is why it was only on 11 March 2022, that the 6th CAA resumed its attack on Izyum. Even then, Ukrainian defences were still so weak that the Russians – supported by about 30 air strikes by Su-30s and Ka-52s – quickly secured most of the town north of the Siversky Donets, and Yershov ordered them across the river. However, poor weather and soft terrain cost him much time – which in turn enabled the ZSU to bring in reinforcements. Amongst the latter was the first Buk M1-equipped unit of the PSZSU known to have been operational in this sector. On 13 March, as the VKS began flying preparatory air strikes to soften the Ukrainian defences in southern Izyum, the Ukrainian unit shot down Su-34 Bort 35 (Registration RF-95010) of the 559th Bomber Aviation Regiment directly over the city. Although one of the two crewmembers was reportedly captured, it seems that both were recovered by the Russians. Two days later, on 15 March, the same Ukrainian Buk M1 unit also shot down Su-30SM Bort 62 (registration RF-81771) from the 14th Fighter Aviation Regiment. This time the crew – Lieutenant Colonel Alexander Pazynych and Captain Evgeny Kislyakov – were killed.

Wreckage of Su-30SM Bort 62 (registration RF-81771), shot down on 15 March 2022 while attacking Ukrainian positions in southern Izyum. (Photo by Anastasia Yushkevich)

Under constant pressure from Moscow, and while bringing the 30th Engineering Regiment and a complete PMP floating bridge into action, Yershov requested additional air support. Once ready, on 17 March he ordered his troops into an assault in the simplest but also the most obvious direction: near the Barvinkivsky Highway Bridge spanning the Siversky Donets. A few days earlier, this had been demolished – together with several Russian combat vehicles – by the SSO during the withdrawal into southern Izyum. However, while approaching the town, one of the Russian BTGs was ambushed by Ukrainians that were roaming the enemy flanks, and suffered heavy losses: undertaken by insufficient forces, the crossing attempt then collapsed amid fierce resistance.[6]

Unimpressed, Yershov organised a new attempt: this time, he ordered the Spetsnaz, a BTG of the 144th Motor-Rifle Division, and the 45th Engineering Regiment through the poorly-defended forests west of Izyum. Eventually, they managed to find two suitable crossing sites and to construct two pontoon bridges across the

By the time the VSRF approached Izyum, the *GenStab* in Moscow had no reservations regarding the deployment of cluster munitions nor incendiaries against densely built-up urban areas of Ukraine. This photograph shows Russian incendiaries in the night sky over Izyum on 23 March 2022. (Ukrainian social media)

A still showing the wreckage of one of about a dozen Russian BMP-3s knocked out in Ukrainian ambushes north of Izyum on 17–18 March 2022. (Public Kharkiv)

Siversky Donets in the Donetske area, three kilometres south-east of the town. Although taken by surprise, the Ukrainians reacted fiercely: their air strikes and artillery destroyed one of the PMPs, knocked out most of the engineering equipment, and caused heavy losses both to the 144th Division and the 45th Engineering Regiment (the latter lost even its commander). Nevertheless, the Russians persisted: they expanded the bridgehead and then bolstered their air defences. When the PSZSU attempted to hit the second bridge, on 22 March 2022, one of its Su-24Ms – Bort 49 – was shot down by Pantsirs, shortly after releasing four OFAB-500ShN parachute-retarded bombs. The jet crashed outside the village of Sulyhivka, about 15km south of the two Russian pontoon bridges: the pilot, Major Oleksiy Kovalenko, was killed, but his bombardier-navigator ejected safely and was captured by the Russians.

Counterattack at Husarivka

Meanwhile, on 16 March, the Ministry of Defence in Moscow claimed to have captured Barvinkove – another major railway and road hub, 40 kilometres south of Izyum, and 80km west of Slovyansk. At the time, Yershov's 6th CAA was still at least a day short of crossing the Siversky Donetsk at any point, and thus this claim could not but be characterised as another wild exaggeration and an attempt to unnerve the defenders of Izyum. Actually, from 17 to 23 March, the ZSU garrison in the town was busy evacuating along the M03/E40 highway in the southern direction, while the 81st Airborne was holding off repeated attempts of the 144th Motor-Rifle Division to seize Kamyanka and the local section of the M03/E40 highway. Eventually, it took Yershov throwing in his last reserve – a BTG of the 59th Guards Tank Regiment and a barrage by TOS-1 Buratino heavy flamethrowers (equipped with thermobaric warheads) – to seize the village on 24 March: around the same time the Ministry of Defence in Moscow proudly announced it was in full control of Izyum.

Actually, the 6th CAA was too short of troops and most of the Ukrainian garrison withdrew in good order: even if shaken, the 81st Airborne retreated to defence positions in Mala Komyshuvakha and Sukha Kamyanka. Thus, when Yershov's regrouped troops resumed their assault, they ran into fierce resistance. Arguably, the *GenStab* in Moscow and the headquarters of OSKs West and South did their best to support his efforts: amongst others, they ordered two BTGs – one each from the 252nd and the 752nd Motor-Rifle regiments – from the 3rd Motor-Rifle Division of the 20th CAA all the way from Svatove in north-western Luhansk to the Izyum area. However, for unclear reasons – possibly related to the need to outflank Ukrainian defences south of Izyum – they were ordered to cross the Siversky Donets in the Balakliya area, seize Husarivka and advance on Barinkove from that direction, instead of being deployed for the advance from Izyum in a southern direction. Considering the distances the two BTGs had to travel, and the fact they were doing so perpendicular to the direction of 6th CAA's axis of advance, it is unsurprising it took them days to complete this manoeuvre. Nevertheless, the plan appeared to work and by 25 March the first of two BTGs crossed the Siversky Donets at Bairak and reached Husarivka.

For a few hours at least, it appeared as if the VSRF had outmanoeuvred the ZSU and the way to Barvinkove was open. Actually, the Russians took too long: a day later, on 26 March, as command elements of the 6th CAA were in the process of setting up their forward headquarters in Husarivka, the place was suddenly hit by a counterattack of the Ukrainian 25th Airborne Brigade. Advancing along the T2110 road from the West, the Ukrainians shot up numerous BTR-82As of the 752nd Motor-Rifle Regiment, then entered the village and destroyed much of both the 95th Command and the 132nd Signal brigades, and even a complete Tor M1 air defence battery. They were stopped only by a counterattack of T-72s from the 252nd Motor-Rifle Regiment. According to the Ukrainian media reports, at that point in time, Yershov was relieved of his command by Putin.[7]

Russian SEAD

While proving unable to conduct more than sporadic strikes by Su-24Ms against the Russian bridgeheads at Bairak and Donetske, the

One of two pontoon bridges constructed by the 45th Engineering Regiment over the Siversky Donets north of Donetske: while the other bridge was destroyed by Ukrainian artillery, this one survived, enabling the Russians to break through towards the south and, eventually, force the Ukrainian garrison of Izyum to withdraw. (Ukrainian MOD)

A BTR-82A of the Russian army seen crossing the PMP bridge over the Siversky Donets River north of Donetske and south-west of Izyum, in early April 2022. Notable around the bridge is the wreckage of sunken trucks, PMP sections, and a T-72 main battle tank – all left-overs from the fierce fighting for this bridgehead on 17–19 March 2022. (Ukrainian MOD)

PSZSU continued bolstering its ground-based air defence assets in the area south-east of Kharkiv and south of Izyum. Between 25 and 28 March, the first Buk M1-equipped unit known to have appeared there was redeployed to support a local counteroffensive of the 92nd Mechanised Brigade, carried out in the area between Malaya Rogan and Vikhivtsi, north of the M03/E40 section connecting Kharkiv and Chuhiv. In three days of fighting, the Russians suffered over 500 casualties, while 50 were captured: according to Ukrainian reports, three Russian BTGs, including the headquarters of the 138th Motor-Rifle Brigade were destroyed. Atop this, the Buk M1 unit supporting the 92nd claimed to have shot down several Orlan-10s and one Ka-52. Meanwhile, the second Ukrainian Buk M1 unit was deployed in support of the 81st Airborne Brigade: on 27 March, it claimed 'two Su-34s' felled over the Izyum area. Eventually one was confirmed: Su-30SM Bort 60 (registration RF-81771) from the 14th Fighter Aviation Regiment, shot down over Mala Komyshuvakha. The pilot, Colonel Serhiy Kosyk, was captured, but the navigator managed to evade and return to the Russian positions. Three days later, on 30 March the same unit then also claimed a 'Russian Mi-35' as shot down in the same area: actually hit was Mi-28 Bort 65 (registration

One of three 9T44 transloaders for the 9K330/331 Tor M1 SAM system of the 3rd Motor-Rifle Division, smashed during the counterattack of the 25th Airborne Assault Brigade on Husarivka, on 26 March 2022. (GenStab-U)

RF-13628): this time, the crew consisting of Major Artem Ogoltsov and Captain Alexander Prikhodko did not survive.

The PSZSU is known to have also suffered a loss on the same day: a Su-24 (versions differ over whether the aircraft was a Su-24M bomber or Su-24MR reconnaissance fighter) crewed by Colonel Maxim Sikalenko (contemporary Deputy Commander of the 7th Brigade) and Major Konstantin Gorodnichev was underway on a mission to mine a road in the area south of Izyum with the use of KMGU dispensers. Over the combat zone, the jet was damaged by a Russian SAM, and the crew decided to attempt saving the precious bomber with an emergency landing at Kanatovo AB outside Kirovohrad. The aircraft crashed outside the base, killing both crewmembers.

Taken by surprise by the activity of the Ukrainian air defences in the Izyum sector, OSK West reacted by ordering the VKS into its first major SEAD (suppression of enemy air defences) operation of this conflict. Involving about 40 aircraft and helicopters, and lasting at least six days (from 28 March until 3 April), this saw the deployment of an A-50, one Il-22M airborne command post, two Ilyushin Il-20M communications/signals and electronic intelligence gathering aircraft, one Ilyushin Il-22PP electronic warfare aircraft, several Su-24MR reconnaissance aircraft, and a squadron each of Su-30s, Su-34s, and Su-35s. Using Il-20Ms and Il-22PPs to triangulate the radar emissions of Ukrainian Buk M1s and Osa-AKMs, as well as the radio and mobile telephone communications of their crews, and with the A-50 for air traffic control, the Russians deployed a number of target drones to prompt into action the PSZSU units they were seeking. As soon as the Ukrainian SAMs powered up, the Il-22M and A-50 would then direct one formation after another of between two and four fighter-bombers into air strikes. Usually, a pair of Su-34s – armed with either eight FAB-250M-62, or four FAB-500M-62, free-fall bombs, or four parachute-retarded OFAB-250ShN or OFAB-500ShN bombs, sometimes with up to four RBK-500 cluster bomb units (CBUs) – was escorted by a single Su-30SM or Su-35S armed with Kh-31P or (rarely) Kh-58 anti-radiation missiles. The latter were deployed first and pre-emptively: fired in the direction of the suspected Ukrainian SAM position to arrive there shortly before Su-34s attacked: the expectation was that if any enemy air defence system powered up, it would promptly attract the anti-radiation missile. As far as is known, such operations were launched up to five or six times a day, every two to three hours, thus keeping the Ukrainian air defences under near-constant pressure.[8]

Dangerous 'Work Behind the Fence'

The effort proved only partially effective. After losing three 9A310M1 transporter erector launchers with radar (TELARs) of their Buk M1 systems, the commanders of the Ukrainian firing units learned to not only operate under total emission control but also to change their positions much more frequently than trained for before the war. In this fashion, they began 'disappearing'. Moreover, the PSZSU went as far as to exploit the Russian preoccupation with hunting SAMs to start setting up ambushes for the Russian fliers.[9]

On 3 April 2022, when the VKS pushed particularly hard, sending even its Il-22Ms into Ukrainian airspace to better guide attack helicopters and fighter-bombers, the PSZSU Buk crews managed to target one of these precious aircraft. The Il-22M piloted by Major Viktor Volodin was damaged while underway at an altitude of 7,600 metres: the proximity-fused warhead peppered the forward fuselage with shrapnel. Retaining control, Volodin rolled the aircraft and rapidly descended to low altitude before distancing away, while his flight engineer and radio operator helped extinguish a fire in the oxygen system: at that point in time, the second Ukrainian missile detonated behind the aircraft, causing damage to the fin. With the fire out, and all engines still working, and although the aircraft 'leaked fuel like a sieve', the crew decided to return all the way to Rostov-na-Donu. Volodin landed his Il-22M safely, and the

A Su-35S wearing the 'Serdyukov' camouflage pattern (colloquially known as 'Negro' within the VKS), and with an icon just behind the cockpit area, seen early during the war, taxiing while armed with four R-77-1s, a pair of Kh-31PDs, and two R-73 or R-74s. The aircraft painted this way belonged to a batch of six delivered to the VKS in late 2012. (Russian Ministry of Defence)

An Il-22PP of the VKS, returning from a sortie over Ukraine to Rostov-na-Donu on 4 April 2022. Equipped with powerful systems for electronic countermeasures, the three Il-22PPs in service at the time were in much demand. (Russian social media)

A still from a video showing a hit on Mi-28 Bort 65 (registration RF-14628) over Holuvivske, in the Popasna area, on 30 March 2022. The helicopter lost its boom as result and crashed seconds later. (ZSU)

An Enix target drone deployed by the VKS in late March 2022 as a decoy in an attempt to prompt Ukrainian SAMs in the Izyum area to activate their radars and thus reveal their positions. (Ukrainian social media)

This still from a video taken early on 3 April 2022, shows the final moments of Major Malov's Su-35S. Gauging by the long trail of smoke, the aircraft was underway at around 2,000 metres altitude when hit. (video by Yurii Kochevenko)

An Il-20M or Il-38 undergoing overhaul at the 20th Aircraft Repair Plant, in Pushkin, south of St. Petersburg. As far as is known, after the Il-22M damaged by Ukrainian Buks on 3 April 2022 was restored to flyable status, it was sent to the same factory for comprehensive repairs and a major update. (20th Aircraft Repair Plant)

ground crews subsequently counted over 200 holes in the wing and fuselage.[10]

Later the same day, at least a pair of Ukrainian Su-24Ms bombed the Russian pontoon bridges on the Siversky Donets: when an enterprising Su-35S pilot, Major Sergey Vladimirovich Malov from the 159th Fighter Aviation Regiment, ventured too far west while trying to catch one of the fast Ukrainian bombers, his jet, Bort 61 (registration RF-81752) was hit by at least one Buk missile and crashed south of Pisky-Radkivski. Malov was captured by local civilians and handed over to the ZSU, while the Ukrainian 'message' was more than clear: although relatively small the concentration of PSZSU and ZSU SAMs in the southern Izyum area had survived the enemy onslaught and remained a threat to VKS aircraft and helicopters.

The crash site of Su-35S Bort 61, registration RF-81752, shot down by Ukrainian Buk M1 SAMs on 3 April 2022. This was the first Russian loss of this type in the war. Notably, the jet came down while still armed with two Kh-58 anti-radiation missiles, and its jammer pod on the left wing-tip remained largely intact. It is very likely that the last was recovered by the Ukrainians for closer inspection. (via Anton Gerashchenko)

3
PLAN C

For the invasion of Ukraine, the Armed Forces of the Russian Federation deployed around 190 BTGs with up to 190,000 troops, of which about 120,000 were inside the country by the first week of March. However, the ZSU had begun mobilising its Operational Reserve 1 on 18 February 2022, and a day or two later it recalled Operational Reserve 2.[1] In grand total, by mid-March, the Ukrainians thus bolstered their manpower to more than 250,000, and then to more than 300,000. Although lacking advanced and heavy weaponry, and especially the firepower of the VSRF's artillery, they began receiving sizeable shipments of modern heavy infantry weapons of Western origin, primarily in the form of light anti-tank guided missiles (ATGMs) and MANPADs. Moreover, due to the geography of the country, and the fact that the Russians invaded simultaneously from the north, east, and south, the ZSU enjoyed the advantage of inner lines of communication: essentially, this meant that it was easier to move troops and supplies around the frontlines, as necessary. Combined, this resulted in the Russian chances of continuing a rapid advance deep into Ukraine and seizing major urban centres waning almost by the hour.

Withdrawal

Nowhere was this more obvious than in the Kyiv area, where not only all the Russian attempts to drive into the city were spoiled, but even the efforts of the 35th Combined Arms Army (35th CAA) to cross the Irpin River at Moshchun, or to isolate the capital through an advance west and south of it were all spoiled: at most, they resulted in weeks-long, bitter house-to-house battles for the western suburbs of Kyiv – a form of combat for which both the VSRF and the VDV lacked training, and for which Putin lacked patience.[2] Moreover, at the high point of the battle for Moshchun, and midway through the attempt of the 35th CAA to widen its salient west of Kyiv through attacks by BTGs of the 5th Tank and 37th Motor-Rifle brigades west of Lypivka, Makariv, Kopyliv, and Motyzhyn, on 15 March the Ukrainians launched a counterattack on Bucha, Hostomel, and Irpin. This not only forced the 35th CAA to stop its attempts to isolate Kyiv from western Ukraine but forced it to withdraw. Indeed, Irpin was cleared of invaders by 22 March, by when also the crossing attempt at Moshchun was literally washed away by flooding caused when the Ukrainians blew up a dam connecting the Irpin River with the Kyiv Reservoir.

Finally, supported by ZSU artillery – which was able to still draw upon sizeable stocks of shells evacuated from depots before these were hit by the Russian air and missile strikes – the ZSU began attacking the western flank of the demoralised 35th CAA all the way from Bucha in the south to Ivankyiv in the north.

The situation overstretched the Russian formations on the approaches to Kyiv east of Dnipro and was becoming even more critical. Although besieging Chernihiv, the 41st Combined Arms Army proved unable to capture the city. Further south, on 18 March, the spearheads of the 2nd Guards Combined Arms Army (2nd GCAA) were bogged down in the mud while attempting to seize Brovary, while their supply columns were continuously savaged by Ukrainian ambushes. Although the commander of this army, Major General Vyacheslav Nikolaevich Gurov, did his best to follow Putin's orders and continue attacking into Brovary as late as 22–23 March, the writing was soon on the wall: another Ukrainian counterattack into the southern flank of the 2nd GCAA forced Gurov to pull back his troops to the Nova Basan area: by 25 March, the ZSU was already on the approaches to Pryluky, where the Ukrainian garrison held out against three weeks of siege.

At that point in time, a major catastrophe befell the deep flank of the 1st Guards Tanks Army (1st GTA): since 21 March, a BTG of its 200th Motor-Rifle Brigade had been assaulting Trostianets. Indeed, the Russians were already in the process of overwhelming defenders and entering the town when suddenly hit by a counterattack by the 93rd Mechanised Brigade, which approached undetected from the direction of Okhtyrka. According to Ukrainian reports, the Russian BTG was completely annihilated, losing 648 troops killed and three captured (two of whom were wounded). From Putin's point of view, this catastrophe 'over-spilled the barrel': he dismissed the commander of the – nominally – most powerful army-level formation of the VSRF, Lieutenant General Sergey Kisel. Of course, this changed little on the battlefield, where the 93rd Mech then liberated the village of Boromlya and launched a pursuit of the withdrawing enemy in the direction of Sumy, capturing scores of abandoned T-80s, MSTA-S and other armoured vehicles of the 2nd Guards Motor-Rifle Division in the process. By 27 March, the Ukrainians had lifted the siege of Lebedyn, of Sumy, and of Romny further west. Finally, on 31 March, the ZSU cleared both the P69 and M01 highways to reach Chernihiv and lift the siege of that city, too. Indeed, by 4 April, the majority of VSRF troops had completely withdrawn from Kyiv, Chernihiv, and Sumy oblasts, leaving behind hundreds of abandoned vehicles, huge amounts of equipment, and hundreds of scattered troops captured by the Ukrainians.

Shifting the Focus

The reason for the apparent collapse and withdrawal of the Russian formations in northern-central and north-eastern Ukraine was that in the meantime Putin had completely changed his strategy: abandoning the plots to topple the government in Kyiv and seize almost all of Ukraine, he ordered a general withdrawal from the three oblasts in the north. The decision in question was probably taken during, or under the impression of, the meeting of the Security Council of the Russian Federation held on 24 March 2022. In the course of this, Putin discussed the situation with Sergei Shoigu, Valery Gerasimov, Nikolai Patrushev (former Director of the FSB, and then the Secretary of the Security Council of Russia, and one of the 'hawks' playing a crucial role in convincing Putin to launch the invasion), and the Director of FSB, Alexander Bortnikov. The televised section of the meeting showed Putin completely ignoring Bortnikov's report and rebuking Gerasimov's complaints about 'significant' losses in troops and equipment by explaining to him that a loss of 30,000–50,000 men is nothing comparable to what Russia would achieve through its victory. The fact that Petrushev (in the part of the meeting that was shown on Russian TV) did report that 'everything is prepared' for a general mobilisation, was indicative of the five men already concluding that Russia urgently needed to downscale the invasion in order to find troops necessary to secure at least all of Luhansk, Donetsk, Zaporizhzhya, and Kherson oblasts. Rather unsurprisingly, Putin thus opted for what

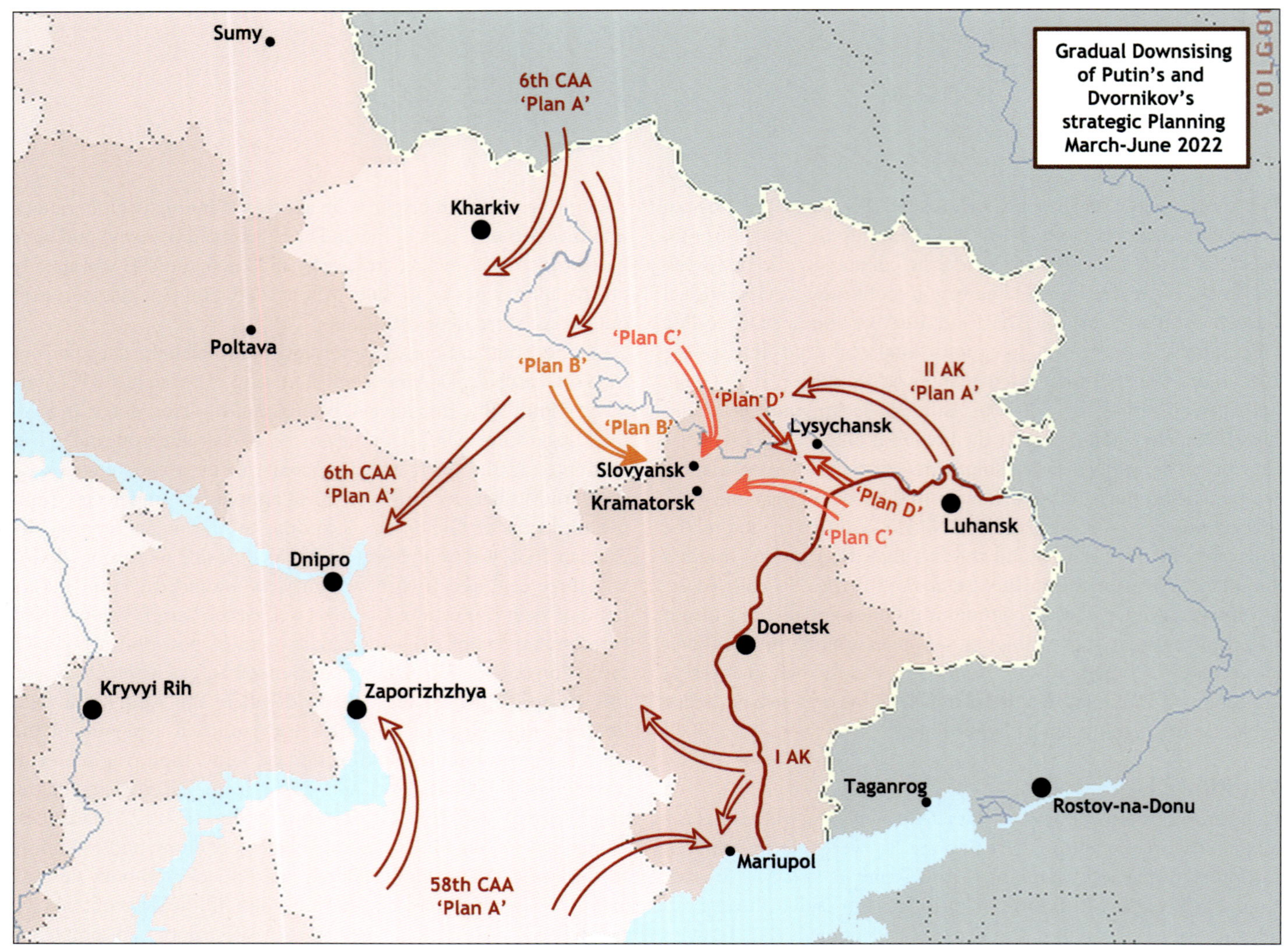

A map depicting the approximate directions of various Russian strategic-level plans for eastern Ukraine – from the original 'Plan A', which envisaged the occupation of Kharkiv and 6th CAA's advance on Dnipro (combined with the advance of the 58th CAA on Zaporizhzhya from the south); via 'Plan B', which led to the crossing of the Siversky Donets and breakthrough at Izyum but was stopped well before reaching Slovyansk; 'Plan C', which began with the combined assault from Izyum towards Slovyansk, and on to Popasna, but resulted in the capture of Lyman; to 'Plan D', described in the next chapter. Notably, due to massive losses in equipment and personnel, every new plan resulted in the gradual downsizing of the overall objective. (Map by Tom Cooper)

can be described as his 'Plan C': refocusing the aims of the war to securing the four eastern and southern oblasts of Ukraine making use of the troops freed through the withdrawal from the north, planned to be completed in two phases, the first of which was to last until 6 April 2022. Typically, the task of informing the Russian public – and thus also the foreign media – about what was actually bad news, fell on Shoygu. On 28 March, he announced that after 'destroying the Ukrainian armed forces' in the Kyiv area, Russia was now about to focus on the 'key objective' of its invasion: the 'liberation of Donbass': at least some of the Russian media went as far as describe this as a 'goodwill gesture'.

Ironically, the withdrawal from northern-central and north-eastern Ukraine not only ended well before the original plan, but resulted in a solution for one of the problems that the Russian armed forces were experiencing during the first month of the all-out invasion: that of – apparently – poor coordination between OSK West (responsible for operations from the Kyiv area to Kharkiv), and OSK South (responsible for operations in eastern and southern Ukraine). Actually, there were no problems between the officers in charge of these two command nodes: instead, their work was repeatedly disturbed by Putin's micromanagement – including telephone calls directly to the commanders of various BTGs, both during the early assaults on Kyiv and Kharkiv as well as during the 6th CAA's drive on Izyum. Therefore, the *GenStab* recommended, and Putin accepted, having just one point of contact for all of his 'queries', and appointed one commander for all the operations in Ukraine: Army General Aleksandr Vladimirovich Dvornikov.

This relatively junior officer became something like a star of the VSRF since serving as the first commander of the Group of Russian Armed Forces in Syria in 2015. While earning himself the reputation of a 'butcher' in the West, mainly for his heavy-handed conduct of operations, application of excessive violence, firepower, and frontal assaults in that country, on return to Russia a year later, Dvornikov was highly decorated and assigned the command of OSK South. In 2021, he published an article emphasising the need for 'thinking outside the box' and for an improvement of the tactical training exercises through competitive force-on-force exercises: something rarely practiced in the VSRF, where after gunnery- and live-fire exercises, the emphasis was on training with use of simulators. Rather unsurprisingly, it was the units under Dvornikov's command – especially the 49th and the 58th CAA – that put up the best performance of all of the VSRF and the VDV during the first two weeks of the invasion.[3]

Unsurprisingly, in Russia, many saw him as the most promising candidate for the position of the Chief of the General Staff, once Gerasimov retired. As the subsequent developments were to

An official, pre-war photograph of Army General Dvornikov: while belittled and disparaged both in Ukraine and the West, he eventually did achieve at least some sort of success for the VSRF in eastern Ukraine in the spring of 2022. The price was the mauling of the remaining intact formations of the Russian army, but, in Putin's own words 'worth the results'. (Russian Ministry of Defence)

show, such expectations were in place, because while still heavily dependent on excessive firepower, in Ukraine through April, May and June 2022, Dvornikov repeatedly demonstrated finesse: if nothing else, he was forced to find a way to outflank various ZSU positions through changing the directions of his attacks.

Return of the 1st Guards Tanks Army

With hindsight, it is certain that Dvornikov wasted no time. As soon as he was in overall command, he focused all of his attention on defeating the ZSU in south-eastern Kharkiv, western Luhansk, and northern Donetsk in the form of a classic *Kesselschlacht* (cauldron): through a concentric onslaught on the agglomeration including Slovyansk, Severodonetsk, Bakhmut, and Kramatorsk from north-west, north, and east, with the aim of encircling a major group of Ukrainian ground forces. The principal formation assigned this task was the 1st GTA, which was to attack from Izyum in the direction of Slovyansk.

This is how it came to be that through late March a miscellany of BTGs began appearing in the Izyum area. The first were three from the 47th Tank Division (including the 26th Tank and the 252nd and 254th Motor-Rifle regiments), which reached the town around 23 March: these were followed by at least two BTGs of the 106th VDV Division – both of which were tasked with securing the Balakliya area. Additional units from the 4th Guards Tank Division and the 27th Guards Motor-Rifle Brigade reached the bridgehead south of Izyum by 1 April. In their way were the Ukrainian 25th Mechanised, 81st and the 95th Airborne Assault brigades, which held positions stretching from Husarivka, via Velyka and Mala Komyshuvakha, Topolske and Kamyanka, to Sulyhivka, Dovhenke and Dolyna in the south, and the Yaremivka-Studenok area on the Siversky Donets. This was to become the scene of the second major showdown between the VSRF and the ZSU in this part of Ukraine.

Always tied to ground operations, the VKS followed in fashion: through the first week of April, it evacuated the majority of around 60 aircraft and 150 helicopters from Belarus to air bases in Kursk and Belgorod oblasts. Just a pair of A-50s and a squadron of Su-35S deployed at Luninets AB continued flying regular operations along the border between Belarus and Ukraine north of Kyiv. They were supported by a major radar station of the VKS at Zyabrovka, in the Gomel area – which included mast-mounted 92N6E and 40B6, one 48Ya6 Podlet, and Kasta-2E2 radars, protected by one S-400 and two Pantsir S1 SAM systems.

To bolster the protection of the major concentration of the 1st GTA (which brought in two of its Buk M3-equipped anti-aircraft missile regiments), and in addition to organic air defence elements of the above-mentioned BTGs – which included such advanced systems as the 9K331 Tor M1 and 9K332 Tor M2Es, Pantsir S1s and S2s, and 2K22 Tunguska M1s – OSK South reinforced the 5th Anti-Aircraft Missile Brigade with the 53rd Anti-Aircraft Missile Brigade. Drawn from the 20th CAA, this Buk M2-equipped unit was notorious in the West for the shooting down of the Boeing 777 airliner of Malaysia Airlines Flight MH17 over Ukraine on 17 July 2014, and thus murdering 298 civilians.

Breakthrough at Izyum

The 1st GTA went into action almost as soon as it reached the Izyum area. On 1 April 2022, supported by about 30 air strikes and several volleys of TOS-1s, it simultaneously assaulted Topolske and Kamyanka. Subjected to vastly superior enemy firepower, the Ukrainians withdrew to Mala Komyshuvakha and Tykhotske (except for a company that held out in Topolske for nearly two weeks, before surrendering on 11 April). By 4 April, the 1st GTA was further reinforced through BTGs from the 2nd Guards Motor-Rifle Division, 4th Guards Tank Division, 47th Guards Tank Division, and then parts of the 35th CAA, and thus became able to widen its frontline. A day later, after the 45th Engineering Regiment constructed yet another bridge over the Siversky Donets, the 38th Motor-Rifle Brigade took the Ukrainians by surprise through suddenly appearing in Protopovika, starting a battle that was to rage for several days. While trying to push the Ukrainians out of the village, the Russians directed one of their BTGs to the south, on Petrivske. Simultaneously, the 13th Tank Regiment assaulted from Brazhkivka against Sulyhivka. An intervention by either the Ukrainian 3rd or 17th Tank Brigade brought this advance to a temporary halt, but further east, the Russian 237th Tank Regiment then punched through and drove all the way to Dovhenke before it was stopped.

All these attacks received significant close air support from Ka-52s and Su-25s of the VKS. While most of the aircraft and attack helicopters flew so-called loft attacks using S-8 unguided 80mm rockets, some Ka-52s were reconfigured for deployment of laser-guided Vikhr and radar-guided Ataka beam-riding ATGMs. Usually, they hovered at very low altitude and sniped at Ukrainian vehicles and fortifications from stand-off ranges. Additionally, Su-34s and Su-35s continued attacking Ukrainian SAM positions at every opportunity and, for example, on 8 April claimed the destruction of an Osa-AKM. The Ukrainians hit back with everything at their disposal, including ATGMs: on 5 April troops of the 95th Airborne Assault Brigade hit a Ka-52 hovering low over trees at Husarivka with a Stugna-P, causing it to crash.[4]

A T-80 of the Russian army crossing one of the pontoon bridges across the Siversky Donets near Izyum on 1 April 2023. (Russian Ministry of Defence)

A Buk M3 TELAR of the VSRF, seen in the summer of 2022. This sub-variant was the primary armament of two anti-aircraft missile regiments deployed with the 1st GTA in the Izyum area in early April of that year. (Russian Ministry of Defence)

Renewed Push

Despite initial success, Dvornikov's advance on Barvinkove and Slovyansk was stopped once again. Therefore, he rotated 'spent' BTGs out of the line, and replaced them with fresh units, rushing forward elements of the 27th Motor-Rifle Brigade, and especially additional BTGs drawn from the 20th CAA (such as the 245th and 752nd Motor-Rifle regiments from the 3rd Motor-Rifle Division), and the 35th CAA (including most of the 64th Guards Motor-Rifle Brigade). On 11 April, supported by about 20 air strikes and an hours-long artillery barrage, these units relaunched the offensive. Led by the 752nd Motor-Rifle Regiment, the western prong of this attack punched through the Ukrainian positions in Petrivske, but when the Russians attempted to cross the Bereka River, troops of the Izyum Territorial Defence Battalion blew up the bridge near Hrushuvakha, together with several Russian vehicles on it. Rather surprisingly, the Russians withdrew.

Further east, a BTG of the 245th Motor-Rifle Regiment attacked Dovhenke with great dash. The Russians actually managed to enter the village by 15 April. However, the Ukrainians hit back with all means at hand, including several air strikes by Su-25s of the PSZSU.

A Ka-52 of the VKS underway low over the forests west of Izyum in April 2022. (Russian Ministry of Defence)

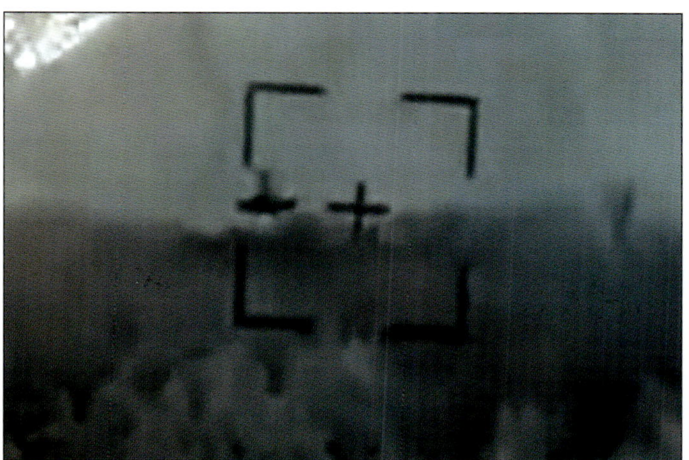

Taken on 5 April 2022, this is a still from a video showing a Ka-52 in the sight of a Stugna-P operator of the 95th Brigade (the operator intentionally held his crosshairs away from the target, in order not to warn the Russian crew too early). Seconds later, the helicopter received a direct hit that caused it to crash. The video showed no ejections by the crew. (95th Airborne Brigade)

Arguably, one of the jets in question – the aircraft flown by Captain Yegor Seredyuk – was shot down and its pilot killed on the same day, but the bitter resistance eventually compelled the surviving assailants to withdraw. Moreover, on 16 April, the Ukrainians hit the command post of the 49th Anti-Aircraft Missile Brigade in the Husarivka area, killing – amongst others – the commander of that unit, Colonel Ivan Ivanovich Grishin.[5]

Demonstrating their ability to adapt to sniping from the Ka-52s, between 15 and 20 April troops of the 95th Airborne shot down two additional Ka-52s using Stugna-P ATGMs. Amongst them was Bort 98 (registration RF-13441), crewed by Colonel Vasily Petrovich Kleshchenko, shot down in the Husarivka area. It is possible that another Ka-52 felled during this period resulted in the first ever successful ejection from a helicopter under combat conditions in the history of warfare. According to Russian sources, the crew in question included Captain Roman Stanislavovich Kobets and Major Ivan Nikolayevich Boldyrev – the same pair that were forced into an emergency landing at Antonov IAP on the first day of the all-out invasion. Correspondingly, this time their helicopter was badly damaged and the two crewmen ejected safely, landed under parachutes and were then recovered by friendly troops while fighting off a group of Ukrainians that attempted to approach their position.[6]

Also shot down – on 20 or 21 April 2022 – was Su-34 Bort 20 (registration RF-95004) from the 559th Bomber Aviation Regiment: this was hit by an Osa-AKM while bombing positions of the 95th Airborne in the Zavody area, a few kilometres north-east of Velyka Komyshuvakha. This time, the crew ejected safely and was recovered by the Russians. Perhaps in reaction to these losses, on 17 April 2022, the Ministry of Defence in Moscow claimed the downing of two Ukrainian MiG-29s over Kharkiv Oblast, including one by an air-to-air missile.

Counteroffensive on Kupyansk

Instead of rotating his units before another assault, at that point in time, Dvornikov was forced to completely stop the operation: once again – for the third time in two months – the reason was a local counteroffensive by the 92nd Mechanised Brigade into his western flank, in the area south-east of Kharkiv. By assaulting from Chuhiv in an eastern direction, the Ukrainians mauled yet another weak BTG of the 144th Motor-Rifle Division and then rapidly liberated Lebyaze, Bazaliivka, Mykhalivka and Shevchenkove, before pushing on Borivske, just 24km short of Kupyansk. Unable to ignore the possible loss of the key railway hub and the crucial bridge over the Oskil River in his rear, Dvornikov was forced to reroute several BTGs into the path of the 92nd. Undeterred, the command of the 92nd Mechanised quickly switched the direction of its attack. On 22 April, it crossed one of the extensive minefields constructed by

A TELAR of the 9K37M1 Buk-M1 system of the 49th Anti-Aircraft Missile Brigade, VSRF, loaded with four 9M38M1 surface-to-air missiles. Notably, the first missile has a crudely applied inscription '*za komandira*' (for [our] commander) – in memory of Colonel Ivan Ivanovich Grishin, killed in the Husarivka area on 16 April 2022. (Russian social media)

Wreckage (the right stub wing with two weapons hardpoints) of Ka-52 Bort 98 (registration RF-13441), piloted by Colonel Vasily Petrovich Kleshchenko, shot down in the Husarivka area by the air defence battalion of the 95th Airborne Brigade, on or around 15 April 2022. (95th Airborne Brigade)

A pre-war photograph of an Osa-AKM TELAR of the ZSU. The system was operated by air defence battalions of a few selected ZSU brigades – including the 95th Airborne – and, although more than 40 years old, proved a thorn in the side of the VKS through March, April and May of 2022. (ZSU)

the Russians north and north-east of Kharkiv, shot down a Russian Orlan-10 reconnaissance UAV using the recently-delivered Martlet MANPADS of British origin, and then surprised and smashed a BTG of the 437th Motor-Rifle Regiment, liberating three additional villages (Bezruky, Slatine, and Prudianka).[7]

Regardless of how limited in their overall scope, these two local counterattacks by a single Ukrainian brigade were sufficient to fully expose all the possible weaknesses of the Russian position in south-eastern Kharkiv Oblast. The shortage of troops was now so critical that – exactly like Yershov before – Dvornikov could only leave a thin screen of badly damaged BTGs to protect his western flank while pushing on Slovyansk. Whenever the Ukrainians attacked in force, the result was such a major crisis that he had to stop assaulting southwards and to reroute his troops, equipment and supplies to the north-west instead.

Shortage of Infantry

Unsurprisingly, the crisis caused by the counterattacks of the 92nd Mechanised forced Dvornikov to rebuild and reorganise some of the battered BTGs before resuming the advance on Slovyansk: during the following days, numerous videos surfaced in Russian social media showing trains carrying T-80 main battle tanks, BMP-1/2 infantry fighting vehicles, dozens of artillery pieces, and even BMPT Terminators of the 90th Tank Division on arrival in the Belgorod area. The availability of equipment, however, did not solve the shortage of infantry: indeed, some of the units he was about to send into combat over the following days were so short on manpower that they had to man their T-72s and T-80s with only two crewmembers.

Dvornikov resumed the advance down the M03 highway on 22 April, by deploying a BTG of the 64th Motor-Rifle Brigade to attack Dovhenke: unusually, this was accompanied by a flanking assault on the hamlet of Dibrovne, a few kilometres further west. In preparation for this new attack, on 20 and 21 April, dozens of air strikes were flown and these followed a new modus operandi. Henceforth, a package was kept on station at high altitude above the target zone: this consisting of one or two Su-34s equipped with the powerful L-175VU offensive/stand-off jammer, escorted by a pair of Su-35s armed with both R-77-1 air-to-air missiles and Kh-31PD anti-radiation missiles. The task of that formation was 'demonstrative' by nature: they were to show themselves on Ukrainian radars and thus prompt PSZSU SAM crews to activate and try to engage. In turn, this supported follow-up attacks by flights of Su-24s or Su-25s, underway at very low altitude, and delivering attacks with free-fall bombs or unguided rockets. In other cases, high-flying formations provided top cover for Su-34s deploying Kh-29 guided missiles. On 21 April, the VKS is known to have targeted Ukrainian forward command posts in Husarivka and Andriivka, and one of its high-flying formations claimed the destruction of one of 25th Mechanised Brigade's Osa-AKM SAM systems in the same area. In turn, and probably on warning from one of the Kolchuga ESM systems of the PSZSU, on the same day, MANPAD teams and Osa-AKM SAM systems of the 95th Airborne claimed a Russian Su-34 and Su-25 as shot down, as they took both an enemy demonstration flight, and

A PTS-2 tracked amphibious transport of the Russian Army, which was abandoned and captured when the troops of the Izyum Territorial Defence Battalion blew up a bridge over the Bereka River near Hrushuvakha on or around 12 April 2022. Just 30 kilometres north of Barvinkove along the T2113 road, this marked the deepest Russian penetration along this axis. (Izyum Territorial Defence Battalion)

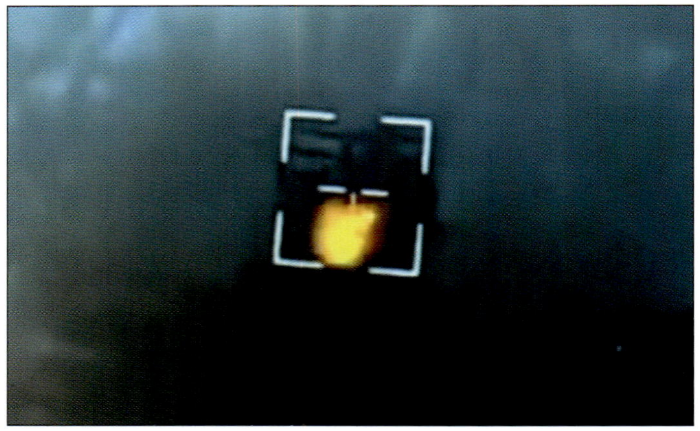

Another still from a video showing a Ka-52 in the crosshair of a Stugna-P ATGM system belonging to the 95th Airborne Assault Brigade, at the moment the missile hit the target, sometime between 15 and 20 April 2022. The helicopter promptly lost power and crashed into the forest below, leaving the crew no time to activate its ejection seats. (95th Airborne Assault Brigade)

the follow-up strike flight under fire. Eventually confirmed was the downing of Su-34 Bort 43 (registration RF-95858) over Dovhenke: the crew of two ejected safely and was recovered.

As the Ukrainian defences held out, Dvornikov rerouted his troops to bypass Dibrovne and attack Nova Dmytrivka and Pashkove, thus reaching an area just 10 kilometres north of Barvinkove. When helicopters of the 11th Aviation Brigade, ZSU, were deployed in attempt to stop this advance on 23 April 2022, the Russians hit one of the Ukrainian Mi-24s: the helicopter crashed outside Oleksandrivka, about five kilometres east of Barvinkove, killing the crew: Captain Serhii Kolisnichenko and Lieutenant Oleg Sklyar. Although subjected to dozens of air strikes and continuous artillery barrages, the 95th Airborne held out in Dovhenke. Moreover, on the western side of this sector, the 25th Airborne and the 81st Airborne Assault brigades were successful in stopping the Russian attacks in the Hrushuvakha area, while the air defence battalion of the former shot down Su-34 Bort 24 (registration RF-95808). The crew ejected safely from a jet that crashed in the Balakliya area, and was recovered by a Mi-8 helicopter.

The problem Dvornikov was facing at that point in time was the fact that the ZSU began bolstering the 81st and the 95th Airborne Assault brigades with battalions of the Territorial Defence and converting every village in his way into a fortified stronghold. This, and the deployment of the Ukrainian 46th Artillery Brigade in the Barvinkove area caused his BTGs such heavy losses that by 27 April he had to stop assaulting. Even though only five kilometres short of that town and less than 30 kilometres from Slovyansk, the involved Russian units were exhausted to the level where they were rendered unable to continue offensive operations. Reportedly, trying to find out what was going wrong with the advance on Slovyansk, on 28 April, even the Chief of the Russian *GenStab*, Army General Gerasimov, visited the troops in the Izyum area. While Ukrainian claims that he was injured by an artillery barrage on one of the VSRF command nodes in the Izyum area, two days later, were exaggerated, it is certain that the Chief of the *GenStab* 'convinced' Dvornikov to give it one more try, regardless of the circumstances. Indeed, on 28 April, the Russians constructed yet another pontoon bridge over the Siversky Donets: this time in the Zavody area, from where they attacked and almost seized Velyka Komyshuvakha a day

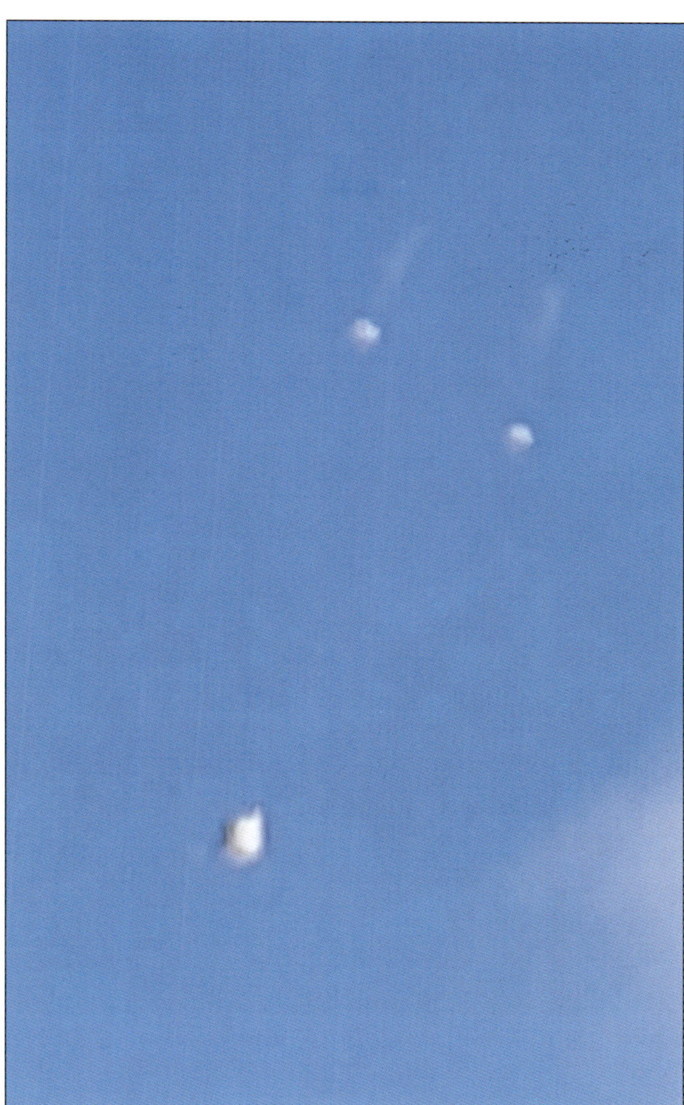

Two stills from a video taken on 20 or 21 April 2022, showing the final moments of Su-34 Bort 20 (registration RF-95004) going down in flames over Zavody. As clear from the second still, the crew ejected safely: the wreckage of their aircraft was discovered by Ukrainian troops only in September of the same year. (fahivetzpity/Ukrainian social media)

A front view of a Su-34 equipped with the large L-175VU offensive/stand-off jammer, installed on a special adapter on the centreline, between the intakes. (Russian Ministry of Defence)

Burned-out remnants of the fin of Su-34 Bort 43 (registration RF-95858), shot down by Osa-AKMs of the 95th Airborne Brigade over Dovhenke on 21 April 2022. (95th Airborne Brigade)

later. Moreover, on 30 April 2022 the Russians managed to hit Su-24M Bort 87 of the 7th Brigade PSZSU while this bombed their new bridgehead: the crew attempted to return to Kanatovo AB, but was forced to eject outside Nova Praha, in the Kirovohrad area, and the jet crashed.[8]

However, that was as much as the VSRF was capable of reaching in this part of Ukraine as of late April 2022. Indeed, the ZSU was meanwhile not only rushing whatever reinforcements it could scratch together, but even started launching new counterattacks. For example, on 4 May, elements of the 14th Mechanised, 17th Tank, and 95th Airborne Assault brigades counterattacked at Protopopivka to recover the village, although suffering losses in bitter house-to-house fighting. With this, the Russian offensive from Izyum on Slovyansk finally ran out of steam. Regardless of bitter complaints by Putin, Dvornikov was forced to develop what can be described as 'Plan D' instead: an attempt to complete his original aim of defeating the ZSU in a cauldron battle, but by crossing the Siversky Donets River at a different point – and in combination with an all-out assault in the Popasna area.

The wreckage of Su-34 Bort 24 (registration RF-95808), from the 47th Composite Aviation Regiment, shot down over the Balakliya area on 25 April 2022. (via The Military Watch)

4
PLAN D

In 2014, Popasna, a town of around 20,000 people in south-western Luhansk Oblast, was another of the places secured by the separatists and then painstakingly recovered by volunteers of the Donbas Battalion. With a population predominantly considered to be at least 'suspect' by the authorities in Kyiv, and 'pro-Russian' by Moscow, it was also an area of many road junctions: relatively close to the LOC, it was repeatedly shelled over the following years and many of the inhabitants left. As of early 2022, it was defended by a battalion of the 24th Mechanised Brigade and well-fortified. Other elements of this brigade occupied an elaborate system of fortifications north and east of the town, including the villages of Troitske, Novooleksandrivka, Hirske, Novotoshkivske, and Zolote. That said, the town was one of many in a similar situation and not the target of major assaults early during the Russian invasion. This began to change only once the 20th CAA invaded northern Luhansk Oblast on 24 February, and over the next two days captured Novopskov, Bilovodsk and Staroblisk – in turn meeting separatist units of II Army Corps (II AK) that were advancing from the Luhansk area over the Siversky Donets River in a northern direction.

The reason was that, starting from 28 February, the Russian invasion of northern Luhansk forced the ZSU units holding fortifications along the LOC in central Luhansk – the 24th Mechanised and the 57th Motorised brigades – to fall back towards Severodonetsk (held by the NATO-trained 4th Rapid Reaction Brigade of the Ukrainian National Guard). Two days later, the Russians reached Svatove: at least in theory, this offered them the opportunity of assaulting the northern sector of the LOC from the rear. Probably due to the lack of troops and the requirement to deploy available units for Plan C, south of Izyum, the *GenStab* in Moscow assigned this task to the separatists commanded by the Russian-staffed II AK, while the 20th CAA continued in the general direction of Lyman. Correspondingly, between 4 and 6 March 2022, the separatist units swung south and began approaching the large urban conurbation of Kreminna, Rubizhne, Severodonetsk, and Lysychansk. This is where both the 20th CAA and II AK became bogged down for the rest of the month: they had failed to secure Kreminna, and in Rubizhne the separatist 2nd and 7th Motor-Rifle brigades suffered horrendous losses to the highly effective defence of the 79th Airborne Brigade.[1]

Concentric Push

When Dvornikov assumed overall command over Russian operations in Ukraine, his staff developed what can be described as 'Plan D' for the Russian all-out invasion. The miscellany of units concentrated south of Izyum was to continue in the direction of Barvinkove and Slovyansk; the 20th CAA was still tasked with securing Kreminna, but was also to support the 1st GTA and the 6th CAA in assault on Lyman; the separatist units subordinated to II AK were to tie down the 4th Rapid Reaction and the 79th Airborne brigades in the Severodonetsk area, while II AK was to find a way to achieve a breakthrough in the Popasna area. Essentially, all of these advances were expected to eventually meet somewhere around Sloviansk and Kramatorsk, thus cutting off a big group of Ukrainian forces north of them.

Elements of the 3rd Motor-Rifle Division of II AK began assaulting from Svatove in a southern direction on 10 March 2022. Initially at least, they failed to enter either Kreminna or Rubizhne. II AK went into action even earlier: supported by Ka-52s and Su-25s of the VKS, and plentiful VSRF artillery, it began assaulting Popasna on 3 March. Indeed, it was in this area that both the Russian fighter-bombers and attack helicopters were observed for the first time deploying unguided 80mm and 130mm rockets by use of the long toss manoeuvre: they would approach to around 5,000–6,500 metres from the target area, then enter a full-power climb at 30 to 40 degrees and ripple-fire all of their S-8 or S-13 rockets. Because pilots frequently flew this manoeuvre in a rather imprecise fashion, it resulted in rockets being spread over a very wide area, which earned this manoeuvre the nickname 'spray-and-pray'. Rather amazingly, as well as praising such attacks as 'methods of enabling the crew to strike with unguided rockets without entering the envelope of enemy air defences', the Russian MOD also boasted of introducing to service B-13 pods for S-13B unguided 130mm rockets, even though these had been in service for at least 15 years. The weapon was used in large numbers on 23 March, when the VKS sought to suppress the Ukrainian air defences through a combination of L-175VU-equipped Su-34s and Kh-31-equipped Su-25s, and repeated low-altitude strikes by Su-25s, to enable two other pairs of Su-34s to deploy not only Kh-29s to hit selected fortifications of the 24th Mechanised, but also Kramatorsk airfield, which was used as a forward operating base by helicopters of the PSZSU, time and again.[2]

Through the rest of March 2022, the 20th CAA and II AK, supported by massive volumes of air strikes and artillery barrages, reinforced their efforts to capture Kreminna and Rubizhne. Initially, the onslaught had little effect: arguably, the Russians and separatists did manage to gradually secure the northern outskirts of both towns, but their attempts to drive in between ZSU positions inside the latter and Severodonetsk all failed. In the Popasna area, the 4th Motor-Rifle Brigade was just as unsuccessful: indeed, on 31 March, while supporting another of its assaults, the VKS lost a Mi-28N attack helicopter to a recently-delivered British-made Starstreak MANPAD. The helicopter is known to have crashed outside Holubivske, in the Alchevsk area, but the fate of the crew remains unknown.

A Ka-52 of the VKS seen firing unguided rockets at Ukrainian positions in the Popasna area – using the 'spray-and-pray' principle – on 14 or 15 March 2022. (Oruzhye i Istoriya)

A Mi-28 in the Popasna area seen pitching up for its rocket attack and releasing flare decoys against MANPADs in March 2022. (Russian Ministry of Defence)

B-13 pod with S-13B 130mm unguided rockets. (Russian Ministry of Defence)

The Wagner Factor

Starting from 1 April, an entirely new party to this war appeared in the Popasna area – the presence of which was soon to be felt strongly. After experiencing severe losses during the first days of the invasion, and facing critical shortages of troops, during an online meeting between Putin and his government, aired on Russian TV on 11 March 2022, Shoygu tentatively recommended the acceptance of '16,000 applicants from various countries…foremost the Middle East… to serve… with liberation movements… in the Luhansk and Donetsk People's Republics' – i.e.: with the Russian armed forces in Ukraine. Indeed, in Syria, rumours about the GRU-linked Wagner PMC – an enterprise involved in Ukraine since 2014 – hiring members of the Syrian Armed Forces loyal to dictator Bashar al-Assad to serve in Ukraine had begun making circles days earlier. This was ironic considering that for years the Ministry of Defence in Moscow, and especially the *GenStab*, had refused to legalise the status of PMCs in Russia: indeed, that the legislation in effect in 2022 explicitly prohibited 'illegal armed formations and mercenary groups'. Still, Wagner not only existed in the form of a network of interacting companies (all controlled by the Concord company group based in St. Petersburg) – but was closely linked to the GRU (its military wing was commanded by Russian military intelligence), while its 'owner' – Yevgeny Prigozhin – was linked directly to two of Putin's top aides, Yuri Kovalchuk and Sergey Kriyenko. Responding that the West was 'openly disregarding international law' through supplying arms and 'mercenaries' to Ukraine, during the same online meeting, the President of the Russian Federation – the very same man that at earlier times denied any kind of link between his government, the Russian Federation, and the Wagner PMC – then officially gave the green light for 'Shoygu's' idea. Reportedly, the first

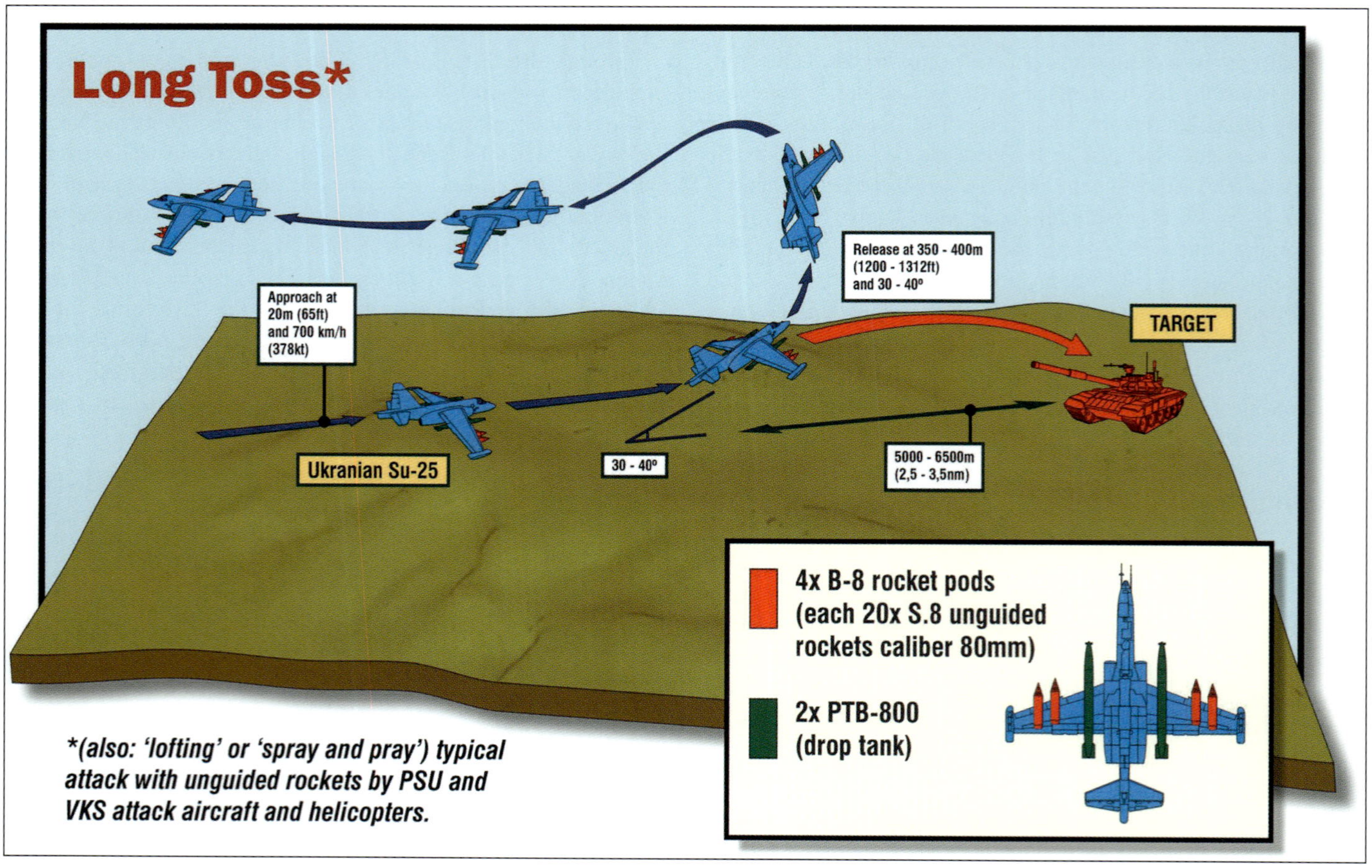

A diagram detailing the long toss, lofting, or spray-and-pray manoeuvre. (Diagram by Anderson Subtil)

A knocked out Russian T-72AV on the streets of Popasna: the Russian multi-wave attack on 3 and 4 April 2022 not only managed to break the Ukrainian defences for the first time, but also became a sort of protype for the Russian assault tactics of the following two years. (ZSU)

group of around 400 Syrian mercenaries arrived in Russia by 15 March 2022.[3]

Before long, there were additional rumours about Wagner hiring Libyan nationals from the areas controlled by 'Marshal' Qalifa Haftar, in the east of that country. Furthermore, on request from Moscow, the Islamic Revolutionary Guards Corps (IRGC) of Iran began hiring Iraqi and Syrian nationals for similar purposes: about 500 of these reached the Russian Federation by the end of March. That said, it took time to recruit enough foreigners to Russia: by the end of March, fewer than 1,000 were around. To bolster its strength to sufficient levels, the PMC had to withdraw some of its own troops from Africa and was given control over extremist paramilitary groups like the Russian Imperial Legion and the neo-Nazi *Russich* Group. Additionally, Prigozhin was granted permission to recruit retired pilots with experience on types like the Su-24 and Su-25, and was provided enough aircraft for these to man something like a small regiment equipped with the two types.[4]

Once in the Popasna area, the resulting two Wagner BTGs made their debut on 3 and 4 April. Operating at the discretion of their own commanders (instead of following plans prepared in Moscow or by the headquarters of OSK South) – they organised a three-wave attack: the first was conducted by units composed of separatists, tasked with spotting Ukrainian positions and minefields; they were followed by troops of the 150th Motor-Rifle Division and the 155th Naval Infantry Brigade. Finally, the third wave included Wagner mercenaries with significant experience in urban combat. Behind them multiple BTGs of the 76th VDV Division and the 90th Tank Division were redeployed to the Pervomaiske area, to wait for an opportunity to exploit a breach in the Ukrainian front line and then to drive on Bakhmut, Kramatorsk, and Sloviansk.

Aerial Onslaught

Supported by immense volumes of artillery fire, on 4 April the Russians managed to advance along the railway line from Pervomaiske into Popasna and capture the railway station and the train depot. Attack helicopters and fighter-bombers of the VKS were heavily involved in this operation: out of more than 250 combat sorties the VKS flew every day during this period of the war, up to 50 included strikes by Su-34s on Ukrainian command posts, and POL and logistics depots in Severodonetsk, Lysychansk, Kramatorsk and Bakhmut, while between 50 and 60 were close air support missions by Ka-52s, Mi-28s, and Su-25s targeting positions of the 24th Mechanised alone. Additionally, on 7 April, Su-34s deployed multiple Kh-29 and Kh-59 PGMs to target trains and depots at railway stations in Kramatorsk, Chasiv Yar, and Bakhmut, and the railway link connecting Barvinkove with Sloviansk, irrespective of these still being used for the evacuation of thousands of civilians: obviously, the trains evacuating civilians towards the west were assumed to be bringing reinforcements and supplies for the ZSU on their way east. That said, gradually, the constantly improving Ukrainian air defences reduced the number of such strikes. Firstly, the VKS was forced to accompany most of the formations sent to strike targets deeper behind the frontline with Su-34s equipped with L-175VU offensive/stand-off jammers, and Su-34s equipped with Kh-31P anti-radiation missiles. Secondly, the Russian stocks of PGMs were always low and industry had a very limited capability to manufacture replacements: as ever-more were spent, ever-fewer weapons like Kh-29s and Kh-59s were available. Correspondingly, through the second half of April and into early May 2022, the VKS was mainly tasked with close air support attacks by Ka-52s, Mi-28s, and Su-25s, using unguided 80mm rockets: while many of these operations were undertaken following predetermined plans, a growing number consisted of 'on call' missions. Although directed by forward air controllers assigned to ground forces – especially forward observers of the 150th Motor-Rifle Division – their overall effectiveness remained low.[5]

Fall of Popasna

The onslaught in the air and on the ground continued: on 6 April, the separatists, followed by elements of the 150th Motor-Rifle Division in addition to the Wagner Group, seized Novotoshkivske, south-east of Severodonetsk, forcing the Ukrainians to fall back to heavily fortified Hirske. In turn, on 8 April, the Ukrainians reported that their artillery destroyed one of the mercenary assault groups. During the following days, Dvornikov directed additional artillery units to the Pervomaiske area and on 12 April the separatists began firing their 9M79 Tockha-U ballistic missiles at the positions of the 24th Mechanised: the MOD in Moscow then claimed the destruction of 14 of its vehicles and 120 troops. Two days later, the MOD continued emphasising the destruction of the Ukrainian brigade, claiming that

The assault on Popasna saw the most intensive deployment of Russian attack helicopters in the war up to that date, as positions of the 24th Mechanised Brigade were subjected to up to 50 air strikes a day. While most of these resulted in the launch of unguided rockets following the 'spray-and-pray' principle, Ka-52s were also targeting Ukrainian fortifications with 9K121 Vikhr ATGMs (ASCC/NATO reporting name 'AT-16 Scallion'). (Russian Ministry of Defence)

A Ka-52 seen on return from a combat sortie in the Popasna area in April 2022. (Russian MOD)

its artillery and the VKS destroyed 'several ammunition depots' and 'five strongholds' of the 24th in the Popasna area, while a Ka-52 crew claimed the destruction of a Ukrainian Buk M1 launcher outside Zolote.[6]

While related information remains scarce, there is little doubt that the massive Russian air and artillery strikes were not only directed at the fortifications and trenches of the 24th Mechanised, but also well to its rear. For example, on 18 April, a volley from BM-27 Uragan 220mm multiple rocket launchers is known to have hit Berestove, about 20 kilometres north-west of Popasna, killing an entire platoon of the brigade. Moreover, once inside the ruined town, the Wagner mercenaries continued to assault using the classic tactics of urban warfare: they first cleared two parallel roads before mopping up the area in between. Hopelessly outmatched just by the sheer volume of the enemy artillery fire – constantly guided by numerous Orlan-10 UAVs – the Ukrainians continued to bitterly resist and during the night of 19 to 20 April ambushed a 25-man assault team largely consisting of Libyans and Syrians. In another case, a strike by a Ukrainian Bayraktar TB.2 UAV killed 19, while an artillery barrage on the headquarters of the 4th Motor-Rifle Brigade in Pervomaiske killed over 50 Russian and separatist officers. The Ukrainian Army Aviation flew air strikes on the advancing Russians too, regardless

A rear underside view of a Ka-52 climbing and unleashing S-8 80mm unguided rockets towards the Ukrainian positions in the Popasna area in April 2022. Theoretically comparable with barrages of BM-21 multiple rocket launchers (which fired 122mm rockets), such attacks proved far less effective because none of the aircraft or helicopters flying the missions had the necessary programmable navigation systems to fly them accurately, while pilots tended to aim by dead reckoning. (Russian Ministry of Defence)

A pair of Su-25s of the VKS passing low over the Horlivka area, underway in the direction of Popasna, on 24 April 2022. (Russian social media)

Undeterred by losses, the invaders continued relentless shelling and air strikes on Popasna and on 20 April, the Wagner mercenaries broke through north-east of the town, sealing its fate. From that day onwards, the 24th Mechanised Brigade was effectively withdrawing from Popasna. This was completed by 7 May 2022, by when the question was if the ZSU still had reserves to establish a new frontline west of the demolished town, or if the Russians would break through towards the Siversky Donets River, thus cutting off a large concentration of ZSU forces in the Severodonetsk-Lysychansk area.

A Su-25 armed with a pair of B-13 rocket pods releases flares over northern Horlivka while returning from a strike on Popasna on 24 April 2022. Ukrainian air defences remained a threat in this area, right until the last days of the Russian onslaught against this town. (Russian social media)

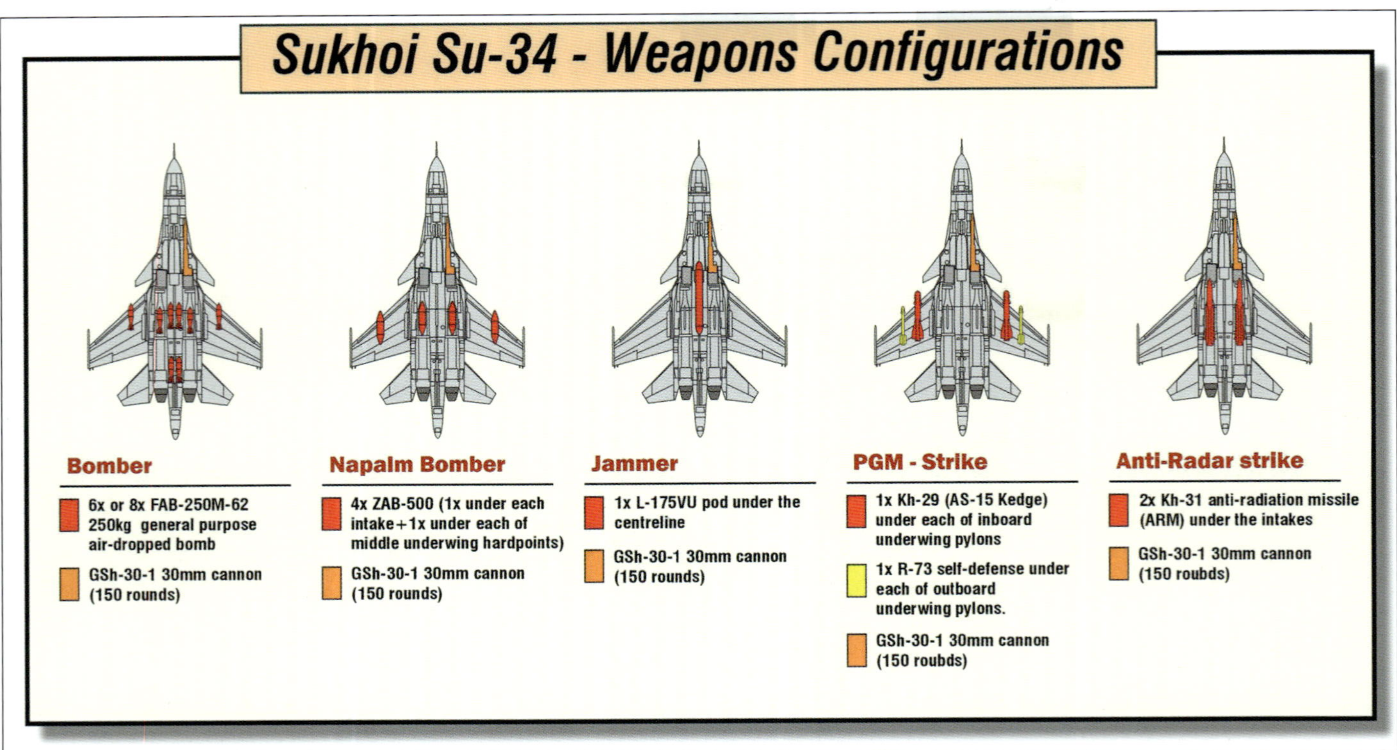

A diagram depicting some of principal weapon configurations of Su-34s during the first few months of the war. (Diagram by Anderson Subtil)

Facing not only a massive concentration of Russian ground-based air defence systems deployed along the combat zone, but also constant combat air patrols of VKS interceptors armed with R-77-1s, the Ukrainian Su-25 pilots were left with little option but to fly as low as possible – both while approaching the combat zone, and while exiting it. Additionally, they tended to do so along major highways, because this not only made navigation easier, but also tended to confuse the Russian radars – which would also detect cars moving at high speeds. (PSZSU)

of the high loses to its attack helicopters. On 23 April, two of these were written off: a Mi-24 of the 11th Brigade crewed by captains Maxim Shendrikov and Pavel Popovich was shot down by Russian air defences during a 'spray-and-pray' strike over Mykolaivka (north of Popasna), killing the crew, while a Mi-24P hit power lines during a similar mission, killing the crew: majors Volodymyr Panasyuk and Mykola Mutyarchuk. In turn, on 30 April, Ukrainian air defences shot down the Su-25 piloted by Colonel Nikolai Markov. This 67-year-old veteran fighter pilot from the USSR and (later Belarus) had served as a mercenary for Wagner PMC in Africa since 2014 and was killed.[7]

Belonging to the second generation of the S-300 SAM system, the S-300PM was introduced to service in 1985 and characterised by the use of MAZ-7910 8x8 trucks to carry its mobile radars and command post, as well as its 5P85 launchers, shown here. Its 5V55R missiles had a range of 90km and semi-active radar homing guidance. Russia acquired around 1,900 launchers for the S-300PT/PS/PMU series: all of its S-300Ps were upgraded to the S-300PM1 standard by 2014, and most of these to the PM2 standard by 2020. However, by 2022, their replacement was lagging badly behind the plan due to the delays in research and development of the S-500 system – which is why numerous VKS units continued operating S-300PM2s during the all-out invasion of Ukraine. Ukraine is known to have operated six S-300PMUs as of 2014, and to have lost 34 launchers during the Russian invasion of Crimea. However, it reactivated so many systems that it should have been able to operate around 100 batteries (each with six launchers) as of 2022, when it received an additional S-300PMU battery from Slovakia. (Artwork by Anderson Subtil)

The S-350 Vityaz SAM system was developed as a replacement for the older S-300PS series, and with the use of missiles developed for the S-400 in mind. Following several delays, it entered service in February 2020 and ever since the VKS has been re-equipping a total of 30 battalions with it. A single S-300 SAM site included one 50N6A multifunctional electronically scanned array radar, one 50K6A command post, and eight 50P6 launchers (like the one shown here): it could simultaneously track up to 200 targets and simultaneously engage 12 ballistic missiles and 16 aircraft and/or helicopters. The S-350 had three types of missiles, including the 9M96E2 (maximum range of 120km), 9M96E (40km), and 9M100 (15km). Notably, since 2012, the VSRF and the VKS abandoned the use of the three-colour camouflage on its vehicles and returned to the practice of painting their vehicles in dark olive green overall. (Artwork by Anderson Subtil)

The S-400 Triumf SAM system was originally developed as an upgrade of the S-300PM series, and eventually became its replacement. Essentially, a single battalion is centred on the 55K6E command post (mounted on the Ural-532301 truck), the 91N6E radar with maximum range of 340km (mounted on MZKT-7930 truck) and up to 12 5P85TE2 TELs (one of which is shown here). However, the system was highly flexible and compatible with a wide range of additional sensors and command nodes, such as Protivnik-GE UHF radars and Moscow-1 passive sensors, or electronic warfare systems, and A-50U airborne early warning aircraft. The S-400 can also be used to control or fire a wide range of missiles, ranging from old V.880s of the S-200 SAM system (ASCC/NATO reporting name 'SA-5 Gammon'), through to various weapons of the S-300 series, to the latest 40N6E, 40N6E2, 40N6E3, 48N6DM, 98M96E, 9M96E2, the ultra-long-range (400km) 40N6E, or anti-ballistic missile weapons like 77N6-N and 77N6-N1. (Artwork by Anderson Subtil)

Envisaged as a refinement of the 2K12 Kub SAM system (ASCC/NATO reporting name 'SA-6 Guideline'), the 9K37 Buk ('SA-11 Gadfly') entered service in the late 1970s. Its third variant appeared in 2008 as the 9K317 Buk-M2 (lower left corner): its TELAR was still equipped with four missiles, and a SAM site with four TELARs could simultaneously track 24 targets and engage four of them. The final version, the 9K317M Buk-M3 (top centre and right side), entered service in 2018: each of its TELARs could carry up to 12 missiles packed in their tubes, and a single SAM site could simultaneously track up to 36 targets while engaging four. As of 2016, Russia had more than 440 9K37/9K317s in service (including 350 with the VSRF and 80 with the VKS), but was rapidly replacing these with 66 Buk M1-2, 36 Buk M2, and 36 Buk M3 SAM systems: indeed, the production of the latter continued through 2022 and 2023, by when 15 additional systems may have entered service. (Artworks by David Bocquelet & Tom Cooper)

The 9K330 Tor was developed as an all-weather, low-to-medium-altitude, short-range replacement for the Osa SAM system, and was designed to be capable of operating its radar and detecting targets on the move, having to stop only to open fire. A typical Tor SAM site includes four 9K332 tracked transporter-launcher (TLAR) vehicles, a mobile Ranzhir-M command post, and Polyana-D4 system enabling automatic interaction with other air defence systems. Each 9K332 TLAR includes a G/H band pulse-Doppler radar (later K band) with a passive electronically scanned array installed on the front of a turret containing eight vertical launchers for 9M330 missiles. Originally, each TLAR could track up to 48 targets and engage one at a time, but the more recent Tor-M1 and Tor-M2E could engage two, and later four targets at once, while guiding up to four and eight missiles, respectively. As of 2017, 116 Tor-M1-2U and Tor-2M2s systems were operational with the VKS: up to 12 have been delivered since. (Artwork by Anderson Subtil)

The Pantsir S1 (ASCC/NATO reporting name 'SA-22 Greyhound') was the primary close-in weapons system of most VSRF tank and motor-rifle formations as of 2022, and for S-300/350/400 SAM sites of the VKS. A single battery included the command post, a surveillance radar, and six combat vehicles, all mounted on KamAZ-6560 8x8 38-ton trucks (the 200th Motor-Rifle Brigade also operated tracked Pantsir-SAs, custom-tailored for operations under Arctic conditions). While the original S1 was the most numerous variant in service as of 2022, the improved S1M was also available in small numbers from 2019. Each of its combat vehicles has its own 1L36 multiple-band target acquisition and tracking radar (range 40km, capable of simultaneously tracking up to 40 targets), 12 ready-to-launch 57E6M-E missiles (range 30km, with a 25kg warhead compared to 20kg of the earlier 57E6-Es), and two twin-barrel 2A38M automatic 30mm anti-aircraft guns. (Artwork by David Bocquelet)

As of 2022, the 48Ya6-K1 Podlet K1 was one of the most advanced Russian-made mobile radars. Operating in the S band (2–4GHz) it was specialised for detecting low-altitude targets and providing early warning and support for such SAM systems as the S-400 and Buk. The mast-mounted system included three antennas, including the primary phased array (large antenna) for detection and tracking, and two smaller arrays used for IFF (identification friend or foe): the slightly bigger one for the international Mark XII signals, and the smaller one for the Russian system. The smaller antenna on the side of the primary array was used as a compensator, for electronic counter-countermeasures. The inset shows the Podlet K1 system when folded up for transit. (Artwork by David Bocquelet)

Designed by Iskra in Zaporizhzhya, the 79K6 Pelikan S band 3D mobile radar with a digital phased array antenna came into being around the same time as the Podlet but was developed only from 2006 and, following testing in 2016, entered operational service a year later. This trailer-mounted, 17,000kg system could go into action within 30 minutes of being deployed and had a maximum detection range for targets operating at high altitudes of 350–400km, or 40km for targets flying at altitudes of 100 metres or less. It served dual roles: early warning/surveillance and support of SAM operations. Equipped with a multibeam klystron, it had a peak power output of 130kW and could track up to 300 targets. (Artwork by David Bocquelet)

Before the Russian all-out invasion, a total of 65 TELARs for Osa-AKMs were operated by the 28th, 39th, 1129th, and 1039th Anti-Aircraft Missile Regiments of the ZSU (each of which comprised 4–6 batteries, and were operationally subordinated to the PSZSU), while additional batteries were assigned to professional ZSU units, like the 1st Tank, or the 92nd Airborne Assault brigades. Starting in March and April 2022, Poland provided up to 32 locally-modernised Osa-AKM-P1s, while the USA sourced several other systems from third parties. This is a reconstruction of a 9A33BM3 transporter erector launcher and radar vehicle of the 9K33M3 Osa-AKM system assigned to the 92nd Airborne Assault Brigade in early 2022: the system had 'command to line-of-sight' guidance and could simultaneously guide two missiles against the same target out to a range of 15km. (Artwork by David Bocquelet)

The primary version of the Buk SAM system in Ukrainian service was the 9K37M1 Buk-M1, some 60 TELARs for which were operational with 15 battalions (or SAM sites) as of 2016, while 12 were stored. The PSZSU had additional systems overhauled and modified to a standard similar to the Buk M1-2, although their primary weapon remained the old 9M38M1 missile. Correspondingly, by 2022, the PSZSU operated Buks with the 11th, 156th and 223rd Anti-Aircraft Missile Regiments, and one regiment of the 208th Anti-Aircraft Missile Brigade, and the number of units increased by at least a brigade following the all-out invasion. This is a reconstruction of a 9A38 TELAR of the Shepetivka-based 11th Anti-Aircraft Missile Regiment. (Artworks by David Bocquelet & Tom Cooper)

While other variants of the S-300 SAM system were envisaged as tactical weapons, primarily suitable for engaging aircraft and helicopters, the S-300V was meant to protect Soviet armies from strikes by NATO's ballistic missiles. It used the chassis of MT-T tracked transports, which made it more complex and expensive, but also offered better cross-country capability. Each 9A82 TELAR could either deploy two big 9M82 dedicated anti-ballistic missiles (maximum range of 100km), or four 9M83 multi-role missiles (maximum range of 76km). While the Russians continued the development of this series in the form of the S-300VM and S-300V4, the Ukrainians initially stored their S-300V1s before – starting from 2014 – overhauling them and returning enough equipment to service to equip one full brigade and one regiment. All three units saw intensive action in 2022, when one S-300V1 SAM site was even deployed in the Kramatorsk area. (Artwork by David Bocquelet)

The primary COMINT/ELINT-gathering platform of the VKS as of 2022 remained the venerable Ilyushin Il-20, 10 of which were brought up to the Il-20MS Retsensent – or similar – standard, illustrated here, and operational as of 2022. Another Il-20M was equipped with the capability to provide secure targeting for the 9-S-7760 Kinzhal missile system. The type was heavily involved in supporting all the assault operations of the VKS early during the all-out invasion of February 2022: subsequently, it was regularly deployed in support of SEAD operations to search for Ukrainian air defence systems. While one Il-22M airborne command post was damaged by Ukrainian SAMs in the course of such an operation on 3 April 2022, as far as is known, none of the Il-20Ms was ever hit. The fleet retained its medium-grey overall livery throughout the war, but most aircraft had all of their serials and service titles removed. (Artwork by Tom Cooper)

After being deployed in the carpet-bombing of Mariupol in March and April 2022, the VKS fleet of Tu-22M-3 bombers was sent into action again in mid-May of the same year: this time equipped with powerful Kh-32 and/or Kh-22M air-to-ground missiles. For this purpose, not only the aircraft of the 52nd and 840th Regiments, but also a handful of aircraft from the Shaykovka-based 40th Composite Aviation Regiment were deployed. Indeed, the two Tu-22M-3s illustrated here – Bort 01 (registration RF-94161) and Bort 46 (registration RF-34112) – both appear to have been not only overhauled relatively recently (around 2018–2020), but also operated by the 40th Regiment as of 2022. Both were last seen wearing relatively new livery and the insignia of the Long-Range Aviation under their cockpits and carrying a single Kh-32 under their left wing. (Artworks by Tom Cooper)

On 14 or 15 March 2022, the Russians deployed the MiG-31K and 9-S-7760 Kinzhal combination in combat for the first time. The sole unit operating this weapons system was the 44th Special Purpose Aviation Regiment, assigned – as made clear by the application of that service's crest on the intake of several of its jets (and as shown here) – to the Long-Range Aviation, and thus directly subordinated to the *GenStab* in Moscow. Officially established on 1 December 2021, the 44th was organised into three squadrons, and may have received total of 36 jets, all former MiG-31DZs, brought up to the MiG-31K standard. Two of these were designated MiG-31I and reportedly served by either launching satellites into orbit or deploying anti-satellite weapons. Gauging by the fact that this jet was subsequently put on public display and participated in the 9 May parade over Moscow, it is possible that Bort 36 was the first MiG-31K to ever fire a Kinzhal in combat. (Artwork by Tom Cooper)

Starting in March 2022, the VKS began rotating detachments of four, sometimes six, MiG-31BM (from the 712th Fighter Aviation Regiment, home-based at Kansk AB) or MiG-31BSM interceptors (98th Fighter Aviation Regiment at Monchegorsk AB) to Balbek AB in the occupied Crimean peninsula. Equipped with the powerful Zaslon-M radar, R-37M (MiG-31BM) and R-33M (MiG-31BSM) long-range air-to-air missiles, and R-77-1 medium-range air-to-air missiles, and capable of super-cruising at Mach 1.23, or accelerating to the speed of Mach 2.83 at high altitude, the type quickly proved untouchable by Ukrainian interceptors and claimed its first aerial victory on 28 April 2022. All were painted in camouflage grey (BS381C/626) overall, with dielectric surfaces in dark gull grey (FS2311). More recently modernised examples have usually received their borts in new fonts, and aircraft of the 712th Regiment had them repeated in white on the rudder. (Artwork by Tom Cooper)

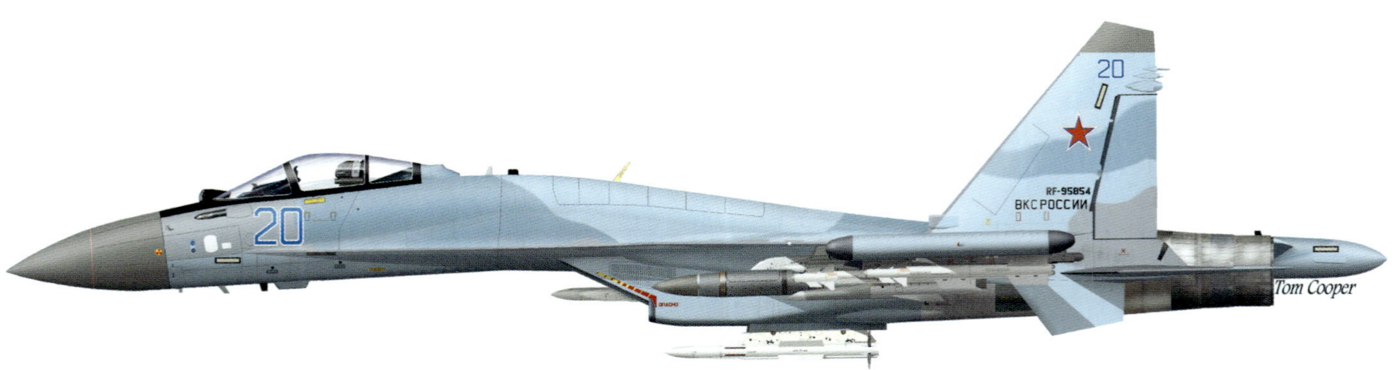

This is a reconstruction of Su-35S Bort 20 (registration RF-95854): one of 12 jets assigned to the 22nd Fighter Aviation Regiment and deployed at Baranovichi AB in early 2022. The others were borts 01, 05, 08, 11, 14, 16, 17, 20, 26, 27, 28, and 35. The unit was operationally subordinated to the 23rd Fighter Aviation Regiment, but its aircraft were flown by pilots from both regiments. Considered the 'favourite mount' of Major Alan Georgievich Datiev – awarded 'Hero of the Russian Federation', and effectively declared the 'leading ace' of the 'special military operation' with a total of 12 officially credited aerial victories – Bort 20 is shown with the typical armament configuration for the first two or three months of the all-out invasion: including a pair of Kh-58 anti-radiation missiles, and four each of R-77-1s and R-74s (where R-77-1s were installed in pairs between the intakes). (Artwork by Tom Cooper)

Unlike the 'famous' Bort 20, Su-35S Bort 61 (registration RF-81752) experienced a shorter, and less successful career. In 2017, it was one of 14 aircraft of this type delivered to the 159th Fighter Aviation Regiment (home-based at Byesovyets AB). Probably deployed in the all-out invasion right from its start, on 3 April 2022 it became the first ever Su-35S to be shot down in combat. The jet crashed in an area – between the villages of Pisky-Radkivski and Nyzhche Solone, in the Izyum Rayon – still controlled by Ukrainian forces, and with much of its weaponry (including Kh-58s, R-77-1s, and R-74s) and sensitive electronics of its L-265M10 Khibiny wing-tip-mounted electronic warfare pods still intact. It is near certain that these were forwarded to the National Air and Space Intelligence Center in the USA for further investigation, thus delivering a major intelligence coup for the USA and Ukraine. The pilot, Major Sergey Malov, ejected safely, and attempted to evade, but was captured about 10km from the crash site. (Artwork by Tom Cooper)

This is a reconstruction of Su-34 Bort 09 (registration RF-93838) in late April 2022, while involved in SEAD operations in the Izyum area. It is illustrated as equipped with the KNIRTI SAP-14 electronic warfare pod. At the time, three variants were known, each custom-tailored for integration on a specific aircraft type: the KC418E (for exported Su-24MK2s), L-175M10-35 (for the Su-35S) and L-175V Khibiny-10V (for Su-34s). Early in combat over Ukraine, the system proved very powerful, often causing Ukrainian radar- and SAM operators to lose situational awareness. However, it also proved inflexible: relying on Digital Radio Frequency Memory, it depended on a threat library updated at regular intervals, targeting radars that worked on a constant frequency. The Ukrainians quickly learned to avoid being disturbed by using frequency-hopping, variating the pulse width, or with no repetitive patterns – in turn making it impossible for L-175Vs to mimic their signals. (Artwork by Tom Cooper)

On 13 March 2022, while flying air strikes in support of the VSRF's offensive on Izyum, the 559th Bomber Aviation Regiment of the VKS suffered its first loss, in the form of Su-34 Bort 35 (registration RF-95010), shot down directly over the town by a Ukrainian Buk M1 SAM (the crew evaded capture). The 277th Bomber Aviation Regiment is known to have operated a jet wearing the same bort, but with the registration RF-81255, as illustrated here. When seen for the last time, in July 2022, this had big eyes applied either side of the forward fuselage, 11 red stars – denoting a total of 110 combat sorties flown over Syria and Ukraine – under the cockpit, white 'V' quick identification markings, and the Russian tricolour over both of its rudders. Moreover, it carried two Kh-29 guided missiles installed on hardpoints under its intakes. Insets show other long-range air-to-ground missiles frequently deployed by Su-34s: Kh-59M Ovod-M (left) and Kh-59MK (right). (Artwork by Tom Cooper)

In similar fashion as over Syria in 2015–2018, most of the VKS's combat sorties over Ukraine were flown by older, but 'less flashy' types, like Su-24s and Su-25s. Indeed, starting in April 2022, the Wagner PMC was given a handful of each to be flown by its crews. In addition to deploying S-8 80mm unguided rockets from B-8M pods in lofting attacks, whenever possible, these venerable bombers were sent into direct strikes. Whenever such opportunities arose – usually because intensive SEAD operations had suppressed Ukrainian air defences to the necessary degree – Su-24s were armed with OFAB-500ShN incendiary parachute-retarded bombs (as shown in the inset on Bort 50), or even with ODAB-1500 fuel-air explosive bombs, as shown on Bort 45 (decorated with a total of 19 red stars for 190 combat sorties flown over Syria and Ukraine). (Artworks by Tom Cooper)

By early March 2022, the Su-25-equipped 266th Assault Aviation Regiment had lost both its commander (Lieutenant Colonel Rusland Rudnev) and his deputy (Lieutenant Colonel Oleg Chervov), while the 18th Assault Aviation Regiment lost five jets and three pilots – all during the fighting in the Kyiv area. Both units were withdrawn to Buturlinovka AB: reinforced by pilots and aircraft from the 999th Air Base in Kant, they subsequently supported the drive on Izyum and Lyman. This is a reconstruction of a Su-25SM-3 of the 368th Assault Aviation Regiment. Home-based at Budyonnovsk AB, but forward-deployed to Millerovo, this regiment operated aircraft equipped with MSP-410/L/S-K25 ECM pods (shown installed on the outboard underwing pylon) and missile approach warning systems (both elements of the L370K25 Vitebsk-25 self-protection suite). They saw intensive action in the assaults on Popasna and Severodonetsk, where several were hit by MANPADS, but all returned safely back to base. (Artwork by Tom Cooper)

The Mil Mi-8MNP-2 was a special tactical reconnaissance version of this venerable helicopter family developed for the GRU and its Spetsnaz formations. This variant had many of its cockpit windows replaced with dielectric covers for various sensors and a large navigation radar under the nose. The bigger turret under the right side of the cockpit included the GOES-342 or OPS-24N-1 electro-optical complex (including a low-light camera), while the smaller one served the GOES-337M3 electro-optical surveillance system, combining a TV camera, IR sensor and a laser rangefinder. Another major difference compared to the fleet standard was the installation of two spindle-shaped pods above the outboard weapons outriggers. Finally, Mi-8MNP-2s were fitted with four missile approach warning systems high on their fuselage. This example (registration RF-23107) is shown armed with a UPK-25 gun-pod and Izdeliye-305 LMUR ATGMs. (Artwork by Tom Cooper)

Early during the Russian invasion, Mi-28s saw less action than either the older Mi-24/35s or Ka-52s: even once they were deployed more intensively, in late March 2022, the type suffered a series of losses. Amongst these were two examples shot down in the Kharkiv area on 30 and 31 March: the first, Bort 65 (registration RF-13628) was brought down in the Elitnie area, and the crew – Major Artem Ogoltsov and Captain Alexander Prikhodko – was killed. The second example, Mi-28N Bort 70 (registration RF-13654, shown here), was shot down near Tsyrkuny: the fate of the crew, including pilot S. T. Kurzhumbaev, remains unknown. Both Mi-28s are known to have worn this standardised camouflage pattern: for illustration purposes, this profile of Bort 70 shows it armed with Izdeliye 305 LMUR guided missiles, introduced to service two months later. (Artwork by Tom Cooper)

With the type not only leading all the advances of ground forces, but gradually beginning to play the role of 'sniper', scouting and then targeting Ukrainian armoured vehicles at long range – usually with use of 9K121 Vikhr laser-beam-riding ATGMs (ASCC/NATO reporting name 'AT-16 Scallion') – losses of the Russian Ka-52s remained high through April 2022. Shot down by Stugna-P ATGM operators of the 95th Airborne Brigade in the southern Izyum area sometime between 15 and 20 April 2022, this example – Bort 98 (registration RF-13441) – might have been the first helicopter from which the crew (Captain Kobets and Major Boldyrev) ejected safely in combat. The two Russians, who had already been shot down during the heliborne assault on Antonov IAP on 24 February 2022 survived and were subsequently awarded the 'Hero of the Russian Federation'. (Artwork by Luca Canossa)

Through the two months of the battle of Popasna, Ka-52s of several VKS units continuously pounded the positions of the 24th Mechanised Brigade with 'spray-and-pray' attacks, using B-8M pods for unguided rockets: indeed, it was in this area that such tactics was observed for this first time, and by the time Popasna fell, literally thousands of such attacks had been flown by Ka-52s, and Mi-28s, Su-24s, and Su-25s. This example – anonymised through crude overpainting of its national markings and other insignia, except for a white 'V' on the side of the engine – was observed while operating from a forward base, probably Lysychansk airport, in mid-April 2022. Notable is the carriage of the drop tank – which occurred early during this battle: later, Ka-52s were regularly loaded with four B-8Ms, indicating their deployment closer to the battlefield. (Artwork by Luca Canossa)

Ukraine placed its first order for 12 of Turkish designed and manufactured Bayraktar TB.2 UCAVs in 2019. By 2022, several follow-up orders may have brought their total to more than 30, however, subsequent deliveries were largely kept secret, and thus it is unclear how many of about 35 TB.2s known to have been delivered since March 2022 were manufactured on pre-war orders. What is certain is that five of them were originally crowdfounded by Lithuanian, Polish, and Ukrainian citizens. Deploying MAM-C and MAM-L laser-guided mini-bombs, Ukrainian TB.2s were highly effective in harassing poorly protected Russian columns in the first few days of the all-out invasion. However, through March, April, and May the Russian air defence operators learned to counter them and Moscow claimed more than 30 as shot down (14 of which were visually confirmed). Consequently, the Ukrainians began deploying the type for observation purposes instead. (Artwork by Goran Sudar)

Through late February and March 2022, fighter units of the PSZSU were regularly scrambled in attempts to intercept at least some of the Russian aircraft underway over northern-central Ukraine. Around 16.10hrs on 25 February 2022, two jets of the 114th Brigade, PSZSU, were scrambled from Ivano-Frankivsk AB. After an air combat with Russian fighters, around 16.40hrs, while returning to the same air base, MiG-29S Bort 35 Blue (usually assigned to the 204th Brigade) then crashed between the villages of Korolevka and Grushka. The pilot ejected safely. Following about a dozen similar experiences, with next to no positive results in return, the Ukrainian air force began deploying its interceptors against cruise missiles instead: it was in this role that both MiG-29 and Su-27s proved more effective. (Artwork by Luca Canossa)

Following numerous negative experiences with friendly fire, by April 2022 both the 7th and the 299th brigades of the PSZSU began painting ever-larger undersurface areas of their aircraft in yellow, to make them easier to recognise as friendly for their own ground troops. Ukrainian Su-24Ms also began deploying old Kh-25ML laser-guided missiles (guided by their internally-installed Kayra-24 target designators) and Kh-25MRs with radio-command guidance. Bort 84 White was one of two jets sent to strike Zmiinyi Island during the night of 25 to 26 June. Around 00.26hrs, shortly after releasing its weapons – probably Kh-25s – it was hit by a Russian interceptor and shot down. The loss and the death of the crew consisting of pilot Colonel Mykhailo Matiushenko and his weapons systems operator, Major Yuriy Krasylnikov, was kept secret for months, until in October 2022 Matiushenko's body was found off the coast of Romania. (Artwork by Luca Canossa)

After suffering an unknown degree of combat damage early during the war, Su-24M 04 White was repaired and completely repainted in dark grey overall (in similar fashion to Su-24MR 11 White). Its undersides were painted in yellow, a national flag applied in front of the intake, and the entire rudder and both drop tanks repainted in Ukrainian national colours. As usual, the jet also had the black dragon – the insignia of the 7th Brigade – on the intake. The final touch included the application of 'mission markings' in the form of small Ukrainian tridents in yellow: the last time Bort 04 was photographed, it had three of these. The highest known number amongst Ukrainian Su-24Ms was 11 mission markings, for a total of 110 combat sorties. (Artwork by Luca Canossa).

Belonging to the group of Su-25M1s that received the 'light' version of the 'pixel' camouflage pattern following overhaul and upgrade, the 40 Blue was another jet of this type that saw only short service during the Russian all-out invasion. Around 13.15hrs on 3 March 2022, it was shot down while attacking a Russian column in the Novooleksandrivka area, halfway between Voznesensk and Mykloaiv. The pilot, Captain Vadim Serhiyovych Moroz, was killed and unlike many other cases his demise did not attract much attention from the Ukrainian public, and he was posthumously awarded only modestly. This reconstruction of 40 Blue shows it armed with four S-25OFM 250mm unguided rockets with explosive-fragmentation warheads: such weapons were usually deployed against hardened targets. (Artwork by Luca Canossa)

Su-25 27 Blue was a veteran of the Afghanistan War in the 1980s, and the Donbas War of 2014. After being stored in 2015, in late February 2022, it was rushed through an overhaul. When reappearing in service with the 299th Brigade in April or May, it was repainted in dark gull grey (FS36231) overall. The undersides of the engine nacelles were then also painted in yellow, and the lower portion of the rudder received Ukrainian national colours. On the nose, the jet wore an emblem denoting it as a veteran of the Afghanistan War, with the number of sorties flown in that conflict. This reconstruction shows it armed with four Kh-25MLs: a laser-guided weapon first observed in operational service with the 299th Brigade in May 2022. (Artwork by Luca Canossa)

The Mil Mi-14 is a version of the Mi-8 family custom-tailored for anti-submarine warfare, with a boat-shaped lower fuselage, and a four-point undercarriage retracting into large sponsons. Its original primary equipment and armament included sonobuoys and a search radar, as well as guided torpedoes and depth charges. Only three Ukrainian Mi-14PLs were evacuated from their home-base in Novofedorvika during the Russian invasion of Crimea in 2014, and a total of four were available eight years later. These were locally overhauled and received a disruptive camouflage pattern in light blue atop their old grey-blue overall livery. This is a reconstruction of Mi-14PL Bort 34, crewed by – amongst others – Colonel Ihor Bedzay – when the helicopter was shot down by a Russian Su-35 on 7 May 2022. (Artwork by Luca Canossa)

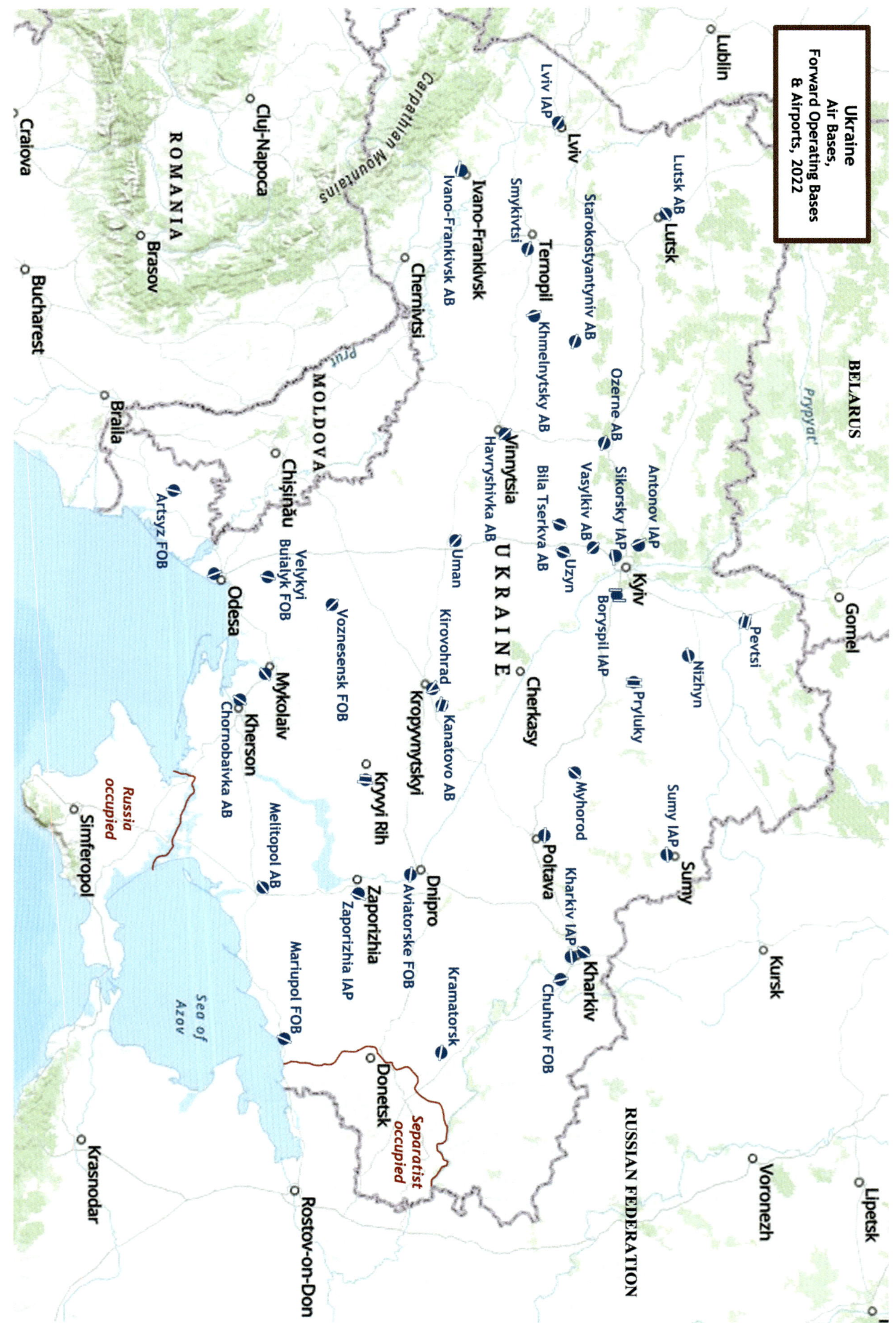

A map of air bases, forward operating bases, and other airports and airfields with tarmacked runways in Ukraine as of March–June 2022. (Map by Tom Cooper)

5
CAULDRON

While closely monitoring the assault by his forces and the Wagner PMC against the 24th Mechanised Brigade in the Popasna area, through the last few days of April 2022, Dvornikov and his staff went to great lengths to reorganise their battered BTGs in the Izyum area, and then reinforced their efforts in this area through an additional attack on Lyman.

Preparations

Finding no other way to quickly rebuild dozens of mauled BTGs of the 1st GTA and the 6th CAA grouped in the Izyum area, during late April 2022, Dvornikov introduced an unusual measure: he re-assigned remaining elements from badly damaged units to those that were still largely intact – irrespective of their original assignment to brigades, divisions, combined arms armies, and thus strategic joint commands. Unsurprisingly, this caused significant confusion both in regards of command and logistics, but: under the given circumstances – especially Putin's constant pressure for the VSRF to advance quicker – there was no other option. The net result was an assault force that included a total of 18 motorised BTGs and four armoured BTGs from the 1st GTA, 20th Guards Combined Arms Army, 35th Combined Arms Army, 36th Combined Arms Army, and LVIII Army Corps. Much more effective was his reorganisation of the VSRF's artillery in this area: the majority of pieces were consolidated into tactical groups established through the combination of available assets. Two additional groups came into being through reactivating sufficient numbers of 2S7 Pion/Malka self-propelled 203mm guns from the 94th Arsenal outside Omsk. Fire control for all these units was exercised directly from the headquarters of OSK South. By early May 2022, about a dozen tactical artillery groups were operational and deployed in a semi-circle stretching from Izyum, around Severodonetsk to Popasna. Each was equipped with between 80 and 90 guns, and responsible for supporting either a single brigade or up to three BTGs.

At least as significant were the Russian preparations carried out in the rear. Amongst others, in late April, the 29th Railway Brigade of the VSRF constructed a new rail bridge across the Oskil River in Kupyansk to replace the one destroyed by the withdrawing Ukrainians. In this fashion, the VSRF reconnected the railway line from Russia via Vovchansk to Kupyansk, thus immensely bolstering its logistic capabilities by an order of magnitude. That said, even this effort was to prove too little. The reason was related to logistics: between 18 and 20 April 2022, the Russians managed to secure Kreminna. However, Lyman remained under the control of the 57th Motorised Brigade, ZSU. Therefore, the VSRF had no railway link directly to the battlefield selected for the coming offensive – which was planned to take place in the middle of the huge Serebryansky forest, stretching between the two towns and the Siversky Donets River in the south. Eventually, this was to prove fatal.

The VKS was prepared to support this operation as well, and on as massive a scale as the artillery of the VSRF – although it changed little in regards of its equipment, composition or tactics. The centrepiece of its activities remained A-50s combined with Il-22Ms and Il-20Ms. Occasionally, Tu-214R intelligence-gatherers were added, but they frequently operated at the discretion of the GRU instead of in cooperation with OSK South. After earlier, unpleasant experiences, all airborne control aircraft always remained inside Russian airspace, parallel to the borders with Ukraine: one station was east of Luhansk, and the other over the Sea of Azov – always at least 70–90 kilometres behind the frontline, to remain safely outside the range of Ukrainian S-300s. Every trio of A-50s, Il-22s, and Il-20Ms was escorted by at least a pair of Su-35S interceptors. The primary task of A-50s remained 'air traffic control': the coordination of movements by other aircraft. The Il-20Ms were trying to track down the work of Ukrainian command nodes: the resulting intelligence was forwarded to Il-22s or downloaded to the headquarters of OSK South, which then distributed targets to controllers aboard A-50s, which in turn provided target coordinates to the pilots of fighter-bomber formations. Only relatively few VSRF units had any forward air controllers deployed with them: most of these were actually busy operating UAVs for reconnaissance purposes.

At the tactical level, and regardless of whether running interdiction strikes or close air support operations, the VKS continued sending high-flying, demonstration flights of Su-34s and Su-35Ss forward, attempting to prompt Ukrainian SAM units to power up their radars and thus unmask and expose themselves to attacks by Kh-31P/PD anti-radiation missiles. Fighter-bombers would usually follow once the PSZSU's positions were unmasked. Generally, the crews of Su-24 and Su-25 fighter-bombers and ground attack aircraft received a set of preselected GPS and/or GLONASS coordinates of their possible targets before their take-off. Once airborne, they would receive the final selection of targets from the A-50s and then conduct their air strikes at tree-top level. Because it often took time for the Il-20Ms to collect the necessary intelligence, and for this then to be distributed to the headquarters of OSK South, or at least to the Il-22M airborne command posts, and then confirm and forward this to controllers on board of A-50s, the endurance of individual fighter jets was at a premium. This is why Su-25s were regularly equipped with four drop tanks, and why there were frequent situations where the VKS had between 15 and 20 fighter-bombers 'on station', circling the skies east and south of the battlefield, and waiting for their assignment. While the majority of air strikes resulted in the release of unguided 80mm or 130mm rockets through the lofting or spray-and-pray manoeuvres, Su-24Ms especially were still, and regularly, sent to deploy free-fall bombs while overflying their targets. Top cover for fighter-bomber operations was usually provided by additional Su-30s and Su-35s.[1]

The Gate to Donbas

While Dvornikov's main push south of Izyum was constantly experiencing delays, other parts of the VSRF's group of forces in the Izyum area were not standing idle. On the contrary, on 13 April, two BTGs of the 201st Military Base (essentially a VSRF brigade home-based in Dushanbe in Tajikistan) managed to take the Ukrainians by surprise through seizing Borova. Weakly defended by elements of the 57th Motorised Brigade and the local Territorial Defence, the town quickly fell. From there, the Russians pressed on in the direction of Lyman – a key railway junction about 20km north of Slovyansk – still known as *Krasny Lyman* (Red Lyman), and even 'The Gates of Donbas' amongst VSRF officers – another Russian 'sentimental' objective.[2]

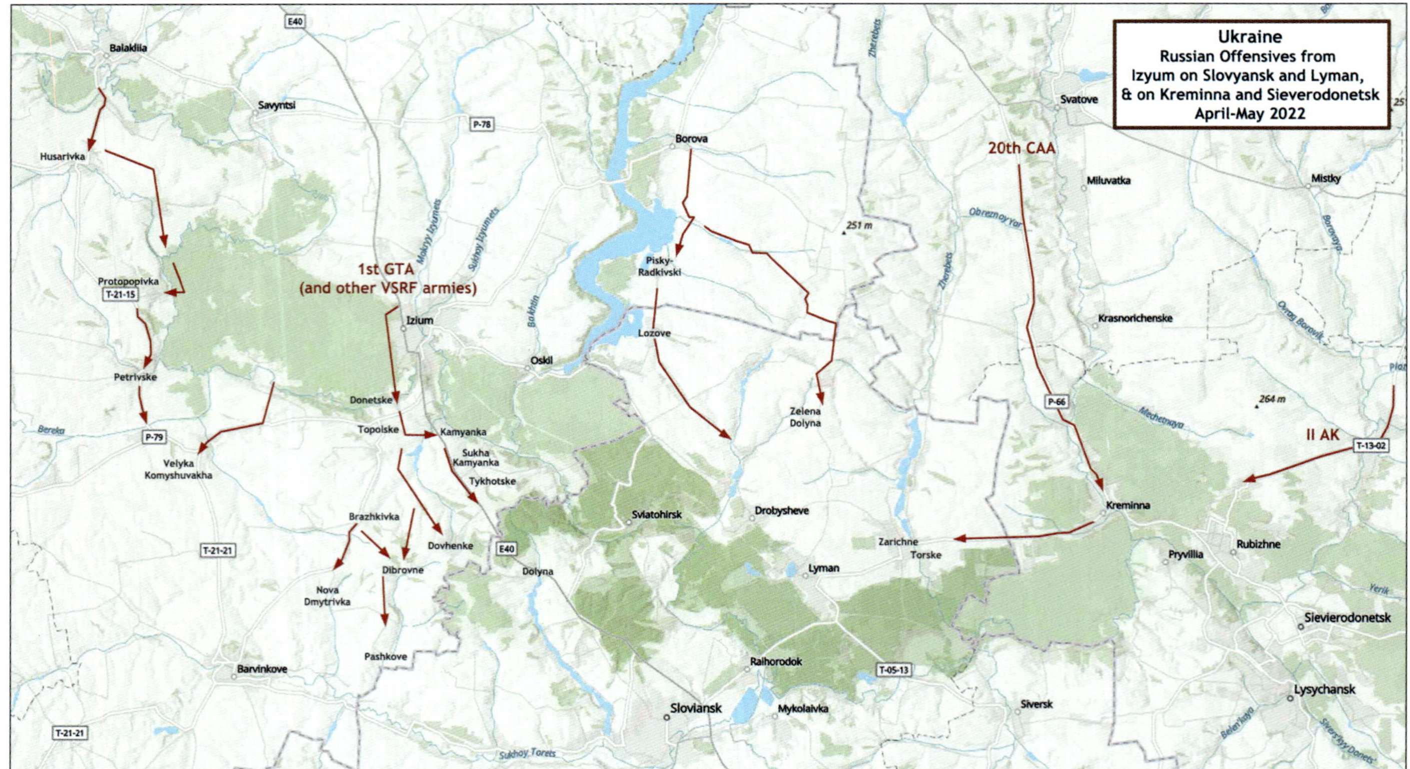

A map of the area between Balakliya (or Balakllia), Lyman, Kreminna, Severodonetsk, and Lysychansk, which became the focus of the Russian offensive efforts from the north – under 'Plan D', in April and May 2022. Notable are several changes of directions of the main assaults of the 1st GTA (and elements from several other VSRF armies) from Izyum towards the south. Eventually, the Russian onslaught was stopped between Dibrovne, Dovhenke, Dolyna and Sviatohirsk, and Dvornikov was forced to replace it with a new assault from Borova and Kreminna on Lyman. (Map by Tom Cooper)

A pair of Russian Su-25s releasing chaff and flares after their lofting strike in the Lyman area on 20 April 2022. (Ukrainian social media)

By 20 April, the 201st Military Base secured Pisky-Radkivski and Lozove. As usual, the VKS operated correspondingly, heavily bombing and rocketing Ukrainian positions along the entire front line in the semi-circle from Husarivka to Lozove. Indeed, this advance and Gerasimov's presence were almost certain to have given Dvornikov the idea of bolstering this effort: on 22 April, one BTG of the 201st Military Base reached the northern outskirts of Yatskivka, thus distracting Ukrainian attention away from a rapid advance of the other formation of this brigade, which seized Zelena Dolyna. In the best traditions of the Russian military doctrine, the successful unit was then rapidly bolstered by a BTG each of the 74th Guards Motor-Rifle Brigade and the 237th Guards Tank Regiment, most of the 7th and 9th brigades of the Luhansk People's Republic, and the 24th Spetsnaz Brigade. Under enormous pressure, the Ukrainian 57th Motorised Brigade was left with little option but to fall back into a defence perimeter around Lyman, stretching from Olekandrivka and Serednie in the west, to Zarichne in the east. This manoeuvre was completed just in time, because on 1 May a platoon of the 24th Spetsnaz Brigade suddenly appeared inside Yampil, five kilometres east of Lyman. Although this Russian attack was spoiled, only a few kilometres further east Dvornikov's troops drove deep into the Serebryansky forest, thus setting the scene for the next showdown.

Battle of the Siversky Donets

The new Russian attempt to cross the Siversky Donets began on 2 May 2022, when multiple teams of operators from the 24th Spetsnaz Brigade crossed the river east of Shypylivka, a village two kilometres west of Lysychansk. While they managed to cause quite some chaos in the rear of ZSU units defending the area, on the morning of 3 May a small task force of the 30th Mechanised Brigade counterattacked. After neutralising several BMPs and a few infantry squads, the Ukrainians also destroyed a PMP ponton bridge that the Russians had constructed on the western side of Shypylivka.

Slowed down by the mud and dense vegetation of the Serebryansky forest, the Spetsnaz took two days to find a new crossing site, thus buying plenty of time for the 30th Mechanised Brigade, reinforced by elements of the 17th Tank Brigade, to mop up scattered survivors of the first crossing attempt in the area between Pryvillya, Novodruzhesk and Bilohorivka, the last of which was a small mining town of about 1,000 people, just four kilometres west of Lysychansk. Late on 5 May, the 12th Engineer Brigade of the VSRF constructed a PP-2205 floating bridge west of Serebryanka (two kilometres west of Bilohorivka). Early the next morning, the VKS flew numerous air strikes on Severodonetsk and Lysychansk, apparently trying to distract Ukrainian attention away from the new crossing site and to pin down the ZSU units there. However, when a BTG of the 35th Motor-Rifle Brigade of the VSRF made a second crossing attempt, the 17th Tank promptly counterattacked, and destroyed the bridge together with a number of BMPs.

Although by now it must have been obvious to everybody in the *GenStab* and Kremlin that the Ukrainians were carefully scouting the Siversky Donets River with their UAVs, Dvornikov, probably under pressure from Putin, decided to continue bolstering a failure. On 7 May, under cover of vicious air strikes by Su-24s, Su-25s, and Su-35s of the VKS – one of which demolished the school in Bilohorivka, where up to 90 civilians were sheltering inside the basement – and severe artillery barrages, his engineers constructed two floating bridges: one PP-2205 and one PP-91.[3]

Both were positioned in a bend of the Siversky Donets about one kilometre north of Bilohorivka: correspondingly, the approaches to them were not only covered by dense vegetation, but the Ukrainians could counterattack from the east only. Early on 8 May, a BTG each of the 6th Tank Regiment and the 35th Motor-Rifle Brigade launched their crossing attempts in full force. However, by that point in time, the ZSU had almost all of its artillery pieces in the area – including the first battery of US-made M777 towed 155mm howitzers – zeroed in on the Russian bridgehead. Their fire was reinforced by several Tochka-U ballistic missiles, and multiple air strikes by Su-25s of the Ukrainian air force. As a result, both Russian BTGs were routed: the most conservative estimates of VSRF casualties during this crossing attempt were for 485 killed and wounded, while visual evidence confirmed the destruction of more than 100 tanks and other armoured vehicles.[4]

Almost certainly under pressure from Putin, OSK South continued trying. During the night of 9 to 10 May, the Russians constructed yet another PP-2205 bridge north of Bilohorivka: however, when their third BTG – drawn either from the 15th Motor-Rifle Brigade or the 74th Guards Motor-Rifle Brigade – attempted to cross the following morning, it was blasted with all available artillery pieces and air strikes of Ukrainian fighter-bombers again. After losing about a dozen T-72s and 50 other vehicles, the survivors of the unit fell back to the northern side of the river. Arguably, the Ukrainian 17th Tank and the 30th Mechanised brigade suffered numerous losses during their counterattacks, and were constantly kept busy with mopping up scattered Russian survivors along the southern bank of the Siversky Donets; however, in grand total, the Battle of the Siversky Donets ended in a colossal Russian defeat, including the almost complete loss of three BTGs. Dvornikov's second attempt to cut off the concentration of up to 40,000 Ukrainian troops holding Severodonetsk, Lysychansk, Slovyansk, Kramatorsk and Bakhmut through combined assaults over the Siversky Donets in the north and Popasna in the south, failed.

Culmination

Simultaneously with the crossing attempt in the Bilohorivka area, Dvornikov resumed offensive operations from the area south of Izyum. Between 2 and 7 May 2022, two BTGs of the 35th CAA assaulted Vinopily and Nova Dmytrivka, On 10 May, the Russians then changed the direction of their attack and assaulted Dovhenke from two sides – but were repelled once again and stopped this prong of their operation. With OSK South preoccupied with developments further east, the VKS only sporadically took part in the fighting in this area – even more so because the PSZSU air defences were still intact. Indeed, the VSRF concentration south of Izyum resumed its offensive only on 28–29 May, with yet another assault on Dovhenke: ironically, by then, the village had been reported as 'liberated' by the

A Su-25 of the PSZSU flying at less than 50 metres altitude, armed with a total of four B-13M pods, seen approaching the combat zone on 7 May 2022. (Ukrainian social media)

Russians at least three times, although they never managed more than to reach its northern outskirts. Simultaneously, the Russians began assaulting Studenok, with the aim of reaching Bohorodichne and then Sviatohirsk. After six days of fighting, the VSRF did manage to reach Bohorodychne – which forced the ZSU to evacuate Studenok – but was repelled at Dovhenke again. Nevertheless, the seizure of Studenok was to prove a major gem, because it enabled OSK South to make use of the railway line from Vovchansk and Kupyansk and thus tranship both supplies and fresh troops of the 29th Combined Arms Army (29th CAA) almost directly to the frontline. As a consequence of the renewed pressure, between 4 and 6 June the Ukrainians also withdrew from good defence positions in Sviatohirsk, on the northern bank of the Siversky Donets.

Early on 7 June, the 29th CAA opened a new assault on Dovhenke, and launched another on Dolyna. Both attacks were initiated by heavy air strikes, followed by massive artillery barrages, reinforced by several volleys from TOS-1 launchers. Arguably, the ZSU withdrew its garrison from the former on 11 June, enabling the Russians to refocus their attention on Dolyna and Bohorodychne instead: however, the Ukrainians held out there, also because all the VSRF attempts to cross the Siversky Donets from Sviatorhirsk to Tetyanivka were destroyed by Ukrainian artillery and 9M79 Tochka-U ballistic missiles. The Russians then refocused on assaulting Dolyna and Bohorodychne, and did so for four days: by 15 June, they were well inside Bohorodichne when the Ukrainians counterattacked by night and mauled one of the enemy BTGs, recovering most of the place. The Russians were more successful in Dolyna though: they seized the village by 16 June, despite multiple air strikes by Su-25s of the PSZSU and Ukrainian claims by the 93rd Mechanised to have shot down another supporting Su-25.

The Fall of Lyman

Meanwhile, in the area east of the Oskil River, the 201st Military Base and two BTGs of the 30th Motor-Rifle Brigade, supported by heavy air strikes, continued advancing via Krymky and Oleksandrivka to Novoselivka, Drobysheve, and Shandryholove, pushing the 57th Mechanised Brigade into a continuously decreasing perimeter around Lyman. Over the following days, the engineers of the ZSU blew up almost all the remaining bridges across the Siversky Donets in the area including two in the Studenok area, one in Bohorodichne,

A still from a video captured by a reconnaissance UAV, showing the Monastery of Svyatohirsk (right side) with the demolished bridge to Bohordichne (left side), on or around 5 June 2022. (Ukrainian social media)

and the one in Ozerne. The Lyman railway bridge – connecting that town with Railhorodok and thus Slovyansk – was dropped by several successive Russian air strikes using Kh-59s.

Despite the loss of about 40 armoured vehicles within just two days, by 13 May, the Russians were assaulting all the way from Olekandrivka and Shandryholove to Novoselivka and captured Yampil. The ZSU meanwhile reinforced the 57th with elements of the 3rd Tank, 79th Airborne, and the 128th Mountain Assault brigades, but these were under attack from BTGs from the 201st Military Base, 90th Tank Division, 15th Motor-Rifle Brigade, 24th Spetsnaz Brigade, and separatists, supported by at least two artillery groups. After a massive artillery barrage and over 200 air strikes mauled one of 79th Airborne's battalions (reportedly inflicting over 100 casualties and causing up to 200 survivors to surrender), on 25 May, the Russians breached the defence perimeter and, by 27 May, secured the northern side of Lyman. By the following morning, shaken survivors of the Ukrainian garrison were withdrawing into the forests of Sviati Hory National Park, further south-west and south, prompting reports in the Ukrainian social media according to which the RFA was 'only 5km outside Slovyansk'. Actually, the dense forests and the broken terrain in this area were to prove ideal for the construction of a new defence line north of the Siversky Donets.

Battle of Severodonetsk

OSK South was still in the process of preparing the onslaught on Lyman when, on 10–11 May 2022, the ZSU forces within the cauldron of Severodonetsk experienced their first major crisis. Once again, the reason was the advance by the separatists of II AK, and Wagner mercenaries in the Popasna area: indeed, when these captured the villages of Oleksandropillia and Komyshuvakha it appeared that the Ukrainian frontline effectively collapsed. In order to restore their defences and construct a new defence line along the T1302 – the 'Road of Life' for ZSU units in Severodonetsk and Lysychansk – the Ukrainians rushed to the scene whatever parts they could spare from a variety of formations, including from the 17th Tank, 80th Airborne, 58th Motorised, 14th Mechanised, the 109th Territorial Defence and the 30th Mechanised brigades. Indeed, combined with the threat of encirclement through simultaneous crossing attempts over the Siversky Donets, the advance from Popasna forced the Ukrainians to withdraw the garrison of Rubizhne. Thus began the battle for Severodonetsk and a period in which the Russian superiority in artillery reached incredible proportions – even more so because there was no way for the ZSU to pack similar amounts of firepower into the cauldron between Slovyansk, Lyman, Severodonetsk, and Bakhmut. This superiority resulted in the PSZSU also withdrawing most of its remaining SAM systems further to the rear: to the area between Kramatorsk and Bakhmut. The fact was that even though reinforced by at least a battery of S-300V1s around 13 May, these could not survive in the face of the combined onslaught of the VKS and the Russian artillery. The result was unavoidable: the number of Russian aircraft and helicopters claimed and confirmed as shot down rapidly decreased, although the intensity of their operations remained high.

Sensing an opportunity, on 18 and 19 May Dvornikov deployed his operational reserve in the Popasna area: elements of the 76th VDV and the 90th Tank divisions. Heavily supported by attack helicopters, these captured Volodymyrivka, and then Nova Kamyanka. The Ukrainians fought back with everything to hand, including air strikes by Su-24s and Su-25s: one of the former – Bort 69 – was shot down by Russian SAMs though, and crashed outside Krasnopolivka, near Bakhmut. The crew, consisting of Lieutenant Colonel Ihor Khamara and Major Illya Nehar, were killed.

Indeed, emboldened by their success, the separatists, the 150th Motor-Rifle Division and a BTG from the Wagner PMC assaulted northwards to seize Lypove while, to increase the ZSU's problems, on 22 May another mercenary BTG assaulted Pylpychatnye. When the Ukrainians deployed a battalion of the 80th Airborne to counterattack and this cut off a part of the assault force, OSK South directed air strikes by all immediately available Mi-8s, Mi-28s, Ka-52s and Su-25s against Ukrainian positions. These flew straight into a virtual 'hornet's nest': several jets and helicopters were damaged by Igla and Piorun MANPADS, while the Su-25 piloted by retired Major General Kanamat Huseinovich Botashev,

On 19 May, at the high point of the Russian breakthrough in the Popasna area, a group of three T-72 main battle tanks and two BMPT Terminator tank-support fighting vehicles of the 90th Tank Division appeared on a hill near Volodymyrivka to shell the T1302 road below them. They were stopped and then forced to withdraw by Ukrainian artillery and air strikes. (Ukrainian social media)

A pair of Ukrainian Su-25s seen early on 20 May 2022 unleashing their S-13 unguided rockets and releasing chaff and flares while trying to stop the Russian advance north-west of Popasna. (Ukrainian social media)

who now served with Wagner PMC, was caused to crash, killing the pilot. Almost unsurprisingly, only days later, reports surfaced in the Russian media about the Vitebsk self-defence suites of VKS helicopters saving dozens of machines and many lives by deflecting up to five Ukrainian MANPADs during every single sortie near the frontlines.[5]

It was probably amid the resulting chaos in the ZSU lines in the Bakhmut area that, on 23 May 2022, the VKS scored a major success against the Ukrainian air defences in this area, when it first detected and then tracked down the command post of an Osa-AKM SAM site with the use of UAVs, and then knocked it out using Kh-59 PGMs launched from Su-34s.

However, while the Ukrainians were busy trying to stop Russian assaults in the Popasna area, a third BTG of the Wagner PMC appeared in the Svitlodarsk area – a village about 25 kilometres south, positioned in between of two artificial lakes on the Luhan River. Usually, this sector of the frontline was held by two battalions of the 30th Mechanised Brigade, but now only a few weak companies were left to guard the area. Taken by surprise, these rapidly withdrew, enabling the Russians to punch through and – after rushing a BTG each of the 40th and the 336th Naval Infantry brigades into the breach – secure Myronivskyi before, by 4 June, seizing the Vuhlehirska Tes thermal powerplant, Ilovaisk, and a longer stretch of the M03/E40 highway in the direction of Bakhmut. Eventually, the ZSU managed to stabilise this sector of the frontline only through deployment of the 10th Mountain Assault Brigade along the eastern side of the cauldron.

Last-Ditch Attempts

Through all of this, Dvornikov kept the Ukrainian garrison of Severodonetsk under severe pressure. In mid-May, the separatist units subordinated to II AK seized Vojevodivka, immediately north of the city. As usual, their assaults were supported by Su-25s of the VKS and Wagner, and Ukrainian MANPAD teams claimed several of these shot down. However, confirmed was only one case: on 16 May, a Russian jet crashed into the Siversky Donets River west of Rubizhne. No ejection was observed. Nevertheless, with additional air strikes, and continuous artillery barrages, by 23 May the Russians ground themselves into the northern and eastern outskirts of Severodonetsk, and then deployed their 2S4 self-propelled 240mm

The scene of the shoot-down of Major General (ret.) Kanamat Huseinovich Botashev's Su-25, outside Pylpychatnye, on 22 May 2022. (Ukrainian social media)

Wreckage of the Su-25 piloted by Major General (ret.) Botashev, found outside Pylpychantnye. (Ukrainian Social Media via TheMilitaryWatch)

As clear from this photograph of a Su-25 returning at low speed and altitude back to Russia, taken late on 22 May 2022, this jet suffered some kind of combat damage during the action over the Severodonetsk cauldron. (Russian social media)

heavy mortars to knock out the last bridge spanning the Siversky Donets and thus connecting the city with Lysychansk.

Indeed, after the above-described success in Lyman, on 28 May, OSK South attempted to repeat the exercise in Severodonetsk: it subjected the city and ZSU positions around and inside it to over 200 air strikes and then an hours-long artillery barrage by several artillery groups, before assaulting from four directions. The Russian firepower eventually focused on a narrow sector in the northern part of the city, enabling ground troops to break through, reach the bus station and the Hotel Mir. During the following night, the Russians then deployed their Spetsnaz to infiltrate Ukrainian positions in southern Severodonetsk, aiming to cut off connections to Lysychansk. This effort was detected early though, and it took the Russians massive volumes of air support by Su-25s, the following morning, to exfiltrate their troops.

However, the vast Russian superiority was marred by two major issues. On one hand, when receiving intelligence updates, officers in the headquarters of OSK South tended to add new targets literally

A still from a video showing four Su-25s of the VKS approaching Severodonetsk at very low altitude on 26 May 2022. Each jet was equipped with a single B-13M pod for 130mm unguided rockets. (Russian social media)

to the bottom of the targeting list and only rarely reassessed their priorities while continuing to work their targeting lists from the top. Therefore, both air strikes and fire missions of the artillery regularly took place at least 20–30 minutes, and sometimes as much as 48 hours *post-factum*. The sole exception were the VSRF artillery units equipped both with MSTA-S self-propelled 152mm howitzers and their own Orlan-10 UAVs: these proved the biggest problem for the ZSU because they regularly opened fire on newly-emerging targets in a matter of three to five minutes from detection. Moreover, Orlan-10s equipped with Leer-3 electronic warfare systems proved highly effective against Ukrainian communications, UAV operations, and battlefield radars: however, the effects of their jamming were also strongly felt by the Russians.

Moreover, close air support operations kept the VKS busy to the degree where – unlike what it had been doing in April – it stopped striking railway stations in Slovyansk, Kramatorsk, and Bakhmut, and that at a time when the importance of Ukrainian railway heads was greater than ever before: because they were the means by which the ZSU was moving the majority of reinforcements and supplies for its forces inside the cauldron. Almost unsurprisingly, by 3 June, the PSZSU deployed one of its battalions equipped with S-300V1 SAMs in the Kramatorsk area, while the ZSU managed to reinforce the garrison of Severodonetsk with a battalion of the 112th Territorial Defence Brigade, reinforced with around 80 foreign volunteers. On arrival, this conducted a counterattack into northern Severodonetsk that pushed the Russians almost out of the city: as was soon to become usual in situations of this kind, OSK South reacted by ordering its Ka-52s and Su-25s into dozens of counter-strikes. On 4 June, troops of the 128th Mountain Assault Brigade shot down a Ka-52 by using a MANPAD: both Lieutenant Pavel Khrebet and Lieutenant Egor Igorevich Nosov from the 18th Army Aviation Brigade were subsequently confirmed as killed. In turn, the Russians targeted Lysychansk with a single 9M79 Tochka-U ballistic missile on 5 June, while Su-34s released at least four Kh-59 PGMs against industrial and storage facilities in the Kramatorsk area. Nevertheless, the Ukrainian counterattack enabled an orderly withdrawal of all units still present in Severodonetsk to the compound of the giant Azot Works, along the northern bank of the Siversky Donets.

The crash of the Ka-52 shot down by the 128th Mountain Assault Brigade north of Popasna on 4 June 2022. (128th Mountain Assault Brigade)

Chain Reaction

Eventually, the fate of Severodonetsk – and that of Lysychansk – was then sealed by developments further south-east. By 15 June, the Russians had not only deployed a fresh BTG of the 31st VDV Brigade to Severodonetsk, but north of Popasna they assigned the 61st Naval Infantry Brigade to the Wagner PMC: together, the two began systematically assaulting fortifications of the 24th Mechanised Brigade in Zolote and Hirske from both east and west. Moreover, in support of these efforts, the FSB and the VKS pressed into service an entirely new air-launched weapon – the Izdeliye-305 LMUR (*Legkaya Mnogotselevaya Upravlyayemaya Raketa,* 'Light Mulitpurpose Guided Rocket'). In a series of strikes flown on 18, 19, and 20 June, LMUR-armed helicopters began systematically targeting any object – hangars, halls and similar – at least resembling a 'storage site' in the Bakhmut area, for example. Additionally, the VKS returned to the practice of targeting similar buildings in the Kramatorsk area: although on 18 June one of its Su-25s (flown by Wagner mercenary, retired Major Andrey Vladimirovich Fedorchukov, who was captured), and a Kh-59M were shot down by Ukrainian air defences, the others caused lots of damage – especially to the ZSU positions in Toshkivka and Myrna Dolyna, two villages five and three kilometres south of Lysychansk, respectively, defended by elements of the 17th Tank Brigade. Indeed, on 20 June, Toshkivka was subjected to another, hours-long, murderous artillery barrage, after which it was stormed by the separatists and Wagner: in a matter of hours, the Russians advanced over the P66 road all the way via Myrna Dolyna to Pidlisne. With this, the ZSU was left with no option but to withdraw not only the surviving elements of the 24th Mechanised from Zolote and then Hirske, but also to abandon the Azot compound in Severodonetsk and thus the entire city.

A long row of Su-25SMs of the 18th Assault Aviation Regiment, VKS, lined-up at Kursk-Vostochny AB on 12 June 2022. Notably, while all wearing the same standardised camouflage pattern (see colour section for details), they all also had their registrations overpainted, and a large white letter 'Z' applied across the fin. Also notable under the wing of the second aircraft from the right is an MSP-410 Omul ECM pod. (Russian Ministry of Defence)

A scene from one of forward operating bases of the VKS in the Luhansk region, where a total of five Ka-52s were being refuelled after their previous mission. (Russian Ministry of Defence)

A pair of Russian Su-25s approaching the battlefield in the Severodonetsk area at extremely low altitude on 15 June 2022. Although the Russians kept all Ukrainian positions in the cauldron under constant artillery barrages and air strikes for weeks, and the PSZSU had to withdraw the majority of its heavy SAMs from the area, thanks to the availability of advanced MANPADs Ukrainian air defences remained extremely dangerous, and pilots of the VKS and Wagner PMC never took their safety for granted. (Russian social media)

Another pair of Su-25s of the VKS seen firing their S-8 rockets in the direction of Severodonetsk and releasing chaff and flares. Although usually exposing themselves to enemy fire for only about a dozen seconds, both Russian and Ukrainian pilots flying such sorties were facing tough odds, and several were shot down during the battle of Severodonetsk. (Russian social media)

A RARE SUCCESS

The Izdeliye-305 LMUR was one of few guided weapons successfully developed for the VKS in the early 2000s. Its development was initiated by the Tactical Missiles Corporation as early as 2007 but abandoned in 2009 for unknown reasons. Two years later, the Russian Ministry of Defence contracted the KB Mashinostoryeniya (KBM) corporation for a new system, originally designated the Izdeliye-79 (Model 79).[6] Although a batch of test missiles was completed by 2013, the results were deemed unsatisfactory and the related contract terminated without testing four years later. However, in 2012, the FSB contracted KBM to develop a slightly different weapon, the Izdeliye-305, for installation on the Mil Mi-8MNP-2: a version of this prolific helicopter family custom-equipped for special operations. Unsurprisingly, the new weapon looked much like the Izdeliye-79 but had a two-way datalink to enable transmission of the optical imagery from its seeker head back to the cockpit, and manual guidance during the terminal flight phase.

Following testing at home and in Syria, the LMUR was claimed to be in series production and deployed in combat by Mi-28NMs of the VKS against Ukraine in June 2022. However, at the time that version of the attack helicopter was not yet in operational service, which led to the conclusion that the FSB and VKS were deploying them from Mi-8MNP-2s. According to Russian sources, the LMUR could be deployed in two operating modes:

- Fire-and-forget: the target was acquired by the missile seeker-head while it was still on its launch rail and, after being fired, the weapon operated autonomously;
- Telecontrol: the missile was preprogramed to strike selected geographic coordinates and fired without a lock-on to the target; when approaching the target, the seeker head was activated, enabling the crew to readjust the aim as necessary.

That said, the second operational mode was described as something like 'missile kung fu': difficult and accomplishable only by well-versed crews. Correspondingly, it was next to never used in combat, although there were a few cases in which the operator switched to a target of opportunity shortly before the weapon was to reach the original coordinates.[7]

The number of deployed LMURs remained relatively low and, although by November 2022 the Russians had released over 40 related videos, it was only in January 2023 that the first videos of them installed on Mi-28NMs appeared. By the end of the same year, a total of 111 documented deployments of this weapon were recorded. While this led to the conclusion that the Izdeliye-305 LMUR was dependent on the installation of Western-made electronic components, like almost all the other Russian high-tech projects of the last 20 years, the weapon was still one of only a handful of new guided systems successfully developed in the Russian Federation of the early twenty-first century.

An Izdeliye-305E seen at an air show in Dubai in 2021. This 1.945m-long 105kg weapon has a reported operational range of more than 14,000m, and a maximum speed of around 450km/h. (Photo by Piotr Butowski)

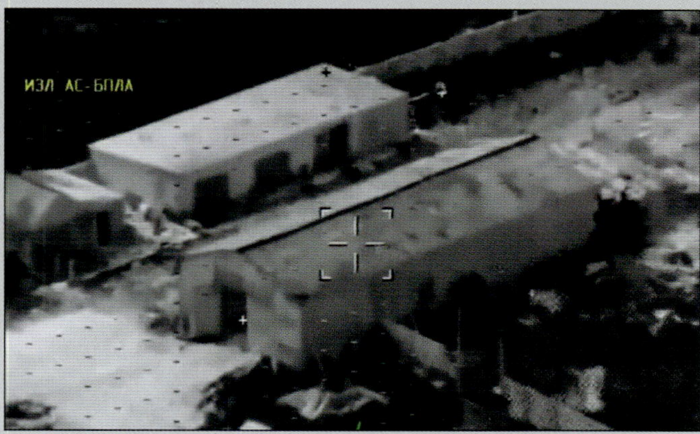

A still from a video taken by the seeker head of an Izdeliye-305 LMUR approaching a target in the Bakhmut area in June 2022. (Russian Ministry of Defence)

6
STANDSTILL

By 23 June 2022, the Ukrainian withdrawal from Severodonetsk was in full swing. Initially conducted by night and in small groups, it included the evacuation of thousands of civilians willing to leave, and hundreds of wounded ZSU troops, usually by small boats over the Siversky Donets. While elements of the 17th Tank, 80th and the 81st Airborne brigades were holding a new, temporary, frontline along the T1302 road, survivors from the 4th Rapid Reaction, 30th Mechanised, 57th Motorised, 79th Airborne, and 113th and 118th Territorial Defence brigades had all left by the morning of 25 June, and then streamed down the narrow corridor via Bilohorivka and Verkhnokamyanka in the direction of Siversk and Kramatorsk. Characteristically, it was precisely during this phase that the ZSU suffered its heaviest casualties in this battle: so much so, some characterised it as one of three biggest Ukrainian defeats.[1]

OSK South – now under the new overall commander of the Russian forces in Ukraine, Army General Sergey Surovikin – reacted promptly: the last Ukrainian troops were still in the process of transiting Lysychansk when the separatists of II AK and Wagner PMC simultaneously assaulted Zolote and Hirske both from east and west. Rather unsurprisingly considering general conditions on the battlefield and the very nature of any withdrawal operation, they captured dozens of troops of the 57th Motorised and the 118th Territorial Defence brigades, which served as rear-guards in this area, and collected a number of damaged armoured vehicles and sizeable stocks of artillery ammunition. However, in grand total, the ZSU managed to evacuate at least 14,000 troops out of the cauldron, and thus despite seizing two major cities and causing significant losses to the Ukrainians, the Russians actually failed to achieve the aim of this operation: encircling and capturing the bulk of ZSU troops in this area. This is why the battle went on and Ukraine soon found itself facing a new crisis.

Fall of Lysychansk

The loss of Severodonetsk came as a severe blow for both the Ukrainian public and the ZSU – even more so because there was no doubt that in three months of fighting for this city the armed forces suffered 'heavy' losses (probably including around 2,000 troops killed or captured). Indeed, the morale of some of the involved Ukrainian units dropped to levels where they began publishing complaints about incompetent officers and lack of supplies on social media. However, while many Western observers expected the force to collapse at any time, the ZSU continued fighting.

Therefore, as soon as his forces found themselves empty-handed in Severodonetsk, Surovikin redirected them to Lysychansk, and reinforced attempts to cut off the remaining ZSU troops in this city through assaults on Vovchoyarivka and Verkhnokamyanka, while heavily shelling the Ukrainian corridor to Bilohorivka. This is what eventually sealed the fate of Lysychansk: although the city was on a slightly higher elevation than Severodonetsk and the areas east of it, and offered strong, natural positions, the Russian advances south of it compelled the ZSU into another withdrawal. Buying time for the evacuation of civilians, the Ukrainian garrison held out for three days before there was no remaining option but to fall back in the direction of Siversk, to a new frontline constructed

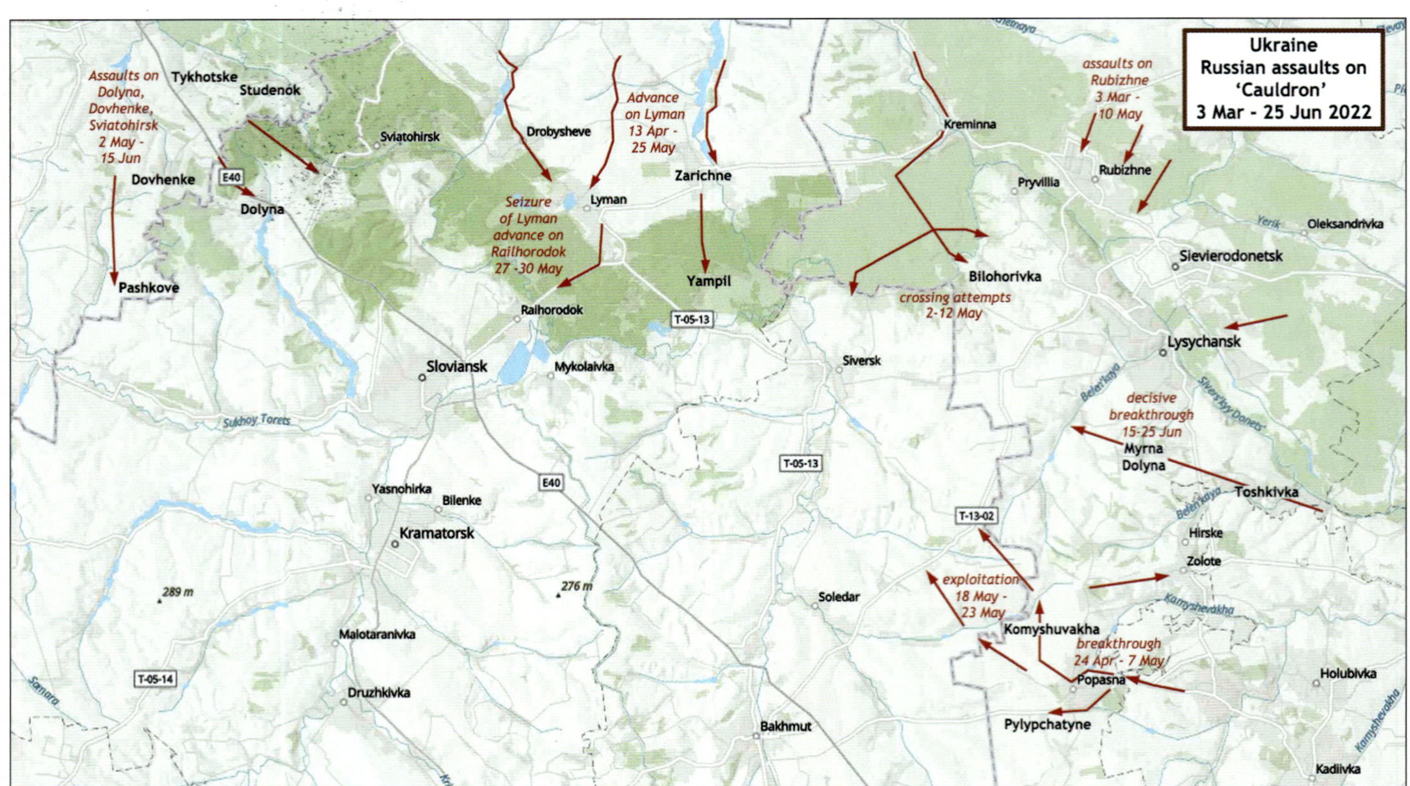

A map depicting the main directions of all the major Russian assaults on the 'Cauldron' between Slovyansk, Severodonetsk, Lysychansk, Popasna, Bakhmut, and Kramatorsk, in March, April, May, and June 2022 – which, ultimately, forced the Ukrainian armed forces into a withdrawal from both Severodonetsk and Lysychansk. (Map by Tom Cooper)

A Su-25 armed with B-8M pods for unguided 80mm rockets, streaking at low altitude over Donetsk, probably in the direction of Avdiivka. Defended by the 110th Mechanised Brigade of the ZSU, the town was exposed to near-constant artillery barrages, ground assaults, and air strikes all through 2022 and 2023. (Russian social media)

One of the non-upgraded Su-25s powering up prior to its next mission. Notable is the armament including four free-fall 250kg bombs, in addition to four drop tanks necessary because of the type's relatively short range. Time and again during the final stages of the battles for Severodonetsk and Lysychansk, Ukrainian air defences were reduced to the level where the VKS could fly direct strikes again. (Russian social media)

A still from a video showing a pair of Russian Su-25s during an air strike flown around 12 June 2022. Notable in the centre of the frame is a B-13M rocket pod: barely visible behind it is a MSP-410 Omul ECM pod, used to disrupt the work of short-range air defence systems. (Russian Ministry of Defence)

A still from a video showing a Ukrainian Su-25 armed with four B-13M pods flying a hard turn while approaching its target in the Lysychansk area around 17 June 2022. (Ukrainian social media)

between Bilohorivka and Zolotarivka: conducted under less orderly conditions than the withdrawal from Severodonetsk, that from Lysychansk was completed during the night of 2 to 3 July.

During the last days of the battles for Severodonetsk and Lysychansk, the PSZSU was forced to withdraw its heavy SAMs outside the range, back to the area between Slovyansk and Bakhmut. Therefore, the VKS was free to support the final advance of ground troops on Severodonetsk and Lysychansk with at least 20 direct air strikes by Su-24s and Su-25s a day. One of the jets in question – a Su-25 piloted by another Wagner mercenary, Andrey Vladimirovich Fedorchukov – was felled by MANAPADs of the 80th Airborne on 18 June, and two days later the same unit claimed to have shot down a Ka-52. The PSZSU hit back with its fighter-bombers, and the flying reached such intensity that on 20 June an air combat between Ukrainian and Russian Su-25s reportedly took place over Vovchovyarivka, though with unknown results. Another Russian Su-25 was claimed as shot down by Ukrainian-operated MANPADs on 24 June, and a third a day later. However, there are no indications that OSK South and/or the VKS recognised the withdrawal of the PSZSU's SAM coverage: on the contrary, the Russian fighter-bomber and attack helicopter crews were slow in switching to direct strikes. Instead, they continued flying largely ineffective 'spray-and-pray' attacks. While at earlier times these did prove at least good enough to pin down the Ukrainians inside their fortifications so that the Russian ground forces could approach, they caused far less damage to ZSU troops withdrawing through the open fields along the Bilohorivka corridor than theoretically possible. A probable reason was the continuous presence of the PSZSU's S-300V-1 SAM site in the Kramatorsk area: although emphasising anti-ballistic missile defence, this system's reported ability to hit targets with a radar cross-section of 0.05 square metres over a range of 30km (19nm), appears to have been taken seriously by the Russians.[2]

The Fourth Counterstrike

Another reason for the restraint of the VKS in operations in the Severodonetsk-Lysychansk agglomeration during the final days of that battle was the fact that by the end of June 2022, the Russian armed forces in Ukraine were generally in a state of crisis: out of 190 BTGs reportedly sent into the all-out invasion on 24 February, fewer than 100 were still operational, and the majority of these was down to around 200 troops. Arguably, the *GenStab* in Moscow meanwhile mobilised and deployed in Ukraine dozens of regiments from the Combat Army Reserve System (Боевой Армейский Резерв Страны, BARS), and numerous other volunteer formations. However, these only helped keep the total number of troops inside the invaded country at around 160,000. Although its losses were nowhere near as heavy as claimed by Kyiv, the VKS was in no better condition: with nearly all of its combat aircraft designed and manufactured for an intensive, but short conflict, after almost exactly 120 days (as of 24 June 2022) of intensive flying, dozens of aircraft and helicopters were out of flying hours, and grounded pending complex overhauls at factories in Russia. The force had lost several dozens of highly experienced crews which could not be replaced by the available training system. While this was one of the reasons for the *GenStab* and MOD granting permission for the Wagner PMC to start recruiting veteran pilots, this proved no solution: not only were older pilots proved less suitable for operations in high-threat areas, but the training of replacement crews under the appropriate system took at least four years.

The proverbial 'nail in the coffin' of Putin's 'Plan D', was the fact that now the remaining formations of the VSRF still deployed in northern Kharkiv were also experiencing a major crisis. This was caused by yet another local counteroffensive by the ZSU, initiated back on 28 April 2022, when the 113th Territorial Defence Brigade attacked Russian-controlled territory in the Slatine area, from the west, while the 92nd Mechanised Brigade (reinforced by the 127th Territorial Defence Brigade) attacked in the east. This two-prong assault took OSK South by surprise. Certainly enough, the 113th proved unable to overcome resistance by four battered Russian BTGs in the Tsupivka area: however, as soon as the Russians rushed reinforcements in that direction, the 92nd attacked from Chuhuiv along the Siversky Donets River towards the north. In a series of clashes, the Ukrainians overwhelmed whatever was left of the 437th Motor-Rifle Regiment and, by 5 May 2022, liberated Stary Saltiv and four nearby villages. OSK South reacted by ordering air strikes by Su-24s and Su-25s on the advancing Ukrainians, and then a counterattack by a BTG of the 61st Naval Infantry Brigade. However, even this unit had been weakened in earlier fighting, and it nearly fell apart in the course of a two-day-long battle. Finding no other solution, Dvornikov then withdrew one of the artillery groups from the Izyum sector: this proved sufficient to bring the Ukrainian advance to a temporary halt, but not to prevent them from mopping up the battlefield to capture dozens of abandoned Russian armoured vehicles. Indeed, next, the Ukrainians reinforced the 92nd with the 40th Artillery Brigade and elements of their SSO before resuming advance in direction of Vovchansk: by 23 May 2022, both Ternova and Rubizhne were liberated and the ZSU was close to the border with Russia. OSK South was still unable to react in any other fashion but with air strikes by fighter-bombers of the VKS. As usual, the Ukrainians claimed several of these as shot down, but only one was definitely confirmed: on 11 May, a Ka-52 was felled and at least one of its crewmembers – Major Egor Yurievich Savelyev – killed.

Eventually, the necessities of the defence of Severodonetsk and Lysychansk forced the ZSU to stop this operation: the ammunition and supplies had to be sent further east. This enabled OSK South to regroup and launch a new counterattack. On 17 May, the 200th Motor-Rifle Brigade assaulted Ternove: a village on an elevation dominating the surrounding terrain and held by a battalion of the 127th Territorial Defence Brigade. As usual, the Russian assault was

IT'S THE PROCEDURES, STUPID

Surprisingly enough, the final assaults on Lyman, Severodonetsk and Lysychansk were undertaken by a new overall commander of the Russian forces in Ukraine: indeed, the assault on Lyman was in full swing when, on 26 May, authoritative Ukrainian sources, citing captured VSRF troops, reported that Dvornikov was dismissed and replaced by Colonel General Gennady Valeryevich Zhidko. Like his predecessor in this position (and his former superior in OSK South) Zhidko spent most of his career serving with motor-rifle troops – where he earned himself the reputation of a highly effective commander and was advanced in rank slightly faster than the majority of his colleagues. After commanding the 2nd Guards Combined Arms Army in the Far East, he was sent on a tour of duty in Syria before, over the last three years prior to the Russian all-out invasion of Ukraine, serving as one of the youngest ever Deputy Chiefs of the *GenStab* and then being promoted to colonel general and assigned the commander of OSK East.[3]

There remains a big question mark over the decisions – certainly sanctioned by Putin – to dismiss Army General Dvornikov from his position, and then Army General Zhidko, around 20 June. Why take such a contradictive decision at such a critical point in time, in the middle of the onslaught on the cauldron in the Severodonetsk area?

Both Ukrainian and the Western military experts, media, and the public, reacted with 'logical' assumptions that their dismissals were caused by factors like 'obvious' military incompetence, fundamental mistakes in planning of the entire invasion, the completely dysfunctional chain of command, and failures to realise the above-described Plans B, C, and D. Others assumed disagreements between Dvornikov and Putin, or between Dvornikov, Shoygu, and Gerasimov – and cited factors like the number of casualties or massive losses of equipment. However, nobody assessed these decisions from the standpoint of the Russian way of fighting wars, nor considered the fact that what mattered for VSRF officers serving within the prevailing system in 2022 were three factors entirely ignored by the outsiders:

a. loyalty to Putin, Shoygu and Gerasimov,
b. complete obedience, and
c. procedures.

Essentially, as long as commanders were following their orders to the last dot and comma, and did not complain, their corruption, incompetence, casualties to their troops, losses in equipment, or even the outcome of their operations did not matter. On the contrary: they were near certain to be decorated, regardless of the results.

Gauging by their earlier methods of command and experience, generals like Dvornikov and Zhidko were as unimpressed by such factors as casualties and losses in equipment as Putin was. Similarly, they were as unlikely to complain about shortages of troops, equipment or supplies: the former was the 'norm', and the latter two 'not an issue', as the staff of OSK South dramatically demonstrated when organising the flawless transhipment of millions of artillery shells to the battlefields of eastern Ukraine through May and June. Finally, while failing to fulfil Plans B and C or to catch the bulk of Ukrainian units deployed in Donbass, and despite murderous losses to many units, eventually, Dvornikov and Zhidko outmanoeuvred the ZSU and, ultimately, they were successful. Although not achieving major breaches of the frontline followed by sweeping attacks into the operational depth, through multiple assaults in different areas undertaken in quick succession, they did manage to capture Lyman, followed by Severodonetsk and Lysychansk.

Almost the same is near certain to be the case for two other top commanders fired by Putin, Shoygu, and Gerasimov at around the same time Zhidko was dismissed: Colonel General Andrey Serdyukov, Commander-in-Chief VDV, and, a week later, Colonel General Alexandar Zhuravlev, the head of OSK West. If either of the two underperformed, then that was by Western metrics only and had occurred well before the war, when grotesquely failing to equip, train and prepare their units for what they were to experience in Ukraine. Moreover, neither was involved in preparing the catastrophic Plan A (the all-out invasion of 24 February 2022) and, with the exception of the 1st Guards Tank Army (from OSK West), their units performed in at least a satisfactory fashion over the following weeks – especially in comparison to the armies that obviously failed (like the 35th CAA from OSK East, or 41st CAA, from OSK Centre), the commanders of which had been dismissed in March.

Some in Ukraine and the West have argued that it was precisely the VKS to blame for both the massive losses of the VSRF and its inability to advance deeper any quicker. To a certain degree, this was true: while designed and equipped for supporting precisely the style of ground operations the VSRF was conducting, the VKS proved unable to neutralise the Ukrainian air defences within the cauldron. As a result, its 'primary tools' – like Su-25s and Su-34s, and even such advanced attack helicopters as the Mi-28s and Ka-52s – were largely reduced to ineffective spray-and-pray air strikes with unguided rockets.

However, as was clear from what Putin did next, neither the president of the Russian Federation, nor anybody from within the circle of his closest advisors was disappointed by the performance of the VKS. On the contrary, on 20 June, the commander of the Aerospace Forces, Army General Sergey Vladimirovich Surovikin, was appointed in place of Zhidko, who was suffering from poor health. Finally, considering Dvornikov continued his career with the VSRF, while Zhidko passed away only about a year later, the reasons for their dismissals must have been of different nature than usually assessed in Ukraine and the West.

A Ukrainian Su-24M approaching the Lysychansk area on 29 June 2022. (Ukrainian social media)

initiated by air strikes and hours-long artillery barrages. However, Ukrainian Buk M1s were still around and one of them hit Su-34 Bort 16 (registration RF-95846), causing it to crash west of Kupyansk, killing one of the two crewmembers (Lieutenant Vladimir Nikolayevich Fetisov),

That said, the 127th was neither as well-equipped nor as well-trained as the 92nd Mechanised, and it took the redeployment of a battalion from the latter to stop this Russian counterattack. Indeed, on 19 May, a MANPAD team from the crack Ukrainian unit then shot down Ka-52 Bort 89 (registration RF-13428) from the 55th Helicopter Aviation Regiment: this time, the crew seems to have survived. Not to be outdone, on 23 May 2022, the Russian MOD boasted of the downing of three Ukrainian Su-25s, and claimed that its Pantsir S1 close-in weapons systems had shot down numerous rockets fired by BM-30 Smerch multiple rocket launchers of the ZSU. However, for all practical purposes, the counterattack of the 200th Motor-Rifle failed: indeed, the Ukrainians not only liberated two additional villages north of Ternova, but also established a bridgehead east of the Siversky Donets, stretching from Metalivka in the north to Khoomiya in the south.

Three weeks later, on 12 June 2022, OSK South again attempted to counterattack Ternova and Rubizhne by deploying six BTGs of the 20th CAA – 'rebuilt' through the addition of separatist units from I and II AK – supported by two artillery groups. During air strikes in preparation for this assault, around 10.00hrs of the same day, the Ukrainians claimed a 'Su-34' shot down by their air defences, and that it crashed in enemy-controlled territory. According to Russian sources, a pair of Su-35S from the 23rd Fighter Aviation Regiment was in the process of engaging three Ukrainian interceptors when attacked by S-300 SAMs. The Russian leader, Major Alan Georgievich Datiev, fired a Kh-31 anti-radiation missile but it was too late: his jet was damaged by shrapnel from a proximity-fusing missile and the pilot was forced to eject. Datiev was recovered by Russian troops and evacuated over the border, but it seems that his combat career thus came to an end.[4]

On the ground, the Russian attack proved more successful: it resulted in the withdrawal of Ukrainian forces from the bridgehead east of the Siversky Donets River, and the loss of Ternova. However, on 17 June, the 19th Missile Brigade of the ZSU introduced to

By May 2022, the first of four Su-25s formerly stored at Ivano-Frankivsk AB and sent to ZDARZ (Zaproizhzhya State Aircraft Repair Plant) for overhauls and upgrades in reaction to the Russian invasion, were returned to service. The jets in question were borts 21, 46, 47, and 48 and they received an overall grey paint scheme with their bellies painted in yellow, for easier identification. (Ukrainian social media)

By June 2022, Ukrainian Su-25s not only had large parts of the underside of their fuselage painted in yellow, like this example, or began receiving large Ukrainian flags on their fins, but then also had the leading edges of their wings painted in yellow and blue. During the fighting in northern Kharkiv Oblast of April–June 2022, the Russians claimed up to eight Ukrainian Su-25s: however, no evidence of even a single loss has been made available. (Ukrainian social media)

A Su-35S of the VKS, seen at low altitude over northern Kharkiv Oblast, in May 2022. In addition to a single Kh-31PD anti-radiation missile, the jet was armed with four each of R-77-1s and R-73/74s. (Ukrainian social media)

service an entirely new weapon – the US-made M142 HIMARS multiple rocket system – to strike the headquarters of the 20th CAA and the 533rd Command and Intelligence Centre of the GRU.[5] The sudden and severe blow, as well as the loss of more than 40 officers came as a rude surprise for the Russians and wreaked havoc within the chain of command of OSK South, effectively bringing further offensive operations in northern Kharkiv to a halt. Indeed, by 20 June, supported by Su-25s of the PSZSU, the Ukrainians recovered Rubizhne, even if failing to liberate Ternova. However, that was as far as both sides could manage at that time in this area: by the end of June 2022, the two parties had fought each other to a literal standstill.

A retouched photograph of Major Alan Datiev: according to official Russian sources, as of June 2022, he was the top 'ace' of the 'Special Military Operation', with a total of 12 'kills'. (Alena Kochkina, Kontingent.press)

7
THIRD RUSSIAN MISSILE OFFENSIVE, APRIL-AUGUST 2022

After reaching its preliminary peak during the first half of April 2022, what can be summarised as the Second Russian missile campaign against Ukraine culminated in the form of the above-mentioned missile strike on the railway station of Kramatorsk, and the massacre of dozens of civilians. Immediately after, it was significantly slowed down for a few days, before being resumed in full, by when the two largest Ukrainian oil refineries – the ones in Kremenchuk and Odesa – were reported by Ukrainian sources as 'completely destroyed'. The question was thus: what might the Russians try targeting next – and what might they be able to find?

Russian Metrics

With both the *GenStab* and OSK South certainly concluding that, overall, their long-range strikes into western, central, and southern Ukraine had failed to impair the ZSU's operations, the *GenStab*'s targeting centre in Moscow received the order to find targets that would do so. Ironically, because of continuous meddling by Putin, and poor methods of intelligence collection and analysis, for weeks and months after, this only resulted in further dissipation of the effort. Indeed, through the spring and summer 2022, three distinct types of targets crystallised:

- objects of a symbolic nature or suitable for psychological warfare through high-profile strikes with weapons of a 'special' nature (like facilities of purely civilian purpose, or objects under closer public scrutiny and thus more likely to be reported if attacked by Russian 'super-weapons' like Kinzhal; apparently attacked on Putin's direct orders);
- objects of strategic importance (like additional POL facilities and the transportation network; probably attacked on advice from the *GenStab*'s targeting centre), and
- objects of tactical importance (like command and control nodes, assembly points, equipment and storage sites of the ZSU; probably attacked on demand from Dvornikov, Zhidko, and Surovikin).

While this is certain to sound banal, and definitely unprofessional from the Western point of view, it is once again the Russian metrics that are important to keep in mind: Putin ordered the all-out invasion on the basis of completely unrealistic views of Ukrainian society and his imperialistic beliefs that the Ukrainians were either confused Russians or nationalists who deserved to be destroyed. He never understood just how resilient Ukraine was, and actually continued ignoring its existence over the following two years. Corresponding 'messages' were indoctrinated into the entire Ministry of Defence, the *GenStab*, the VSRF – and thus the VKS.

Slow Recovery of the Ukrainian IADS

As described in Chapter 1, through early April 2022, the *GenStab* put Ukraine's POL facilities high on its targeting list. From time to time, gas production facilities were struck as well. Combined, these actions shut down the country's production of refined fuels and caused a shortage felt through the rest of that month and well into May. Eventually, Kyiv solved the problem through acquiring thousands of tanker trucks in the EU: these not only served to tranship imported fuels, but also for storing them, while being extremely hard to track for the Russian intelligence services. The Russian mauling of the Ukrainian POL sector thus proved insufficient to impair the ZSU's capability to defend the country, or to significantly disrupt the economy or civilian life. Therefore, following another pause, on 10 April 2022, the *GenStab* thus initiated an even more intensive offensive with ballistic and cruise missiles. Early that morning, up to seven unidentified weapons hit Aviatorske AB/Dnipro IAP, destroying a Su-25 of the 299th Brigade on the ground, together with a civilian aircraft, and killing one ground crew and injuring five others, damaging the runway and 'destroying infrastructure'.[1]

On 11 April, the Russian MOD claimed the destruction of 20 'enemy targets by high-precision weapons': Kyiv later confirmed the second deployment of Kinzhal air-launched ballistic missiles but generally remained silent, making it rather obvious that the PSZSU was unable to stop this onslaught. During the night of 14 to 15 April, it was the turn on fighter-bombers of the VKS: deploying Kh-59 PGMs, these – according to Moscow – struck 13 'military targets', including two ammunition depots and 10 'areas of concentration of Ukrainian weapons and military equipment', all of them by night. Arguably, most of the missiles hit. The problem was what they had hit: most of the intelligence collected by the GRU from its informants in Ukraine, and forwarded to the *GenStab*'s targeting cell was still rather poor. Essentially, it resulted in the VKS targeting whatever hangars, halls, or other types of storage facilities were within its reach, and it could target. Here it should be kept in mind that its Su-30 and Su-34 crews regularly deployed Kh-59Ms from the maximum effective range of 120km. In order for the missiles to reach that far, they had to be released from an altitude of around 12,000 metres and a speed of around 1,050km/h (Mach 0.95). Combined with VKS crews depending on radio communications with the usual trios of A-50s, Il-20s and Il-22s for conducting their missions, and the majority of their radio traffic was in clear, their flight altitude meant that they were regularly detected by Ukrainian early warning radars in time for the PSZSU to at least sound an alert, if not to prepare its defences. As a consequence, and although gradually, a growing number of Kh-59Ms was shot down, while others malfunctioned, primarily because most had been manufactured back in the 1980s and 1990s.

A Kh-59M precision guided missile caught in flight by the TV camera of a Ukrainian air defence system. (PSZSU)

A still from a Ukrainian security camera, showing a Kh-59 (right centre) approaching the storage facilities of a large agricultural enterprise in the Dnipro area on 2 May 2022. (Ukrainian social media)

Another still from the same video, showing the impact of the Kh-59. The missile actually hit the ground few metres short of the building it was aimed at. (Ukrainian social media)

'Retaliation' Strikes

In reaction to the Ukrainian missile strike that sank the guided missile cruiser *Moskva* – the flagship of the Black Sea Fleet – on 13 April (see Chapter 8), early the following morning the Russians fired a total of 36 ballistic and cruise missiles at Ukraine, and the Ministry of Defence in Moscow claimed the same number of targets to be 'destroyed'. As far as is known, two of the weapons in question were Iskander-M missiles that struck Myhorod AB, where the Russians claimed to have destroyed two Mi-8 and two Mi-24 helicopters. The 'retaliation' operations were continued on 15 April, when the Vizar Machine Building Plant in the Vyshneve District of Kyiv – a facility for the production and repair of anti-aircraft- and anti-ship missiles – was targeted by a total of eight missiles. As far as is known, five scored direct hits, seriously damaging a workshop, an administrative building, and about 50 vehicles parked outside.[2] Immediately after, the MOD in Moscow publicly declared that 'The number and scale of missile strikes on targets in Kyiv will increase in response to any terrorist attacks or acts of sabotage on Russian territory committed by the nationalist regime in Kyiv'. Furthermore, another strike was claimed on Aviatorske AB/Dnipro IAP, and this resulting in 'destruction of one MiG-29, a Bayraktar, and a Mi-8 helicopter'.

On 16 April, the Russians hit the POL facilities in Mykolaiv and Poltava oblasts, while a day later they switched objectives again, and hit the railway marshalling yard in Lviv, and the railway stations in Synelykovo and Pavlohrad (Dnipro Oblast), claiming to have destroyed a 'shipment of Western arms'. Finally, on 18 April, at least four cruise missiles hit a military warehouse in Lviv, killing seven people and injuring 11. The PSZSU appeared to now be excelling in the early detection of incoming Russian attacks. On 19 April, it detected and warned of Tu-95MSs on station over the Caspian Sea very early, enabling its air defences to shoot down two cruise missiles approaching Ivano-Frankivsk AB. However, in grand total, the force still struggled while trying to recover and reintegrate its air defence system. Moreover, after massive losses of its stocks of missiles in pre-war sabotage of its major ammunition dumps, and heavy losses suffered in earlier fighting, it began experiencing shortages of units, equipment, and ammunition. Correspondingly, through the rest of April and then May and June, it still had only enough assets available to provide relatively good radar coverage of the action above the front lines and major urban centres. However, only the most important of the latter, and most critical sectors of the front line were actually covered by its heavy SAMs: indeed, along the front line, the majority of PSZSU SAMs were concentrated in four groups covering sectors south of Izyum, and around Kramatorsk, and between Kherson and Mykolaiv. Elsewhere, ZSU brigades were forced to make do with whatever air defence systems they had to hand.

Round Two

The next round of Russian strikes switched back to the railway infrastructure: around 19.55hrs on 21 April, three Kh-555 cruise missiles hit the marshalling yard of Novomoskovsk (Dnipro), while others hit the line connecting Kharkiv with Poltava, interrupting traffic for several hours. Two additional cruise missiles missed the Preobrazhensky Railway Bridge in Zaporizhzhya, but while one detonated closely enough to shatter windows on a train passing by, the other demolished a sanatorium on the island of Khortytsia. On 22 April, two Kh-59s hit unknown objects in Druzhkivka and Dopropillia, north of Rodynske, in western Dnipro, while around 14.35hrs on 23 April, eight Kalibr cruise missiles approached the Odesa area: the Ukrainians later claimed that six were either shot down by air defences, or missed their targets, while one hit an apartment block killing eight civilians and wounding up to 20. The last missile hit the local airport, where the Russians claimed to have 'destroyed a warehouse containing US and European weapons systems'.[3]

On 24 April, the Ukrainians claimed the downing of two Kalibrs that approached the Odesa area, and two that were approaching Yuzhne. However, other Russian missiles then hit the Kremenchuk oil refinery and the local thermal power plant, killing at least one person.[4]

Determined to strike back at every opportunity, during the night of 24 to 25 April, the 383rd Regiment PSZSU attacked multiple points in western Russia with Bayraktar TB.2 unmanned combat aerial vehicles (UCAVs). Amongst others, these hit two oil storage depots (both used for civilian and military purposes) in Bryansk, 150 kilometres inside the Russian Federation, causing a massive conflagration. However, on the way back, one of the slow UCAVs – registration S49T – was shot down.

The Russians reacted only a few hours later: around 08.20hrs, Tu-95MSs released two dozen Kh-101 and/or Kh-555 cruise missiles, targeting an industrial facility in Zaporizhzhya and six railway stations in central and western Ukraine after approaching from the south. Reportedly, three approached Zaporizhzhya: while one was shot down near Spasivka, two others hit an aluminium plant in the city. The PSZSU claimed two cruise missiles that were approaching a major railway hub in Zhmerynka (Vinnytsia) as shot down, but another is known to have hit this facility and caused casualties. Yet another then hit a railway station in Koziatyn (also in the Vinnytsia area), one missed the railway station in Korosten (northern Zhytomyr), one hit a traction substation providing power to the Krasne railway station (eastern Lviv), while three others struck Zdolbuniv railway station near Rivne (at least one of these missed, but its detonation still blew away rooves and windows of about 20 buildings). While at least five Ukrainians were killed and 18 injured, this strike also managed to cause hours-long delays to up to 30 different trains, 16 of which were carrying civilians evacuated from the east of the country.

During the night of 27 to 28 April, the 383rd Regiment PSZSU attempted to simultaneously hit POL dumps in Kursk and Belgorod oblasts of the Russian Federation, but this time air defences were ready, and two TB.2s were shot down. The following day, as the Secretary-General of the United Nations, António Guterres, was visiting Kyiv (only a day after he visited Moscow to meet Putin), two Kh-59 guided missiles hit and badly damaged the administration buildings of the Artem missile enterprise in the Shevchenkivskyi district of the Ukrainian capital, damaging a 25-storey residential building nearby and killing at least one person in the process. However, constructed underground, production facilities remained intact.[5]

Finally, on 29 April 2022, a Project 636.3 Varshavyanka-class diesel-electric attack submarine (ASCC/NATO reporting name 'Kilo') of the Russian Black Sea Fleet carried out the first submarine-launched cruise missile strike of the war, when firing four 3M14 Kalibrs (ASCC/NATO reporting name 'SS-N-30A Sagaris') at a POL depot outside Donets.[6]

Odesa Under Pressure

Attempting to operate according to the RUK (*razveyvatelno-udarnnyy komplekx*, Reconnaissance Strike Complex) concept, on 30 April and 1 May, the Russians deployed multiple reconnaissance

AN EYE FOR AN EYE

The 'Tactical Operational Missile Complex' -21 (abbreviated in Russian as 'OTR-21'), was a Soviet-designed tactical ballistic missile with a maximum range of 70km. Entering production in 1973, and operational service in 1975, the OTR-21 (or 9K79 Tochka) was designed to be deployed in support of ground forces by striking command nodes, bridges, storage facilities, troop concentrations, and forward operating bases. The 6.4-metre-long weapon had a mass of 2,000kg on launch, and was originally equipped with a high-explosive warhead of 420kg. Before long, submunition and then nuclear warheads were developed and deployed as well.

The improved Tochka-U was introduced to service in 1989. Thanks to new propellant, it could carry a 480kg conventional warhead over a range of 120km, while its circular error probable (CEP; the radius centred on the target within which 50 percent of warheads would be expected to land) was reduced to 95 metres. In addition to a unitary warhead and a submunition dispenser, it could be fitted with an anti-radiation warhead, an electromagnetic pulse warhead, and two different types of nuclear warheads. The 9M79 Tochka-U missiles (ASCC/NATO reporting name 'Scarab-B') were fired from 9P129 or 9P129-1M TELs. Rocket brigades operating them usually comprised three battalions, each including a mobile command post, six TELs, one 9T218 or T9128-1 transport and loading machine, four 9T222 or 9T238 transport vehicles, and testing and support equipment.

Upon independence, Ukraine inherited 38 TELs and up to 500 9M79 Tochka-U missiles: they were operated by the 19th Missile Brigade: based in Khmelnytskyi, this comprised four battalions equipped with 12 TELs, and one battalion equipped with BM-30 Smerch multiple rocket launchers (additionally, the 27th and the 107th Rocket Artillery brigades operated multiple rocket launcher systems like the BM-27 Uragan and BM-30 Smerch). During the times of the USSR, multiple enterprises from Ukraine were involved in the design and production of intercontinental ballistic missiles and cruise missiles. However, the country possessed no capability to manufacture weapons like the Tochka-U. In 2014, the KB Pivdenne design bureau launched the development of its own equivalent to the Iskander, named Grom-2. While the project was halted for a few years, it was relaunched in 2022 and, at least according to the Russian Ministry of Defence, in 2023 it was deployed several times in combat (and always shot down).

Through late February and early March 2022, the 19th Missile Brigade was mainly busy supporting the defences of Chernihiv, where its Tochka-Us are known to have mauled several Russian BTGs. Towards the end of the month, the unit switched its focus to operations against the Russian advances into southern Zaporizhzhya. Later in March 2022, the 19th refocused its attention to the southern frontlines, where it several times targeted the port of Berdyansk, eventually sinking a Tapir-class (ASCC/NATO reporting name 'Alligator') landing ship. On 30 March, early in the morning, at least one Ukrainian Tochka-U hit the Russian forward ammunition depot outside the village of Okybarskoye, near Belgorod, blowing it up.

Eventually, by May 2022, the high expenditure of Ukrainian Tochka-Us threatened to render the 19th Missile Brigade non-operational. Correspondingly, the General Staff in Kyiv demanded, and the Pentagon granted permission for, delivery of M142 HIMARS and M270 MLRS multiple rocket launchers and associated rockets to Ukraine. These arrived late the same month and, following rushed training, the ZSU's sole unit operating tactical ballistic missiles was back in business, this time almost completely rearmed, and starting an entirely new episode of this war.

A pre-war photograph of three OTR-21 Tochka-U TELs of the 19th Missile Brigade. (ZSU)

A pre-war photograph of a Kh-555 cruise missile, shortly before its installation on a Tu-95MS bomber. This upgrade of the original Kh-55 was easily recognisable by the additional fuel tanks added either side of the fuselage. (Russian Ministry of Defence)

Wreckage of the Ukrainian TB.2 coded S49T found in the Bryansk area on 25 April 2022. (Russian social media)

UAVs over Odesa, to search for targets suitable for strikes by Oniks missiles of the K-300P Bastion-P anti-ship system. The Ukrainian air defences claimed at least two of these unmanned aircraft shot down. Nevertheless, the Russians fired several missiles including one that – around 18.30hrs local time – slammed into the runway of Odesa IAP. The offensive was further intensified during the night of 2 to 3 May, when another Oniks blew up a hall storing nitrate in the local port. Immediately after, the Russians then deployed their UAVs to search for a Ukrainian S-300 SAM battery deployed in the Odesa area, and then targeted this with a combination of Iskander-K and Oniks missiles. The Ministry of Defence in Moscow claimed it was destroyed, while Kyiv reported only a hit on an apartment building where a 14-year-old child was killed and several civilians injured. The assaults passed and, during the morning of 3 May, aiming to disrupt the flow and distribution of supplies and Western weapons, Tu-95MS bombers flew one of the biggest strikes on Ukraine up to that date: underway over the Caspian Sea, these released a total of 18 Kh-101 and Kh-555 cruise missiles against electricity substations for the railway system. As far as is known, the targets were the Preobrazhensky railway bridge in Dnipro, three substations in Kirovohrad, one in Vinnytsia, one in Odesa (on the railway line to Romania), and one in Volovets (Zakarpatia). At least three stations were hit, causing delay to 50 different trains around the country.[7]

The Russians maintained pressure by firing four sea-launched Kalibr cruise missiles on 4 May. However, by then the Ukrainian air defences had improved sufficiently enough for such attacks with a small number of weapons to be easily repelled: according to Kyiv, three 3M54s were shot down. Another large wave of Kh-101 and Kh-555 cruise missiles entered Ukrainian airspace during the night of 4 to 5 May. According to Kyiv and the local media, one was shot down in the Brovary area, west of Kyiv, but another hit a residential neighbourhood in the centre of Kramatorsk, injuring 25. That said, most were directed against southern Ukraine: one missile was claimed shot down by the PSZSU while approaching the Bilhorod-Dnistrovsky area (Odesa), and one while approaching Mykolaiv. However, two others hit unknown objects in the Odesa area, a third hit an unknown object in Ochakiv, and one crashed into an empty field in Pokrovske (Dnipropetrovsk region).

On 9 May 2022, amid celebrations all over Russia for the Victory Day in the Second World War, the 44th Special Purpose Aviation Regiment launched its first two 'group strikes'. In the afternoon, three MiG-31Ks each launched a Kinzhal against unknown targets in the Odesa area. The second wave followed later in the evening, as the city was receiving a visit by the President of the European Council, Charles Michel, and Prime Minister of Ukraine, Denys Shmyhal: as far as is known, around 22.35hrs the weapons homed in on three warehouses and a shopping centre in the village of Fontanka, outside the city, killing one person, and injuring five.[8]

The launch of a 3M14 Kalibr cruise missi e from an attack submarine of the Russian Black Sea Fleet, reportedly on 29 April 2022. (Russian MOD)

The launch of an Iskander-M missile. The front of the missile can be seen emerging out of its launcher, which also serves as its transport container. (Russian Ministry of Defence)

One of the warehouses in Odesa, ruined by Kinzhal strikes on the evening of 9 May 2022. (OdesaCityOfficial)

Wreckage of a submarine-launched 3M14 Kalibr cruise missile shot down by the PSZSU in Vinnytsia Oblast on 21 May 2022. (Ukrainian social media)

The Kalibr and Kh-22 Season

On 12 May 2022, the *GenStab* in Moscow upped the ante by ordering the first known air strike by Tupolev Tu-22M-3s armed with Kh-32 supersonic missiles – an overhauled and upgraded variant of the venerable Kh-22 anti-ship missile (ASCC/NATO reporting name 'AS-4 Kitchen'). A total of four bombers approached from the south before releasing the same number of missiles, all four of which homed in on the already damaged Kremenchuk oil refinery. On the same day, the VKS also targeted a school in Novhorod-Siversky (Chernihiv) with two Kh-59s: the weapons completely demolished the building, killing three people and injuring 19. While this phase of strikes with air, ground, and sea-launched cruise missiles peaked on 15 May, with strikes on military infrastructure in the Lviv area, for the rest of that month, the Russians continued attacking Ukraine primarily with ballistic missiles.

Through 13 and 14 May, the VKS busied itself trying to track down and destroy a Ukrainian S-300 SAM system recently deployed in the Sumy area. Eventually, the MOD in Moscow claimed the destruction of its early warning radar and two launchers, while Kyiv claimed one of the involved VKS fighter-bombers as shot down. However, neither side provided any kind of evidence in support of such reports.

Early on 15 May, the Russians switched their targets again: this time, four cruise missiles targeted an unknown ZSU base in the Yavoriv area. Moreover, around noon two Kalibrs approached the Lviv area from the south but were both shot down.

On 16 May, the VKS attempted to strike the Zatoka Bridge on the railway line from Odesa to Romania again, while during the following night Tu-95MS bombers attempted to strike a military base in the Zatoka area again, though with unknown results. Early on 18 May, the PSZSU claimed the downing of all four Kalibrs approaching the Lvivi area from the south. On 17 May 2022, an Iskander-M ballistic missile – probably guided by a Forpost UAV – hit the ZSU base in Desna, outside Chernihiv, killing 63 and injuring 39 military personnel, while another 68 were eventually declared 'missing'. This became the biggest single loss of life in the ZSU of 2022.[9]

Tu-22M-3 bombers of the VKS flew their second known strike on 21 May, when firing Kh-32s at the bridges spanning the Dnipro in the city of Zaporizhzhya: both constructions seem to have survived and the Ukrainians reported only additional damage to the sanatorium on the island of Khortytsia. The Russians also attempted to hit the railway station of Vinyansk, north-east of Zaporizhzhya, but a wave of four submarine-launched 3M14 Kalibr missiles was shot down while passing Vinnytsia Oblast.

On 23 May 2022, the MOD in Moscow claimed to have hit the railway station in Zhitomir and the base of the 10th Mountain Assault Brigade in Ivano-Frankivsk, while the PSZSU claimed all four Kalibrs approaching Malyn railway station, in north-western Zhytomr, as shot down – although the resulting debris damaged up to 150 private homes and killed one railway worker. Moreover, two days later Moscow claimed that its interceptors shot down a Ukrainian Su-27 shortly after it took off from Aviatorske AB/Dnipro IAP: the claim might have been indirectly confirmed by locals reporting a large detonation in that area.

After returning their submarines to Sevastopol to reload, the Russians attacked early on 25 May again. Four Kalibr cruise missiles approached Zaporizhzhya: one was shot down, but the other three hit the part of the Motor Sich Works manufacturing engines for UAVs. A day later, another wave of four Kalibrs was detected by the PSZSU: two were shot down by a MiG-29, while the fate of the other two was never reported. Around the same time, at least a pair of Tu-22M-3s was deployed to strike tactical targets in the Kramatorsk area with Kh-22s

Claims and Counter-Claims

The long-range action continued only on 1 June 2022, when the Russian Black Sea Fleet launched four Kalibrs at the Stryi area of Lviv Oblast: all three missiles found their mark, striking the railway tracks and two or three minor bridges, injuring five workers and causing sufficient damage to stop the railway traffic in that part of Ukraine for 24 hours. A day later, the MOD in Moscow claimed its 'high-precision missiles' had completely destroyed the base of the 406th Artillery Brigade in Mykolaiv, including '12 US-made M777 (towed) howitzers': Kyiv only claimed that its air defences had shot

A Tu-95MS of the VKS with no registration is visible, underway over the Caspian Sea, sometime in early May 2022: this is from where the Russians launched the majority of their Kh-101 and Kh-555 cruise missiles during that period. Tu-22M-3 launched their Kh-22s primarily from the skies above the Sea of Azov. (Russian Ministry of Defence)

By May 2022, the primary task of MiG-29s of the PSZSU became intercepting Russian cruise missiles. This jet of the 40th Brigade was photographed while scrambling for an air defence sortie and carrying its full standard weapons load, including two R-27R medium-range air-to-air missiles, and four R-73 short-range air-to-air missiles. Notable is the large-scale application of Ukrainian national colours as the means of quick visual identification intended to prevent 'blue-on-blue' incidents. (PSZSU)

down three cruise missiles over the Mykolaiv area, and one over the Odesa area.

On 5 June 2022, five Tu-22M-3s armed with Kh-22s approached Ukraine via Belarusian airspace: four of their missiles are known to have homed in on the Darnytskyi Railway Car Repair Plant of Ukrzaliznytsia, in Kyiv. According to the MOD in Moscow, the target of this strike was 'T-72 tanks and other armoured vehicles supplied by Eastern European partners that were located in the premises of the car repair plant'. However, multiple Ukrainian official sources denied the presence of military vehicles and even invited foreign journalists to visit the factory. On the same day another obscure incident involving the 831st Brigade of the PSZSU occurred over southern Zaporizhzhya Oblast: during the visit by President Zelensky to the frontlines in the Donbas region, a single Su-27 demonstratively passed over that area, before continuing towards the frontlines of southern Zaporizhzhya. Shortly after the Ukrainian army claimed to have shot down a Russian 'Su-30 or Su-34' over the Orikhiv area, and that the pilot was killed. As it transpired a few days later, the jet in question was actually Su-27P1M Bort 38 returned from overhaul only in December 2021), piloted by Lieutenant Colonel Dmitry Vilgelmovich Fisher. It is possible that Fisher was shot down by a Su-35S of the 23rd Fighter Aviation Regiment piloted by Lieutenant Colonel Ilya Andreyevich Sizov: he is known to have been awarded the title 'Hero of the Russian Federation' and highly decorated for – amongst others – 'shooting down two nationalist aircraft over a range of 150km', even though the Russian sources quoted 7 June 2022 as the date of this success. If so, this would have been the first

FROM 'THE TERROR OF US NAVY AIRCRAFT CARRIERS' TO 'THE TERROR OF UKRAINIAN CITIES'

The original Tupolev Tu-22 bomber (ASCC/NATO-codename 'Blinder') was a supersonic aircraft developed in the late 1950s. Weighing up to 92,000kg on take-off, it was about 42 metres long and could reach speeds of up to 1,500km/h. However, it was armed with free-fall bombs only, proved a maintenance nightmare, was heavy on the controls and troublesome to fly. Moreover, as ground- and sea-based air defences became ever-more effective, the question was how to convert it into an effective weapons system.

At the time, the USSR was facing many threats – including that of aircraft carriers of the US Navy: these were equipped with bombers armed with nuclear weapons. When searching for a way to counter this threat, the *GenStab* concluded that aircraft carriers were protected so well that the only means of targeting them was with very fast guided missiles launched from as far away as possible. Because the weapon was expected to carry a nuclear warhead, precision was of secondary importance. Thus came into being the requirement that led to the development of the Raduga Kh-22 missile

The original Kh-22 Burya (Storm) was about 11.5 metres long and weighed almost 6,000kg. The liquid-fuelled weapon was capable of accelerating to Mach 2 and reaching a range of between 400 and 500km. It became the centrepiece of the Komplex-22: a Tu-22K bomber equipped with the Leninets targeting radar, and capable of carrying one Kh-22 semi-recessed under the centre fuselage. The Kh-22's seeker head was relatively primitive and required a target cross-section of at least 600 square metres – something the size of an aircraft carrier – to lock-on to and guide. Moreover, the US Navy studied it extensively and began developing an entirely new generation of manned interceptors and surface-to-air missiles as a counter. In turn, the Soviets initialised work on a new 'version' of the Tu-22, capable of carrying up to three Kh-22s. This is what resulted in the design of the Tu-22M, then the Tu-22M-2, and finally the Tu-22M-3 bomber.

Meanwhile, the Kh-22 was upgraded as well: while retaining its original dimensions and the launch weight, it received a guidance section programmed to operate at a speed of 3,675km/h and above the engagement envelope of the new, multi-layered air defence weapons of the US Navy. Moreover, the new variant was primarily equipped with a conventional, shaped-charge 960kg warhead, expected to punch holes 12 metres in diameter in any US warship they could hit.

The end of the first Cold War saw the withdrawal from service of all the original Tu-22s and early sub-variants of the Tu-22M family. Eventually, even all the units of the Russian Naval Aviation equipped with Tu-22M-3s – and trained to operate against US Navy's aircraft carriers – were axed and integrated into the Strategic Aviation. While there was much talk about an upgrade of around 250 surviving Tu-22M-3s to the Tu-22M-4 standard, the sole prototype ended in a museum. By 2022, only two regiments still operated the type: out of around 70 available airframes, fewer than 30 were fully mission capable at any point in time: how many of around 3,000 Kh-22s and Kh-22s originally manufactured were still around, and how many had been upgraded to the Kh-32 standard, remains unknown.

When not only the all-out invasion of Ukraine went wrong, but it turned out that there was going to be no quick and easy victory, and VKS stocks of modern cruise missiles decreased below all acceptable levels, in May 2022 the *GenStab* ordered the Tu-22M-3s of the 52nd Guards Heavy Bomber Aviation Regiment (based at Shaykovka AB), and the 840th Heavy Bomber Aviation Regiment (based at Soltsy AB) into action armed with Kh-22Ms and upgraded Kh-32s. As of 2022, additional Tu-22M-3s were operated by a single squadron of the 40th Composite Aviation Regiment (40th SAP): the unit in question also flew transport aircraft and helicopters (including Mil Mi-26s), and was able to draw upon some 40 bombers stored in the open at its home-base at Olenyegorsk AB.

Unlike the US Navy, and although operating three major types of SAMs, each with a different maximum engagement range, Ukraine in 2022 had no multi-layered air defence system. Nominally at least, it possessed weapons such as the S-300V-1 and Buk M1 theoretically capable of intercepting Kh-22Ms and Kh-32s during their terminal flight phase. However, these had to be almost perfectly positioned to operate effectively: preferably right next to the missile's target. In a country as large and including as

Tu-22M-3 Bort 45 (registration RF-94223) seen taking-off armed with a single Kh-32 under its left wing. The Kh-32 represented an upgrade of the Kh-22 and was deployed in significant numbers in 2022. (Russian Ministry of Defence)

Three stills from a video showing the release of a Kh-32 missile from the left underwing station of a Tu-22M-3 bomber in 2022. (Russian Ministry of Defence)

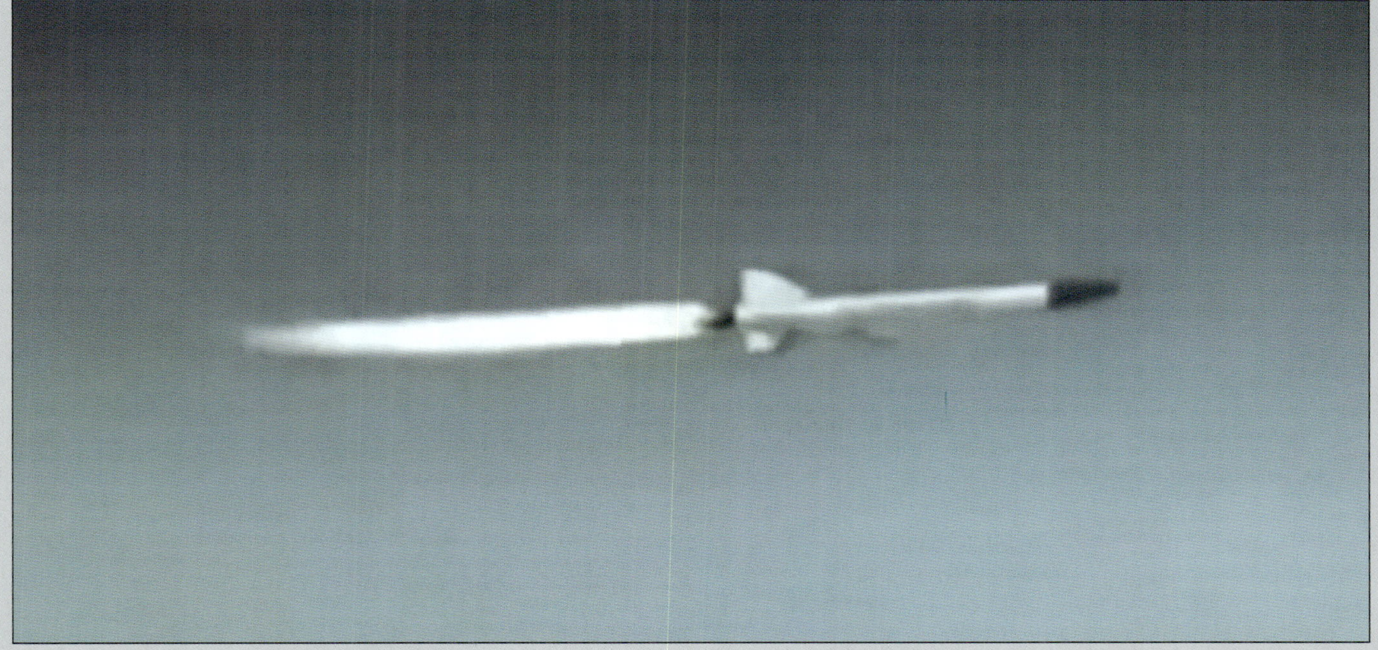

A Kh-32 seen milliseconds after the activation of its Isayev S5.33M twin-chamber liquid-propellant rocket motor and starting to accelerate away. (Russian Ministry of Defence)

many potential targets as Ukraine, this proved near-impossible. As a consequence, regardless how old, tricky to handle and operate (especially because of their highly-toxic fuel), and even unreliable, Kh-32s and Kh-22Ms were to prove highly effective through the rest of 2022 and most of 2023. Arguably, with their seeker-heads still requiring a target with a radar cross-section of at least 600 square metres, they were ill-suited for strikes on targets in a dense urban environment – and thus anything but the 'high-precision' weapons claimed by Moscow. Seemingly, this factor was considered to be 'unimportant' by the *GenStab*.

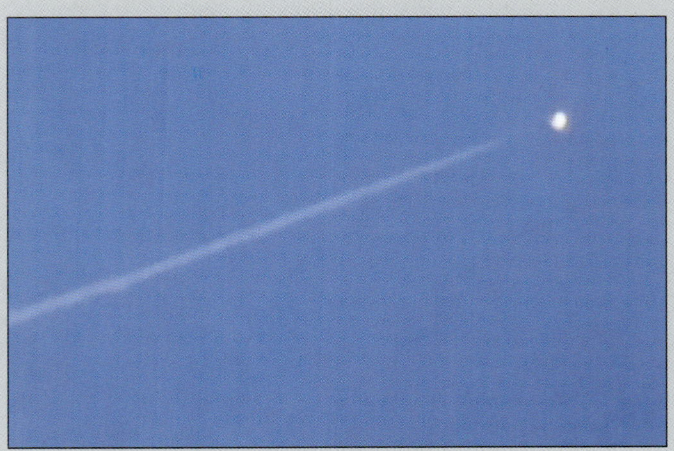

A Kh-32 accelerating and climbing following its release from a Tu-22M-3 towards Ukraine in June 2022. (Russian Ministry of Defence)

A view of the pilot of a Ukrainian MiG-29 at the moment he fired an R-73 short-range air-to-air missile (visible to the right). (PSZSU)

confirmed case of combat deployment of the R-37M long-range air-to-air missile from a Su-35S.[10]

During the night of 9 to 10 June, Tu-22M-3s of the VKS returned to strike air bases/airports in Dnipro and Kryvyi Rih again, and 'production facilities rebuilding weapons and military equipment' in Kharkiv. Whether they actually hit anything remains unclear: the Ukrainian authorities reported damage was exclusive to civilian facilities and emphasised civilian casualties. The following morning, the Russians attempted to attack the Ukrainian Navy landing ship *Yuri Olefirenko*, anchored near Ochakiv, but missed. Slightly later, the Ministry of Defence in Moscow reported shooting down four Ukrainian Tochka-U ballistic missiles as they were approaching the Donetsk area. However, the missiles in question appear to have been rockets of the M142 HIMARS system, of which the ZSU deployed dozens at that time, all with the aim of destroying forward field headquarters and ammunition depots of the VSRF. For example, one is known to have obliterated a football stadium in Stakhanov, which was used as a base by a BTG of the Wagner PMC.

Late on 11 June 2022, four Kalibr cruise missiles entered Ukrainian airspace from the south-east: two hit the Kryvyi Rih area, smashing an apartment block and a warehouse, killing 13 people. The other two continued all the way to Chortkiv in Ternopil Oblast, where one struck a pumping station of a gas pipeline, and another demolished an apartment building nearby: the Ukrainian authorities reported that 23 civilians were injured. Ukrainian air defences operated much more effectively on 14 June, when three out of four Kalibrs were shot down shortly after crossing the coast in the Mykolaiv area: unofficial Russian sources subsequently reported the first combat deployment of the modified Kalibr-M cruise missile.

HIMARS and Mugen UAVs

In the early hours of 16 June 2022, the 19th Missile Brigade of the ZSU took the Russians by surprise through firing a combination of least three 9M79 Tochka-Us and several volleys of M142 HIMARS. Amongst others, these hit the ammunition depot of II AK in Krasnyi Luch, causing a major conflagration and dozens of secondary detonations of S-8 unguided rockets used by Russian attack aircraft and helicopters. Another hit the local train station, prompting the Russians to remove numerous trains parked there. Also blown up was a hall next to the Donbass Arena in Donetsk, blowing up yet another ammunition dump. The *GenStab* in Moscow reacted viciously. Early on 18 June a total of 12 Russian missiles – described by the Ukrainians as 'S-300 SAMs fired in surface-to-surface mode', but more likely 9M55 rockets from BM-30 multiple rocket launchers – targeted an industrial zone in Mykolaiv, damaging a window factory and a sausage plant.[11] Around the same time, six Tu-22M-3 flew air strikes on oil depots in Dnipro and Kryvyi Rih, each of which was hit by three Kh-22s that killed one firefighter and injured 13. Even more was to follow: by the mid-morning, about 20 Kh-101s and Kh-555s hit the oil depot in Andriivka (Kharkiv), the Novomoskovsk Oil Terminal in Dnipro, the oil refinery of Lysychansk, the non-operational refinery of Kremenchuk, and the local thermal power plant. As if this was not enough, on 19 June, the Ministry of Defence in Moscow reported the destruction of a 'military command post' in Shiroka Dacha (Dnipro), by a Kalibr cruise missile that supposedly killed over 300 Ukrainian troops, including '50 generals and other officers' – while a day later the VSRF targeted Ukrainian positions north of Kharkiv with a total of six Iskander-M missiles.

Lacking missiles capable of reaching deeper within the Russian Federation, yet remaining keen to strike back as often as possible, in the second half of June 2022, the Ukrainians began deploying their next new weapon: the Mugin-5 UAV. Made in the People's Republic of China, with a body and wings consisting of carbon-fibre, weighing 85kg on take-off (including a payload of 25kg) and having a flight endurance of seven hours, this type was to serve as a 'prototype' for a large number of similar projects of domestic origin that were to follow. On the morning of 22 June 2022, one of these was flown into the distillation tower of the Novoshakhtinks oil processing plant, north of Rostov-na-Donu, about 150 kilometres from the nearest point on the frontlines in Ukraine. As a consequence, the facility was out of commission for more than four months.

The Russians attacked Mykolaiv on 24 June again, when six or seven Kh-22 missiles hit the main base of the 59th Mechanised Brigade and numerous apartment blocks nearby, causing dozens of casualties. As now usual, the 19th Missile Brigade of the ZSU retaliated by firing three Tochka-Us at unknown targets in the Donetsk area: 'in retaliation', between 03.45 and 05.30hrs local time of the following morning, the Russians then launched one of their first coordinated and concentric long-range air- and missile strikes in months; indeed, the kind of operation the VKS and other branches had been expected to conduct right from the start of the all-out invasion. According to official Ukrainian accounts, the first of more than 50 missiles were 3M14 Kalibrs launched by submarines of the Russian Black Sea Fleet that reached the air defence zone of Zhytomyr around 04.15hrs. The PSZSU claimed up to 10 of these as shot down, but several are known to have hit almost every military facility in and around the city, killing several soldiers. Around the same time, two Russian missiles were claimed as shot down while approaching the Yavoriv Training Centre, and two others in the Khmelnytski area. Over north-eastern Ukraine, a strike group of Su-34s escorted by Su-35s, released about 20 Kh-31 and Kh-59 missiles, mostly targeting the ZSU bases in Desna and in Sumy. Over southern Ukraine, a formation of Tu-22M-3s targeted an industrial facility in Konstantinovka, about 80km west of Donetsk with up to

A secondary detonation at the ammunition dump in Krasnyi Luch, Luhansk Oblast, hit by a combination of Tochka-U ballistic missiles and M142 HIMARS rockets early on 16 June 2022. As a consequence of this strike, the area in question was scattered with hundreds of unexploded S-8 rockets. (Ukrainian social media)

The Mugen drone that struck the distillation tower of the oil processing plant in Novoshakhtinsk, on 23 June 2022. (Russian social media)

A near-simultaneous launch of three Tochka-Us of the 19th Missile Brigade, against a target in the Russian-occupied Luhansk Olbast, on 24 June 2022. Such grouping of missiles was necessary to increase their survivability when striking targets protected by a combination of Russian systems like S-300, Tor, and Pantsir: several times through June and July 2022, Tochka-Us were also used in combination with US-made M142 HIMARS rockets. (ZSU)

12 (though more likely nine) Kh-22s, while the VSRF added several Iskander-M and Tochka-Us launched at Mykolaiv from the area of the city of Kherson. Finally, Mykolaiv was also hit by several Oniks anti-ship missiles.[12]

After smashing the headquarters of the 20th CAA on 17 June – which the VKS 'avenged' by striking Mykolaiv with multiple Kh-22s on the same day – the Ukrainian 19th Missile Brigade continued striking the Russian command nodes and forward depots with a combination of Tochka-Us and M142s. Early on 25 June, it hit an ammunition depot in Svatove, causing a fire that lasted for nearly 24 hours. Apparently, this 'provoked' the *GenStab* in Moscow into the next series of long-range strikes. On 26 June, Tu-95MSs released about a dozen Kh-101s from their usual 'station' above the Caspian Sea: several targeted the Artyom Factory in Kyiv; two hit Cherkasy, while two that approached Lviv were both shot down. A day later, two Tu-22M-3s from the 52nd Guards Heavy Bomber Aviation Regiment launched from Shaykovka AB, in Kaluga Oblast, released at least two Kh-22M or Kh-32s at the road paving equipment factory in the Kredmash Industrial Complex of Kremenchuk: one missile hit the storage area while another went completely astray and smashed the Amstor Shopping Mall, massacring 21 civilians and injuring 59. At 05.30hrs in the morning of 28 June, six 3M14 Kalibr cruise missiles hit Dnipro, where one is known to have blown up the Avtodiesel car repair shop.[13]

The PSZSU attempted to retaliate by launching one Tupolev Tu-142 UAV at Kursk-Vostochny AB, but with unknown results.

A still from a video showing a pair of Kh-22s moments before smashing an industrial facility in Mykolaiv on 17 June 2022. (Ukrainian social media)

Two stills from a video showing a Tu-160 bomber of the VKS underway high in the sky, about 50km east of the border with Ukraine, on 26 June 2022 – by when it is possible that the Russians had begun deploying this type for combat operations, or at least for demonstration purposes. As clear from the second still, the big bomber eventually banked hard right and turned away, without launching any kind of weapons. (Russian social media)

Contrails left by a Tu-22M-3 and its Kh-22Ms or Kh-32s during a strike on a target in Zhytomyr Oblast on 25 June 2022.

A still from security camera, showing a Kh-22M or Kh-32 missile milliseconds before it hit the rear side of the Amstor Shopping Mall, killing more than 20 civilians, on 27 June 2022. (Ukrainian social media)

Instead, it was the Russians who delivered the next blow: at 04.00hrs of 28 June, the Tu-22M-3s flew the first in a three-wave strike on Mykolaiv and Ochakov. Their first three Kh-22 missiles hit the base of the 79th Airborne Assault Brigade, and caused a great deal of material damage, but – reportedly – no casualties. At least one missile released during the second wave then struck the naval base in Ochakov, while another hit a stadium in Mykolaiv. The same stadium was reattacked in the afternoon, when at least three civilians were killed and six injured.

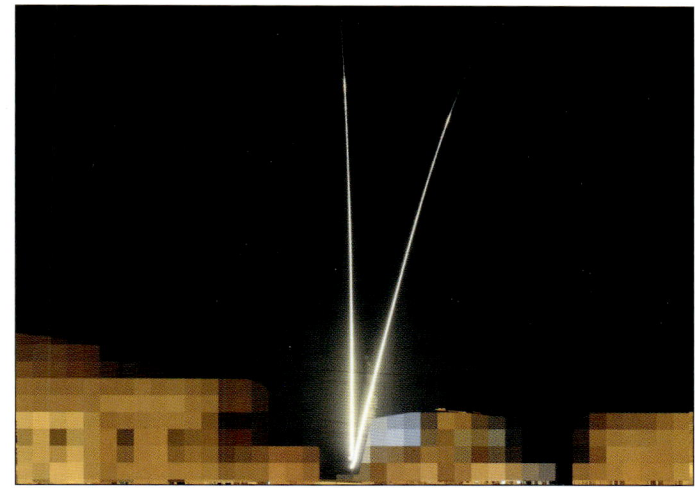

The launch of two Iskander-Ms from the Belgorod area late on 29 June 2022. (Russian social media)

GAMES WITH ZATOKA BRIDGE

One of the better examples of all the Russian problems with targeting and poor efficiency of their ballistic and cruise missiles were their attempts to knock out the Zatoka Bridge. Constructed near Zatoka, a sleepy beach resort on the coast of the Black Sea about 60km south of Odesa, the bridge was constructed in 1955 on two narrow spits of land that form the mouth of the Dniester River. The 500-foot-long rail and road bridge with a vertical lift connected Odesa with a region known as Budjak: the southernmost part of historical Bessarbia and Ukraine's southern gateway to Romania.

The first Russian air strike on this area was recorded on 3 March 2022, when a single Su-30SM dropped four cluster bomb units on a military facility outside Zatoka, only to be shot down by a MANPAD (as described in Volume 6). Nine days later, several warships of the Russian Black Sea Fleet shelled Zatoka and three nearby towns, while apparently trying to fake an imminent amphibious landing in this area. The bridge came under the first direct attack around 12.25hrs on 26 April 2022, when it was targeted by four 3M54 Kalibr missiles: one malfunctioned and crashed harmlessly into the water; another missed entirely; the third hit the berm east of the bridge, causing only minor damage, but the fourth did hit the bridge, destroying a part of its road section. A follow-up strike took place at 06.45 on the morning of 27 April: this time, Kyiv declared the bridge to have been 'destroyed' – although it remained operational for railway traffic, even if at diminished capacity.

Realising they had been fooled, the Russians attacked the bridge again on 2 May, this time with P-800 Oniks missiles: once again, the Ukrainian authorities declared it to have been 'destroyed' – while strictly prohibiting any kind of reporting or photographing from that area – and this time the *GenStab* in Moscow took only a week to realise the ploy. Therefore, the Russians reattacked the Zatoka Bridge on 10 May once again. Certainly enough, once their satellite intelligence revealed the bridge was still standing, they repeated the attack on 16 May, when one of two Kh-59s crashed into the sea short of the target, while the other missed it. While it is possible that this important structure was seriously damaged and has been out of use ever since, considering its importance it is very likely that the Ukrainians attempted to repair it. An attack by a suspected Russian naval drone, undertaken on 23 February 2023, was at least indicative of the FSB, GRU, and the *GenStab* in Moscow not taking any chances in this regard anymore.[14]

An aerial view of the Zatoka road and railway bridge from before the war. (Ukrainian social media)

Damage caused to the road section of the Zatoka Bridge during the Kalibr strike on 26 April 2022. (Ukrainian social media)

8
THE ISLAND OF SNAKES

The strategically important Zmiinyi Ostriv (Snake Island), lies approximately 40 kilometres offshore where Ukraine's and Romania's borders meet the Black Sea.[1] The rock measuring just 560 by 615 metres, with no natural shelter, became important because Moscow aimed to blockade the Ukrainian coast and connections between the ports of Odesa and Mykolaiv, with Izmail on the Danube, the Romanian port of Constanta, and the Turkish Straits. Moreover, the island offered an excellent forward position for radar stations, and electronic warfare and air defence systems. Unsurprisingly, it came under attack on the first day of the all-out invasion.

Russian Occupation

As of 24 February 2022, the Ukrainian garrison of Zmiinyi comprised 80 troops, including 30 Border Guards, 40 troops of the 35th Naval Infantry Brigade, and several soldiers from the ZSU and the PSZSU. Additionally, a group of civilians maintained the local lighthouse. Around 09.00hrs local time, the Russian patrol ship *Vasily Vykov* approached the island and requested that the garrison surrender. When there was no reply, a few hours later the most powerful warship of the Russian Black Sea Fleet, the guided missile cruiser *Moskva* (former *Slava*, the lead ship of the Project 1164 Atlant-class), appeared on the scene: both Russian vessels then opened fire with their guns. Over the next three hours, Zmiinyi was heavily shelled from the sea, and hit by several air strikes flown by Su-34 fighter-bombers. The crews of two Ukrainian speedboats braved the enemy fire to reach the island, but only three civilians agreed to evacuate. The shelling and air strikes continued into the evening, interrupted for only a short while, when the Russians radioed another request for the Ukrainians to surrender. One of the Border Guards snapped back 'Russian warships, go fuck yourself' – and the shelling and air strikes went on. Around 22.00hrs local time, the ZSU then lost the contact with the garrison and thus ordered the civilian search and rescue ship *Sapir* to sortie in that direction: early the following morning, the vessel and its crew of 19 were captured by the Russians. By then, the Ukrainian garrison – which, according to the Russian Ministry of Defence, numbered 82 – decided to surrender: they were brought by ship to Sevastopol, and then flown out to Russia aboard an Ilyushin Il-76 transport. Moreover, Moscow claimed that a Ukrainian counterattack by 16 speedboats was repelled and all the vessels destroyed.[2]

Threat to Odesa

After quickly seizing Zmiinyi, numerous warships of the Russian Black Sea Fleet appeared off the coast of Odesa. Their principal task was that of imposing a sea blockade of the Ukrainian coast, attacks on international merchants caught anchored off the ports of Odesa and Mykolaiv, and to sow mines. However, they also shelled several places along the coast with their artillery. Moreover, radar systems and the S-300F long-range SAM system of the *Moskva* were not only protecting the naval vessels from the Ukrainian air force, but also helped the Russians track the movement of PSZSU aircraft in the area between Odesa, Mykolaiv, and Kherson.

However, considering what is now known about the technical state of the cruiser, there are big question marks over the Russian decision to deploy *Moskva* in a combat operation at all. As far as can be reconstructed on the basis of both pre-war reporting about the state of the ship's systems, and reports, photographs, and videos that subsequently surfaced in the social media, the ship was anything but combat ready at the time. Her Lesorub-1164 fire-control system was a hybrid of analogue and solid-state components: it was manpower-

Ziyni Ostriv – or Snake Island – viewed from the west before the war. (Ukrainian Ministry of Defence)

A Boeing P-8 Poseidon maritime patrol aircraft of the US Navy, as photographed by the VKS over the Black Sea. Unofficial Ukrainian sources confirm that the USA supplied intelligence collected by P-8s over the Black Sea, but deny their involvement in such Ukrainian operations as the strike on the guided missile cruiser Moskva. (Russian Ministry of Defence)

intensive to operate, while the training of the crew – which largely consisted of conscripts – was poor. *Moskva* had received very few weapon and sensor updates over time: indeed, as of mid-February 2022, the cruiser was in a poor technical state: four out of six of her gas turbine generators were in need of repair; the S-300F SAM system had problems keeping targets illuminated and had no serious capability to counter missiles like Neptune; both fire-control directors for the Osa-MA SAM systems were non-operational, one of the AK-630 close-in weapons systems was down, and all three MR-123 fire-control directors for AK-630s had technical difficulties. Finally, the ship had far fewer firefighting systems than comparable Western vessels. The combination of these factors effectively rendered *Moskva* defenceless against attacks by sea-skimming anti-ship missiles.

Nevertheless, the Russians relied on the cruiser for air defence of their operations off the coast of Odesa, and for protection of their garrison on Zmiinyi, and thus the vessel was almost constantly kept on station. This was the case during the last few days of February 2022, when a task force of warships – including three amphibious assault vessels – approached Odesa closely enough to be seen by the naked eye. Concerned that the Russians might be preparing an amphibious assault, the local commanders of the ZSU requested the deployment of a Neptune anti-ship missile system. Developed by the State Kyiv Design Bureau Luch, and manufactured by Artem, the R-360 Neptune was based on the Soviet-made Kh-35U anti-ship missile: as such the weapon was turbojet powered, weighing 870kg on launch, and carried a warhead of around 147kg over a maximum range of 200km. A firing unit consisted of a single Mineral-U targeting radar, four launchers with two, later four tubes each, reloading vehicles and other support equipment, all mounted on Czech-made Tatra trucks. Initiated in 2016, the development of the Neptune system was 'put on hold' in 2020, and it was only late in that year that Luch and Artem received the funding to manufacture the first system. Entering service in 2021, as of February the following year there was still only one operational firing unit: indeed, this received its first Neptune missiles only once it reached the Odesa area, sometime around 27 February 2022.

On 3 April, as the Russian warships appeared off the coast of Odesa again, the Neptune unit was brought into position north-east of the city and fired two missiles. Usually, R-360s were programmed to fly extremely low over the sea surface. However, because the weapons in question first had to cross the city, in this case they were programmed to fly at an altitude of 120 metres or higher. Unsurprisingly, both were detected and shot down by the Russian air defences – which was just as well because, subsequent inspection of the remaining R-360s revealed a fault with their fusing: as a consequence, a team of technicians from Artem was sent to Odesa, to rework the entire stock. Nevertheless, the appearance of Ukrainian anti-ship missiles did take the Russians by surprise, and henceforth all of the warships kept their distance from Odesa.[3]

Moskva down[4]

After waiting for weeks for another opportunity, on the afternoon of 13 April, around 15.40hrs, the Mineral-U radar of the Ukrainian firing unit – redeployed closer to the shore – detected a 'major target' about 120km south of Odesa. Usually, the radar could not detect surface targets that far: however, that day heavy rain clouds covered the sky. While reducing visibility above the water to just a few kilometres, they helped the Ukrainians because they reflected radar emissions onto the water surface, which in turn reflected them back to the clouds and to the emitter. Essentially, the weather conditions that day enabled the Mineral-U to act as an 'over-the-horizon' radar. Moreover, low clouds and poor visibility lessened the alertness of the Russian crews because bad visibility hampered the work of Ukrainian UAVs. Following several minutes of consultations amongst the staff, at 15.51hrs, the commander of the Ukrainian firing unit decided to open fire.

Around 16.00hrs local time, while roughly 50km east of Zmiinyi Island and underway in a north-eastern direction, *Moskva* was hit by two R-360 Neptune guided anti-ship missiles. After approaching from the port front quarter, the sea-skimming weapons homed in on the part of the ship with the highest radar cross-section – roughly the part of the hull between the forward and rear radar mast of the ship. One struck the hull low over the waterline, at, or just aft of the forward engine room. The second impacted slightly higher, below the two AK-630 mounts positioned underneath the rear radar mast. Whether one or both warheads detonated might never become known. What is certain is that the two hits caused a conflagration that might have caused a magazine explosion – either that of the two AK-630s, or even one of the 16 P-1000 Vulkan anti-ship missiles installed in launchers either side of the superstructure: reportedly, everybody on the bridge, including the skipper, was killed. At least as important was that the hits disabled all propulsion and electrical power, and demolished the damage control centre (constructed atop

The guided missile cruiser *Moskva*, seen afire and listing heavily. Notable are at last two large fires in the area below its funnels, and numerous scorch-marks along the centre hull, denoting extensive internal fires. (Russian social media)

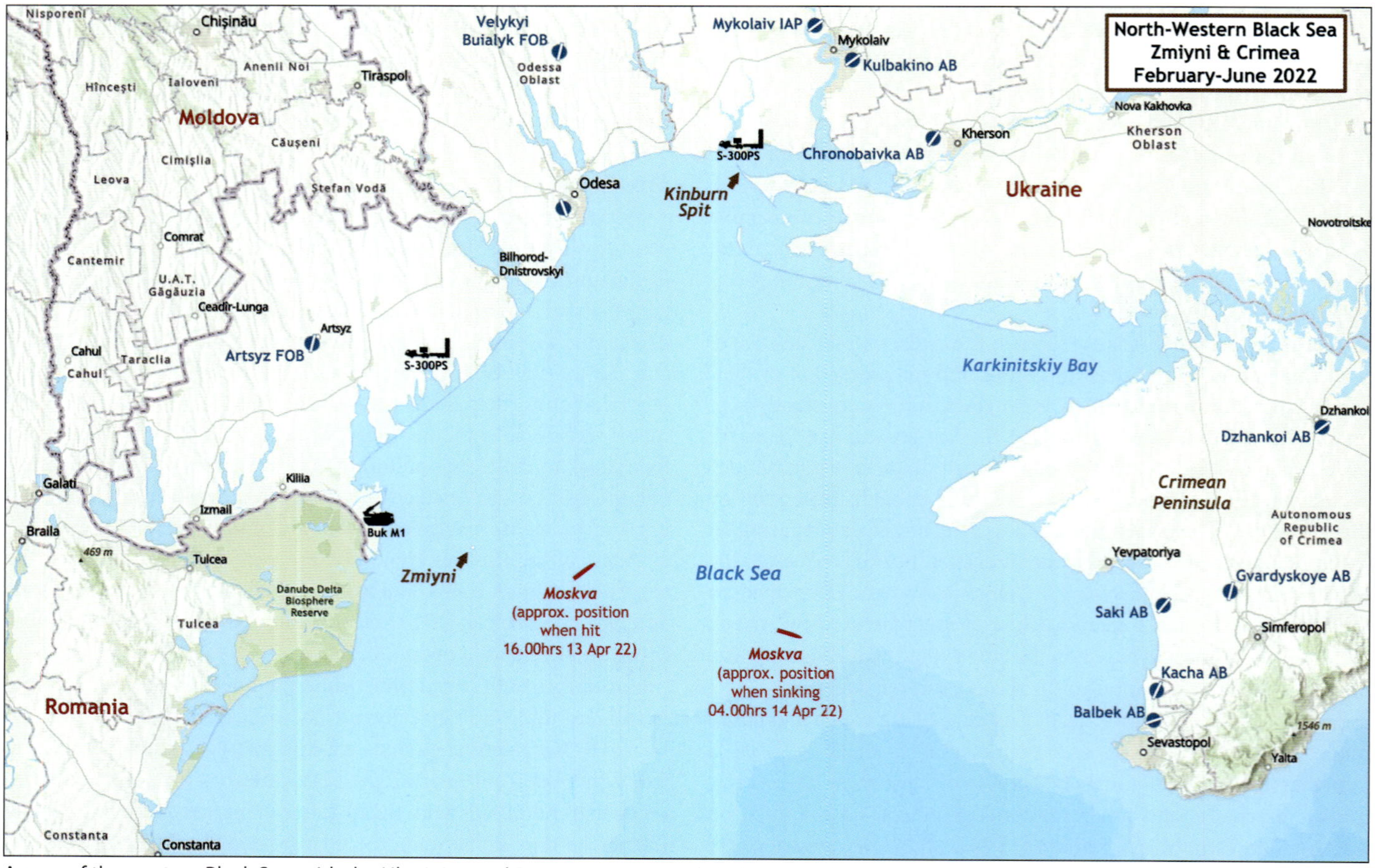

A map of the western Black Sea, with the Ukrainian and Romanian coast and Zmiinyi Island, as well as the approximate position of the *Moskva* at the time she was hit and when she sank. Also shown are approximate positions of principal Ukrainian ground-based air defence units in this area, as reported by the Russian Ministry of Defence. (Map by Tom Cooper)

of the machinery spaces): *Moskva* was thus left dead in the water and burning.

Because the attack took the crew completely by surprise, none of the watertight doors was closed. The fire thus spread through the hull towards the rear, while disorganised firefighting attempts by the poorly-trained crew then caused a list of at least 15° to the port. The Russian Ministry of Defence subsequently reported that attempts were launched to tow the ship to Sevastopol, and Ukrainian sources seem to have confirmed this with the claim that they tracked the cruiser as it was still moving in the direction of a nearby offshore oil rig. According to the Ministry of Defence in Moscow, salvage efforts were then spoiled by an unexpected local storm and heavy seas. Actually, it appears that the fire spread aft, all the way to silos for the S-300F missiles, and then to the helicopter hangar, while the

A MiG-31BM armed with R-77-1 (under the wing) and R-37M air-to-air missiles, seen at Balbek AB in occupied Crimea, in March 2022. (Russian Ministry of Defence)

Designed by Scientific and Technical Centre for Electronic Combat, the Repellent-1 was installed on the chassis of a MAZ 6317 or KAMAZ truck and entered service in 2016. The primary purpose of the system was the suppression of UAV operations: according to Ukrainian reports, it proved effective out to a range of 30–35 kilometres. (Russian Scientific and Technical Centre for Electronic Combat)

Wreckage of the TB.2 coded S51T, shot down on 30 May 2022. (Russian social media)

list caused progressive flooding. The four other Russian warships nearby, and a tugboat dispatched from Sevastopol, could neither extinguish the fires nor solve the problem of the increasing list: together with a Turkish civilian vessel that appeared on the scene, they collected the survivors from the crew of 485–534 (sources differ) before *Moskva* capsized and sank during the morning of 14 April 2022. As far as can be gauged from all the related Russian reporting, 45 crewmembers were killed or declared missing.

Interdiction

Regardless of how much mis-explained and then hushed up by Moscow, the loss of the guided missile cruiser *Moskva* was a severe blow for the Black Sea Fleet. From 14 April onwards, the fleet moved its warships even further away from the coast, in turn enabling the Ukrainians to start planning the recovery of Zmiinyi. In turn, the Russians were compelled to not only reinforce their garrison on Zmiinyi, but through late March and April, they began deploying air defence systems on the island, including a battery of Strela-10 SAMs, and a Repellent-1 electronic warfare system. Therefore, when the Ukrainians decided to recover Zmiinyi, they first had to find a way to disable both the Russian air defences and electronic warfare systems, in order to enable operations of their reconnaissance UAVs.

Starting from 26 April, the ZSU began targeting the Russian garrison with 300mm rockets from BM-30 Smerch multiple rocket launchers. On 28 April, the PSZSU attempted to increase the pressure with a strike by two Su-24s, escorted by at least one Su-27. However, according to unofficial Russian sources, the ingressing formation was detected early by an A-50 AEW aircraft, which in turn guided a MiG-31BM to intercept them and one Su-24 was shot down over the sea. While it is possible that this intercept saw the first combat deployment of both a MiG-31BM and the R-37M long-range air-to-air missile, no firm Russian claims in this regard, nor any corresponding Ukrainian loss, have become known. Instead, two days later, the Russians were successful in shooting down a Bayraktar TB.2, coded S51T, west of Zmiinyi, as it was targeting their garrison. Unimpressed, Kyiv claimed that by 1 May, two Russian Strela-10 air defence systems and a single Repellent-1 electronic warfare system had been destroyed on Zmiinyi. Over the following 24 hours, they additionally claimed the destruction of two Raptor-class patrol boats and a Serna-class landing craft underway to Zmiinyi.[5]

Failed Ukrainian Counterattack[6]

Emboldened, on 7 May, the Ukrainians launched a combined operation of the SBU and the Navy, in the form of a heliborne and amphibious assault. The heliborne component included four Mi-8s and four Mi-24s provided by the Army Aviation, while the Navy contributed both of its Centaur-class assault boats and several other vessels. The operation was coordinated from a Mi-14 helicopter (an anti-submarine warfare variant of the Mi-8) of the 10th Brigade, Ukrainian Naval Aviation, on board of which was also Colonel Ihor Volodymyrovych Bezday, commander of the 10th Brigade, Ukrainian Naval Aviation, and deputy commander of the Ukrainian Navy.

As the helicopters and assault vessels moved out, TB.2 UCAVs of the Ukrainian Naval Aviation approached the island to conduct reconnaissance and detected the presence of a Tor M1 SAM site. One of the Tor TELARs was knocked out first, followed by the second – which was being unloaded from another Serna-class vessel. Finally, the Bayraktars destroyed a Mi-8 helicopter that landed and was unloading reinforcements and supplies. Next, two Su-27s of the 831st Brigade, each armed with a pair of OFAB-500ShN parachute-retarded bombs, approached the island flying in a trail formation at around 100 metres altitude. The leader released his bombs as planned, but his wingman reached Zmiinyi just as one of two weapons detonated almost directly underneath him, showering his aircraft with shrapnel and causing his weapons to miss by a wide mark. That said, one of the bombs did hit a Russian ammunition dump, causing several secondary explosions. Undaunted, the helicopter formation and amphibious component attempted to assault – but then it turned out that yet another Tor M1 was still operational. Moreover, the Russian garrison called for help, and the VKS and the Russian naval aviation scrambled numerous fighter-bombers from their bases in occupied Crimea. Gauging by the bodies of killed Ukrainian troops subsequently shown on Russian TV, at least a part of the force did manage to reach the island and land. However, interceptors of the VKS then counterattacked and, according to claims of the Ministry of Defence in Moscow, shot down three Mi-8s, one Su-24 and one Su-27, two Bayraktar TB.2 UCAVs, and struck a landing craft.

As far as can be reconstructed on the basis of Ukrainian sources, it seems that Bezday recalled the operation and requested top cover from the PSZSU. This came too late, but Su-27s managed to distract the Russian interceptors long enough for most of the helicopters to withdraw without losses. Nevertheless, the Russians shot down one of the Ukrainian Navy's TB.2s (Bort 72, coded T188; the wreckage of which was found off the coast of Sulina, in Romania, two days later). They repeatedly attacked the relatively slow surface vessels and sank the amphibious assault boat *Stanislav* (DSHK-1), killing at least 10 SBU operators. Finally, Lieutenant Colonel Ilya Sizlov, flying a Su-35S from the 23rd Fighter Aviation Regiment, VKS, tracked down Bezday's Mi-14, Bort 34, and caught it underway low over Pervomaisky Island, between Kinburn Spit and Mykolaiv. Once there, Sizlov dived to attack with his 30mm internal gun, fired two bursts that missed, made a tight turn and then reattacked with a single R-74 (or R-73) air-to-air missile. The weapon scored a direct hit, crashing the helicopter into the sea: five crewmembers and passengers were killed, including Bezday, and one survived.

Moscow claimed additional clashes over Zimyni on the next morning as well. Correspondingly, through the night of 7 to 8 May, interceptors of the VKS claimed another two Su-24s, one Mi-24, and a third TB.2 UCAV as shot down 'south of Odesa'. Moreover, on 9 May, the Ministry of Defence in Moscow claimed the destruction

A Russian Mi-8 helicopter seen in the sight of a Ukrainian TB.2, shortly after landing on Zmiinyi Island and milliseconds before it was hit by a PGM released by the unmanned aerial combat vehicle of Turkish origin. (ZSU)

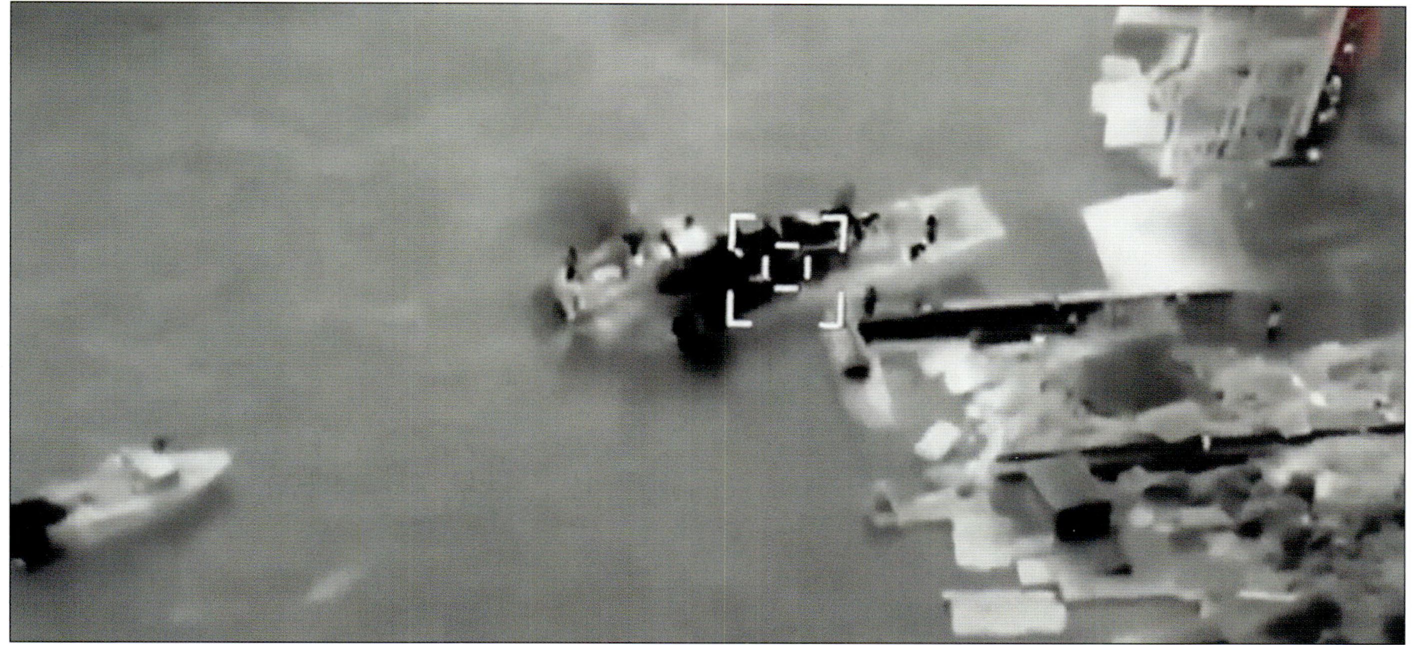

A Serna-class amphibious assault vessel unloading a Tor M1 air defence vehicle on Zmiinyi, moments before both were obliterated by PGMs released by a Ukrainian TB.2. (ZSU)

of six Ukrainian Mi-8s and Mi-24s during a strike by P-800 Oniks missiles on Artsyz FOB, and the downing of four additional Bayraktars. Gauging by the lack of any kind of evidence supporting such claims, it is near certain that all such reports were massively exaggerated.

Artillery and UAVs

Regardless of the reason for the failure of the Ukrainian attempt to recover Zmiinyi, there is no doubt that this was a serious, large-scale operation, including all three branches of the armed forces – and that it fully exposed the much-weakened Russian position following the loss of *Moskva*. The VKS was unable to maintain the permanent presence of its interceptors over the island, which was also too small for the deployment of longer-ranged SAM systems. Therefore, after the failed Ukrainian counterattack, the Russians reinforced their garrison on Zmiinyi with a new Tor M1 SAM site and such an amount of electronic warfare systems that neither Baryaktars nor Matrix or Mavic UAVs could approach to less than 30 kilometres without losing connection with their bases. Nevertheless, the UAVs continued interdicting Russian naval traffic and on 12 May TB.2s hit the logistics ship *Vsevolod Beborv* as it was underway to Zmiinyi with a Pantsir system on board: set on fire, the vessel had to be towed back to Sevastopol. Five days later, the Ukrainian Navy launched two US-made RGM-84L Harpoon missiles, part of a batch recently delivered from Denmark, the Netherlands, and Great Britain, to strike the Russian tug *Spasatel Vasily Bekh* as it was approaching

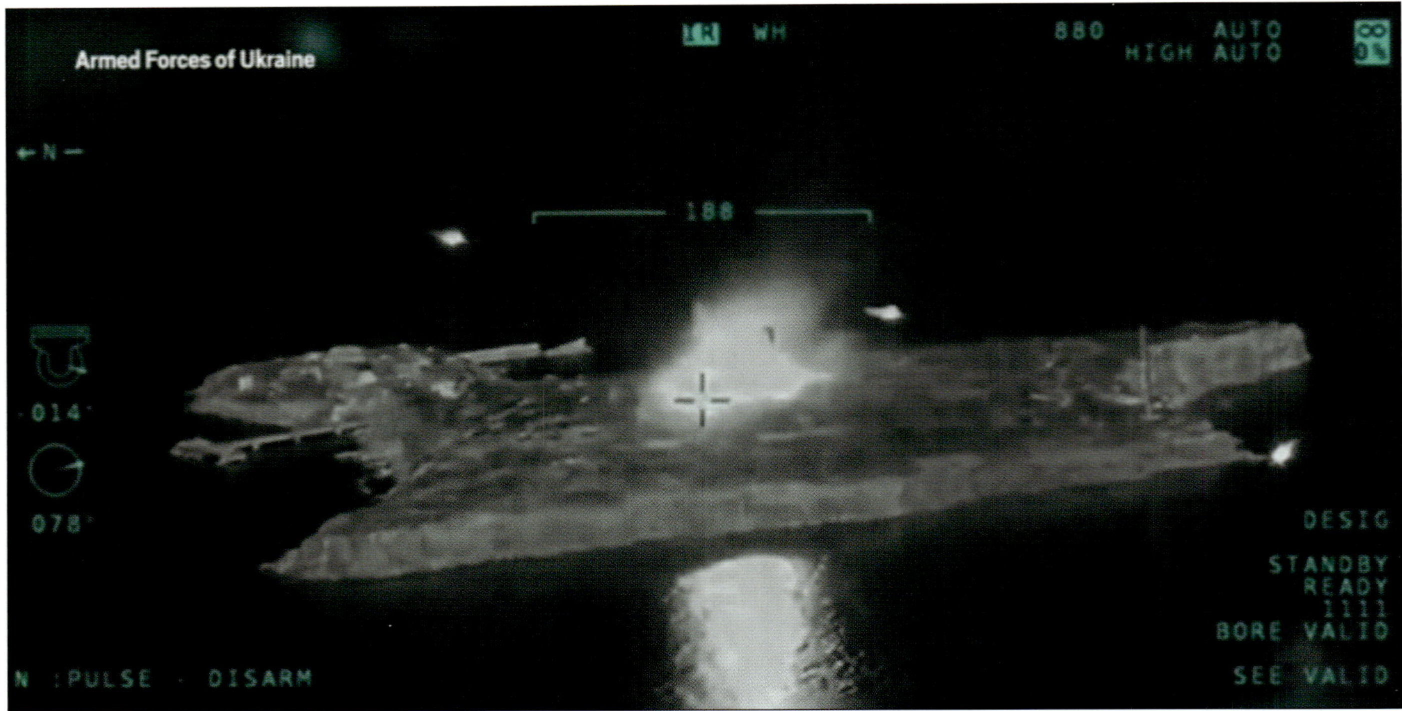

A still from thermal imagery taken by a TB.2 of the Ukrainian Armed Forces, showing the pair of Su-27s during their botched strike on Zmiinyi Island on 7 May 2022. The lead fighter-bomber is visible to the left, the detonation of its bombs in the centre right underneath the second Su-27. As a consequence, the Ukrainian wingman's weapons missed by a wide mark, and his jet was peppered by shrapnel from his leader's bombs. (ZSU)

The Ukrainian assault attempt on 7 May 2022 prompted a vicious reaction from the VKS and Russian naval aviation. Fighter-bombers like this Kh-29-armed Su-34 – photographed over the Black Sea in June 2022 – repeatedly attacked the withdrawing vessels of the Ukrainian Navy and are known to have sunk at least one. (Russian social media)

Zmiinyi: the vessel was sunk and, according to the Russian Ministry of Defence, lost 10 of the crew missing and the other 23 injured. Over the following days, the Ukrainians also targeted gas platforms near the island, reportedly because the Russians had installed electronic warfare equipment there.

That said, attempts to strike positions directly on the island with a combination of Tochka-Us fired by the 19th Missile Brigade and Verba 122mm multiple rocket launchers proved unsuccessful: according to both Russian and Ukrainian sources, these were all shot down by Tors and Pantsirs protecting the garrison.

Therefore, the ZSU decided to continue striking the island with long-range artillery. For this purpose, it ordered the sole prototype of the Bohdana self-propelled 155mm howitzer to the scene. Although undergoing development since 2016 and put on display during the 2018 Independence Day parade in Kyiv, at the time of the all-out invasion it was dismantled and stored inside a hangar of the PrJSC Kramatorsky Heavy Machine Tool Building Company (part of the National Association of Ukrainian Defence Industries) in Kramatorsk, where its barrel and a few other major parts were manufactured. Evacuated to Zhytomyr on private initiative, the prototype was reassembled and then sent to Kryvyi Rih: from there, and together with a similar French-supplied Caesar self-propelled 155mm howitzer, it was brought to the Vylkove area, and then moved down the Danube River to the seashore with use of motorised barges. Following extensive preparations – including the deployment of a single Buk M1 SAM site for their protection – the two pieces went into action on 19 June 2022.

Still unable to correct their fire with UAVs – because of the Russian electronic warfare system on Zmiinyi – the Bohdana and the Caesar could not be particularly precise. Nevertheless, the

The TB.2 coded T188 belonging to the Ukrainian Navy, known to have been shot down by Russian interceptors on 7 May 2022 during the Ukrainian attempt to recover the Snake Island. (Ukrainian Navy)

A still from a video with Sizlov's Su-35S passing above the Bezday's Mi-14 after missing with its internal GSh-30-1 30mm cannon, and before turning around for a final attack with R-73/74 air-to-air missiles, over Kinburn Spit on 7 May 2022. (Russian social media)

following morning, the Ministry of Defence in Moscow claimed the destruction of 15 different Ukrainian UAVs and two TB.2s, four Tochka-Us and 21 artillery rockets – just over the island – and an S-300 SAM site in the Ochakov area, as well as the downing of a US-operated Boeing RQ-4 Global Hawk. In the same report, and because the Ukrainians targeted the 'Boyko Towers' (the BK-1 and Krym-1 offshore oil and gas drilling platforms about 70km south of Odesa, occupied by the Russians since 2015), the Russians then targeted the 'hangars for Ukrainian Bayraktar UAVs' at Shkoly AB, outside Odesa, and an S-300 SAM site outside Tuzla.

Whatever Moscow claimed for 19 June, the Russians were certainly successful during the night of 25 to 26 June, when the PSZSU sent two of its Su-24Ms to attack the Repellent-1 station on Zmiinyi. However, either after firing their Kh-25s, or after releasing their bombs and – reportedly – destroying one Pantsir S1 close-in weapons system, they were intercepted by Russian Su-35s. Around 00.26hrs, the lead jet – Bort 84 – was shot down: the pilot, Colonel Mykhailo Matiushenko, was killed, while his weapons system operator, Major Yuriy Krasylnikov, was initially declared missing in action, but was never found.[7]

Goodwill Gesture

Lacking UAV support, the two Ukrainian artillery pieces took days to zero-in their fire on the Russian garrison on Zmiinyi, but once they did, by 27 June, they knocked at least one Pantsir. Over the following two days, they also destroyed one of the Russian radars and then the Repellent-1 electronic warfare system, thus making the area free for operations by reconnaissance UAVs. While the Ministry of Defence in Moscow reacted by claiming its Pantsirs had shot down 12 Ukrainian rockets and a Su-25, and although Su-30s and Su-35s of the VKS and the Russian Naval Aviation three times attempted to strike the firing positions of the two Ukrainian artillery pieces and the Buk M1 SAM site protecting them with Kh-31PD anti-radiation missiles and Kh-38 anti-ship missiles, the writing was on the wall: exposed to regular and increasingly precise artillery shelling, and with resupply efforts interdicted by Ukrainian anti-ship weapons, the position of the Russian garrison became untenable. Late on 30 June, the survivors were withdrawn in what Moscow declared a 'goodwill gesture' to demonstrate its will to lift the naval blockade and enable Ukraine to resume wheat exports.

The battle for Zmiinyi went on for several days longer: around 18.00hrs on 1 July, a pair of Russian Su-30s plastered the island with incendiary bombs, apparently aiming to destroy abandoned equipment. The Ukrainians landed their troops and reported Zmiinyi as liberated on 4 July: three days later, Russian Su-30s flew the final attack of this campaign, when deploying Kh-38 anti-ship missiles to badly damage the pier. It was only at that point that the campaign for the recovery of Zmiinyi was concluded. Even then, the Ukrainians did not garrison the island: just like the Russians, they concluded that doing so would cause them too many problems.

Taken by a TB.2 from very long range (probably more than 30km), this still from a video shows one of two RGM-84L Harpoon anti-ship missiles about to strike the Russian tug *Spasatel Vasily Bekh* of the Project 22870-class, some 33km east of Zmiinyi, on 17 May 2022. (ZSU)

The sole Bohdana prototype in action against Zmiinyi Island on 30 June 2022. (GenStab-U)

Another still from a video taken by a Ukrainian UAV, this time showing Zmiinyi covered by dense columns of smoke following the heavy artillery barrage of 30 June 2022. (ZSU)

MEAGRE REINFORCEMENTS

A still from a video showing a train transporting elements of the Slovakian S-300PMU SAM system to Ukraine in April 2022. (Ukrainian social media)

From 2014, Ukraine received small amounts of heavy infantry arms – mainly FGM-148 Javelin anti-tank missiles, and Piorun and FIM-92 Stinger MANPADS – from the USA and different NATO members. However, in attempt to appease Putin, the West refused any of Kyiv's requests for deliveries of heavy arms. Renewed talks in this regard began immediately after the Russian all-out invasion, but the initial results were meagre. Eventually, the ZSU received the first significant shipments of heavy arms only during the second week of March 2022, and then in the form of Soviet/Russian-made missiles for Osa-AKM and S-300 SAM systems, acquired by the USA from third parties. By April, the USA also delivered a total of 1,400 FIM-92 Stinger MANPADS, while through April and June 2022, these were followed by additional MANPADS, including Soviet/Russian-made 98K34 Strela-3s, and the first two out of 21 US-made, trailer-mounted AN/MPQ-64 Sentinel pulse-Doppler 3D surveillance radars with a range of 40km (25nm), usually deployed to cue short-range air defence systems.

In April 2022, the USA began delivering the first of 17 Russian-made Mil Mi-17V5 helicopters originally acquired for the Afghan Air Force (five of these are known to have been in the country as of the 13th of that month): their number was eventually increased to 20 Mi-17V5s and one Mi-8MT. Turkey continued delivering PGMs for its Bayraktar UCAVs, five TB.2s crowdfunded by Lithuanian, Ukrainian, and Polish citizens, and 30 Mini-Bayraktars. However, despite protracted discussions between Kyiv and NATO headquarters in Brussel, as well as several European capitals, the much-expected – and often announced – deliveries of MiG-29s and Su-25s from Bulgaria and Slovakia did not take place. Instead, the Czech Republic delivered eight Mi-24Vs starting in May 2022, and four Mi-17s and one Mi-2 in June. All of these were assigned to the Army Aviation of the ZSU.

Starting in June 2022, the USA began delivering a total of 21 trailer-mounted AN/MPQ-64 Sentinel radars. Amongst others, these were deployed to coordinate and control the air defence systems of the ZSU's brigades in areas with lesser presence of ground-based air defence assets of the PSZSU. (bemil.chosun.com)

One of 21 Mi-17V5s, originally acquired for the Afghan Air Force, but then rerouted to Ukraine in April–June 2022. Most of them were assigned to the 18th Brigade of the Ukrainian Army Aviation (the insignia of which is shown on the lower right corner of the photograph). (PSZSU)

BIBLIOGRAPHY

Benedek, W., Bilkova, V., Sassoli, M., *Report on Violations of International Humanitarian and Human Rights Law, War Crimes, and Crimes Against Humanity committed in Ukraine since 24 February 2022*, OSCE, 13 April 2022

Boyd, A., *The Soviet Air Force since 1918* (London: Macdonald and Jane's Ltd., 1977)

Butowski, P., *Flashpoint Russia; Russia Air Power: Capabilities and Structure* (Wien: Harpia Publishing, 2019)

Chung, W., J., *War in Ukraine, Volume 4: Main Battle Tanks of Russia and Ukraine, 2014–2015; Post-Soviet Ukrainian MBTs and Combat Experience* (Warwick: Helion & Company, 2023)

Chung, W., J., *War in Ukraine, Volume 5: Main Battle Tanks of Russia and Ukraine, 2014–2015; Soviet Legacy and Post-Soviet Russian MBTs* (Warwick: Helion & Company, 2023)

Collins, L., 'In 2014, the "decrepit" Ukrainian army hit the refresh button. Eight years later, it's paying off', *The Conversation* (online), 8 March 2022

Cooper, T., *Moscow's Game of Poker: Russian Military Intervention in Syria, 2015–2017* (Warwick: Helion & Company, 2018)

Cooper, T., Fontanellaz, A., Crowther, E., Sipos, M., *War in Ukraine, Volume 2: Russian Invasion, February 2022* (Warwick: Helion & Company, 2023)

Crowther, E., *War in Ukraine, Volume 1: Armed Formations of the Donetsk People's Republic, 2014–2022* (Warwick: Helion & Company, 2022)

Crowther, E., *War in Ukraine, Volume 3: Armed Formations of the Luhansk People's Republic, 2014–2022* (Warwick: Helion & Company, 2023)

Dabrowski, K., *Defending Rodinu, Volume 1: Build-up and Operational History of the Soviet Air Defence Force, 1945–1960* (Warwick: Helion & Company, 2022)

Dabrowski, K., *Defending Rodinu, Volume 2: Build-up and Operational History of the Soviet Air Defence Force, 1960–1989* (Warwick: Helion & Company, 2023)

Defense Intelligence Agency, *Russia Military Power; Building a Military to support Great Power Aspirations* (DIA, 2017)

Elfving, J., *An assessment of the Russian Airborne Troops and their Role on Tomorrow's Battlefield* (Washington DC, The Jamestown Foundation, 2021)

Facon, I., *La nouvelle armée russe* (Paris, L'Observatoire franco-russe, 2021)

Fiore, N. J., 'Defeating the Russian Battalion Tactical Group', *Armour*, No. CXXVIII,⊠ Spring 2017

Francois, D., *Operation Danube: Soviet and Warsaw Pact Intervention in Czechoslovakia, 1968* (Warwick: Helion & Company, 2020)

Grau, L. W. & Bartles, C. K., *The Russian Way of War; Force Structure, Tactics, and Modernization of the Russian Ground Forces* (Fort Leavenworth, Foreign Military Studies Office, 2017)

Grau, L. W. & Bartles, C. K., 'Getting to Know the Russian Battalion Tactical Group', *The Royal United Services Institute* (online), 14 April 2022

Gressel, G., 'Waves of Ambition: Russia's Military Build-up in Crimea and the Black Sea' (European Council on Foreign Relations, 2021)

Gunston, B. & Spick, M., *Modern Air Combat: The Aircraft, Tactics and Weapons employed in Aerial Warfare Today* (London: Salamander Books Ltd., 1983)

Gunston, B. & Spick, M., *Modern Fighting Helicopters* (London: Salamander Books Ltd., 1986)

Harris, C., Kagan F. W., *Russia's Military Posture: Ground Forces order of battle* (Washington, Institute for the Study of War, 2018)

Holcomb, F., *The Order of Battle of the Ukrainian Armed Forces: A key component in European Security* (Washington, Institute for the Study of War, 2016)

Lambeth, B. S., *Russia's Air Power in Crisis* (Washington D.C.: Smithsonian Institution, 1999)

McDermott, R., N., Bartless, C., K., *The Russian Military Decision-Making Process & Automated Command and Control* (German Institute for Defence and Strategic Studies, October 2020)

Milyukov, I., *The Soviet War in Afghanistan, 1979–1989* (Warwick: Helion & Company, 2023)

Ministry of Defence of Ukraine, *White Book 2013*; The Armed Forces of Ukraine (Kyiv, 2014)

Ministry of Defence of Ukraine, *White Book 2014*; The Armed Forces of Ukraine (Kyiv, 2015)

Ministry of Defence of Ukraine, *White Book 2015*; The Armed Forces of Ukraine (Kyiv, 2016)

Ministry of Defence of Ukraine, *White Book 2016*; The Armed Forces of Ukraine (Kyiv, 2017)

Ministry of Defence of Ukraine, *White Book 2017*; The Armed Forces of Ukraine (Kyiv, 2018)

Ministry of Defence of Ukraine, *White Book 2019–2020*; The Armed Forces of Ukraine (Kyiv, 2021)

Mladenov, A., 'Tough Days for Ukraine's military Helicopter Community', *Kiakaha Medias*, 23 August 2020

Muzyka, K., *Russian Forces in the Western Military District* (Arlington, CNA, 2021)

Sandler, E., *Battle For Grozny, Volume 1: Prelude and the Way to the City, 1994* (Warwick: Helion & Company, 2023)

Watling, J., Danylyuk, O. V., Reynolds, N., *Preliminary Lessons from Russia's Unconventional Operations During the Russo-Ukrainian War, February 2022 – February 2023*, RUSI, 29 March 2023

Zhirokhov, M., *Airwar in Ukraine, February-May 2022* (Kyiv: Vizitochka, 2023)

Zhirokhov, M., *Hot Skies over Ukraine: Aerial Warfare, June-December 2022* (Kyiv: Vizitochka, 2023)

Zhirokhov, M., *Fire in the Sky: Airwar over Ukraine, January-August 2023* (Kyiv: Vizitochka, 2023)

Zhirokhov, M., *Sukhoi Su-24 in Service* (in Ukrainian) (Chernihiv: Knizhni Bal, 2023)

Zhirokhov, M.., *Sukhoi Su-25 Frogfoot* (in Ukrainian) (Chernihiv: Knizhni Bal, 2023)

Zhirokhov, M., *Su-27 Guardians of the Ukrrainian Sky* (in Ukrainian) (Chernihiv: Knizhni Bal, 2023)

NOTES

Chapter 1

1 Figures based on cross-examination of Google Earth imagery.
2 PSZSU, 'Thanks to modern Aircraft and Western Technology, 2023 could be a Turning Point in Ukraine's War with the Global Aggressor' (in Ukrainian), *Facebook.com*, 8 April 2023.
3 One of the reasons for the high effectiveness of the Ukrainian Kolchugas through 2022 was the fact that for navigation purposes most Russian fighter-bomber pilots preferred to use US-made Garmin hand-held GPS receivers, or Chinese-made Baofent radio systems, instead of the Russian-made avionics and Azarts radios of their aircraft. As it became known, later on, both could be detected, tracked, and read in real time.
4 L. O. (veteran PSZSU officer), interviews, 03/2022 & 04/2022; 'An Officer from the Rostov Region died during the Special Operation in Ukraine', *bloknot-rostov.ru*, 9 March 2022.
5 Bohdan Ben, 'Fallen Pilots who saved the Ukrainian Air Force', *EuromaidanPress.com*, 1 May 2022. Colonel Kovalenko was a former commander of the 7th Brigade, while Captain Kazimirov was a reservist: both returned to active service with the PSZSU on 24 February 2022. The third Ukrainian jet lost around the same time was Su-25 Bort 29, crewed by Captain Aleksander Bogdanovich: he crashed while taking off (as a Number 2) from Starokostyantyniv AB and was killed.
6 A. B. (officer of the PSZSU), interviews, 01/2024, 03/2024 & 04/2024.
7 A. B. (officer of the PSZSU), interviews, 01/2024, 03/2024 & 04/2024.
8 'In Kharkiv, a memorial plaque was opened for the fallen Guardsmen of the 5th Slobozhan Brigade', *Suspilne Kharkiv/suspilne.media*, 5 March 2024; 'The Russian Ministry of Defence reported that eight Planes and two Helicopters were shot down in Ukraine in one Day', *TASS*, 6 March 2022.
9 Resolution of 08/24/2023, No. 283/2122/23 Malynsky District Court, verdictum.ligazakon.net, 25 August 2023 & 'Intercepted Radio Communications: Crew of the crashed Su-34 of the VKS survived' (in Ukrainian), *Projekt MotolkoHelp/Youtube.com*, 21 April 2022.
10 A. K. (veteran VVS/PSZSU officer), interviews, 05/2022, 06/2022, 08/2022 & 04/2024; Resolution dated 21.04.2022, No. 296/1885/22 Korolev District Court of Zhytomyr, verdictum.ligazakon.net, 22 April 2022 & Ukraine State Emergency Services, Telegram post, 7 March 2022.
11 V. J. interviews, 03/2022, 04/2022, 05/2022; 07/2022 & 06/2024.
12 V. J. interviews, 03/2022, 04/2022, 05/2022; 07/2022 & 06/2024.
13 'Russian unmanned Forpost shot down over Zhytomyr Oblast' (in Ukrainian), *Zhitomir-online.com*, 11 March 2022.
14 'Airport completely destroyed due to missile attacks by invader in Vasilkiv, Kyiv Region – Mayor', Interfax-Ukraine, 12 March 2022; 'Zelensky vows to keep negotiating with Russia', Associated Press, 13 March 2022; 'Russia claims to kill "180 foreign mercenaries" in Strike in western Ukraine', *Times of Israel*, 13 March 2022; 'Update on Yavoriv Air Strike: 35 Dead, 134 Wounded', *Ukrinform*, 13 March 2022; Alex Horton, 'Attack on Ukrainian Base came from Warplanes inside Russia', *Washington Post*, 14 March 2022; Resolution dated 12.09.2023, No 935/2908/23 Korostyshiv District Court, verdictum.ligazakon.net, 12 September 2023.
15 Elena Pocelueva, 'Heroes Z: Ilya Perepelkin', kontingent.press, 29 March 2022.
16 Russian MOD, Facebook post, 19 March 2022; Paul Kirby, 'Russia claims first use of hypersonic Kinzhal Missile in Ukraine', BBC News, 19 March 2022; 'Russia recognises first crew to use hypersonic missile in Ukraine, *TASS* reports', *Reuters*, 4 September 2023.
17 'Russian Su-34 uses Kinzhal hypersonic missile in special op – official', *TASS*, 4 September 2023.
18 Alexey Ramm, Bogdan Stepovoy, 'Missile Association: Iskander Brigades have increased Firepower', *Izvestiya/iz.ru*, 16 December 2019.
19 In a speech televised in March 2018, Vladimir Putin described the Iskander-K as a 'low-flying, difficult-to-detect cruise missile carrying a nuclear warhead, with a practically unlimited range and an unpredictable flight path, which can bypass lines of interceptors, is invincible in the face of all existing and likely future systems of both missile defence and air defence…'.
20 V. J. (veteran VVS/VKS officer), interviews, 03/2022 &, 04/2022.
21 The 13th brigade equipped with Iskanders was set up in Karelia, in early 2024, as a part of the new Leningrad Military District, established in response to Finland joining NATO (see Kasperi Summanen, 'Russia is said to be bringing Iskander Missiles to Finland's Border' (in Finnish), verkkouutiset.fi, 22 April 2024).
22 'Russia picks MiG-31 Fighter as a Carrier for cutting-edge hypersonic Weapon', *TASS*, 6 April 2018; 'Russian Fighters armed with Kinzhal hypersonic missiles hold Drills with Strategic Bombers', *TASS*, 19 July 2018; 'New Russian Weapons to guarantee Security of the Country without increasing costs and involvement in the Arms Race'; eng.mil.ru., 20 February 2019; 'MiG-31K Fighter Jet fired a Kinzhal hypersonic Missile at an unknown Target in Syria' (in Russian), avia.pro, 9 July 2021; ('War Criminals of the Russian Federation', Main Intelligence Directorate of the Ministry of Defence of Ukraine/gur.gov.ua, 12 May 2024.
23 'Military Database', scramble.nl & 'War Criminals of the Russian Federation', Main Intelligence Directorate of the Ministry of Defence of Ukraine/gur.gov.ua, 12 May 2024. According to the latter report, the MiG-31K of the 44th Regiment may have worn registrations RF-03230, RF-03231, RF-03234, RF-20862, RF-20867, RF-20882, RF-20883, RF-42251, RF-42253, and RF-94268. However, gauging by what is known about registrations of MiG-31Ks confirmed by photographs, most of these were misread: the first of the five digits of all known MiG-31K registrations is always 9.
24 Paul Kirby, 'Russia claims first use of hypersonic Kinzhal Missile in Ukraine', BBC News, 19 March 2022.
25 Watling et al, p. 32.
26 'Ukraine Kremenchuk Refinery destroyed after Attack – Governor', Reuters, 3 April 2022; Issam Abdallah, 'Missiles hit Ukrainian Refinery, Critical Infrastructure near Odesa', Reuters, 3 April 2022.
27 Evgeny Vakulenko, 'Anniversary of the Shelling of the Kramatorsk Station', 8 April 2024, *FreeRadio.com.ua*; 'Kramatorsk Train Station Massacre sparks international Outrage', *Le Monde*, 10 April 2024; Michael Sheldon, 'Russia's Kramatorsk "Facts" Versus the Evidence', *Bellingcat*, 14 April 2022. Notably, the claim that the 47th Rocket Brigade of the 8th Combined Arms Army was still operating OTR-21s as of October 2021 is almost irrelevant. Not only had the VSRF repeatedly deployed 9M79 ballistic missiles against Ukraine since 24 February 2022 (when one of these was used to damage a hospital in Vuhledar; see 'Russian Military commits indiscriminate attacks during the Invasion of Ukraine', Amnesty International, 25 February 2022), but, as described above, the 47th was re-equipped with Iskanders in early 2022 (see: 'The Southern Military District Missile Unit received a Brigade Set of the Iskander-M Missile System' [in Russian], *TASS*, 21 January 2022). Nevertheless, the 47th certainly still had some 9M79s and related TELs as of April 2022, and even if not: their replacement by Iskanders would have freed a corresponding complement of Tochka-U equipment for 'other tasks'.
28 Case No. 283/2122/23, District Court of Malinsky, *verdictum.ligazakon.net*, 25 August 2023.
29 'Death of two Aviators that served in Lutsk became known', *suspilne.media*, 25 March 2022; V. J., interviews, 04/2022 & 05/2022; D. Z., interviews, 11/2023 & 04/2024;
30 Maxim Streletsky, 'Heroes Z: Alan Datiev', *kontingent.press*, 22 March 2024. For what Moscow has published about Datiev's other achievements, see further below.

Chapter 2

1 For details on the Russian invasion of Kyiv, Chernihiv, Sumy, Kharkiv, Zaporizhzhya, and Kherson oblasts, see volumes 2 and 6 of this mini-series.
2 The Russian objectives for this theatre of operations are based on V. J., interviews, 03/2022, 04/2022, 06/2022 & A. K., interviews, 05/2022 & 06/2022.
3 'NATO Envoys arrive in Balaklia to assist in humanitarian demining', *Unian.info*, 25 March 2017.
4 V. J., interviews 03/2022, 04/2022, 06/2022 & A. K., interviews, 05/2022 & 06/2022.
5 For details on this battle, see *Volume 2*, p. 49.
6 'Broken and trophy Equipment under Izyum: Footage from the Battlefield' (in Ukrainian), *Public Kharkiv/YouTube.com*, 21 March 2022.
7 Julia Sheredeha, 'The General Staff of the Ukrainian Army named the Russian Generals who lost their Jobs or Lives since the start of the War in Ukraine', *babel.ua*, 31 March 2022.
8 V. J., interviews, 03/2022, 04/2022 & 04/2024; A. B., interviews, 01/2024, 03/2024 & 04/2024.

9 A. B. (officer of the PSZSU), interviews, 01/2024, 03/2024 & 04/2024.
10 Air Force of the Army of Ukraine, Telegram release, 3 April 2022; 'Russian Pilots lands Plane after two Buk hits' (in Russian), mk.ru, 10 September 2022.

Chapter 3

1 For details of Operational Reserves 1 and 2 of the ZSU, see Volume 2.
2 For details of the Battle of Moshchun, see Volume 6.
3 Aleksander Dvornikov, R. R. Nasybulin, 'Topical Lines of Improving Combat Training of Troops based on the Experience obtained in Syria' (in Russian), *Voenaia Misl*, July 2021. For details on the advances of the 49th and 58th CAAs into southern Kherson, Zaporizhzhya and Mykolaiv oblasts in late February and through early March, see volumes 2 and 6.
4 Although frequently claimed as the 'first ever deployment of anti-tank guided missiles against helicopters', this was far from true. The first confirmed helicopter kills by anti-tank guided missiles were scored by aviators of the Islamic Republic of Iran Army Aviation, in January 1981, against Iraqi Mil Mi-25s. By the end of that conflict more than 20 such aerial victories were claimed by both sides, combined. During the Syrian War (raging since 2011), several helicopters of the Syrian Arab Air Force were shot down in similar fashion: the last known case occurred in April 2017, when US-supported insurgents deployed a BGM-71 TOW anti-tank guided missile to shoot down an Aerospatiale SA.342 Gazelle light helicopter of the Syrian Arab Air Force.
5 'Grigoriev, Seredyuk, Tsyuryk, Tsyupak, Martsenyuk: Five more Heroes of Ukraine, Posthumously' (in Ukrainian), *Novynarnia.com*, 21 April 2022; 'A Bust of the 49th Brigade Commander Ivan Grishin, who died in the SVO Zone, was unveiled in Smolensk' (in Russian), *smolensk.er.ru.*, 23 February 2023.
6 Elena Pocelueva, 'Heroes Z: Vasily Kleshchenko', *kontingent.press*, 14 November 2022; Elena Pocelueva, 'Heroes Z: Ivan Boldyrev', *kontingent.press*, 14 April 2022 & Elena Pocelueva, 'Heroes Z: Roman Kobets'; *kontingent.press*, 14 April 2022.
7 'The Ukrainian Armed Forces demonstrated a "hunt" for Russian Orlans using Martlet LMM MANPADS' (in Ukrainian), *Dialog.ua*, 22 April 2022.
8 Resolution dated 04.05.2022, Case No. 405/1868/22, Leninsky District Court/*verdictum.ligazakon.net*, 5 May 2022.

Chapter 4

1 For details, see posts by Leon_spb67, from March 2022 (leon-spb67.livejournal.com).
2 Description of the attack on Kramatorsk airfield as per V. J., interview, 04/2022.
3 Andrey Sharogradsky, Alexander Gostev, Mark Krutov, 'Syrian losses of the Slavnoic Corps' (in Russian), Radio Svoboda (svoboda.org), 29 March 2016; 'Reincarnation of Robin Hood: How the legend of Wagner PMC was born' (in Russian), *Economics Today*, 24 March 2017; Eveny Krutikov, 'The US is trying to punish the mythical Russian PMC' (in Russian), *Vzglyad Delovaya Gazeta* (vz.ru), 21 June 2017; Mark Galeotti, 'Moscow's mercenaries reveal the privatisation of Russian Geopolitics', *OpenDemocracy.net*, 29 August 2017; 'Jabbar' (retired officer of Syrian Military Intelligence), interview, 07/2022; 'Rechtsextreme betailigen sich an Angriff auf Ukraine', n-tv.de, 22 May 2022; 'Sources say that the leadership of the Power Bloc has made a final decision to hastily shut down the Cook Project' (in Russian), *Russkiy Kriminal*/Telegram, 17 March 2023; Elena Rykovtseva, 'Behind him is Kiriyenko, behind Kiriyenko is Kovalchuk' (in Russian), Radio Svoboda/svoboda.org, 16 March 2023.
4 Lilia Yapparova, 'Roughly speaking, we started the War' (in Russian), *Meduza*, 13 July 2022.
5 According to V. J., requests from forward air controllers of the 150th Motor-Rifle Division were usually forwarded to Il-22M airborne command posts. In turn, these tasked A-50s with directing selected formations into attacks on predetermined coordinates. If flown – which, gradually, became a rarity or something undertaken in emergency only – direct attacks with free-falls bombs were flown by Su-24s and Su-34s.
6 Ivan Boyko, 'Ukrainian Artillery near Popasna covered the Russian Mercenaries of the Wagner PMC' (in Ukrainian), *Unian.ua*, 8 April 2022; daily press releases by the Russian MOD & Leon_spb67, 1 May 2022 (leon-spb67.livejournal.com);
7 Stefan Korshak, 'Ukrainian Officials: Dozens of RF Mercenaries from Libya, Syria, Russia killed in Popasna Attacks', Kyiv Post, 21 April 2022 & Leon_spb67, 1 May 2022 (leon-spb67.livejournal.com); Report on the shoot-down of a Su-25 of the Wagner PMC, *TheMilitaryWatch/Facebook.com*. CHECK Zhirokhov.

Chapter 5

1 V. J., interviews, 04/2022, 05/2022, 06/2022, 07/2022.
2 V. J., interviews, 04/2022 & 04/2024
3 Notably, based on reports by the Governor of Luhansk Oblast, Serhiy Haidai, the Russian air strike on the school in Bilohorivka was widely reported as having killed over 60. However, the number of those trapped under the rubble must have been much lower than originally assessed: while two fatalities were officially confirmed, 30 are known to have been rescued. For one example of related reporting, see 'Bombing of school in Ukraine kills two, dozens more feared dead, governor says', *Reuters*, 8 May 2022.
4 'Successful strikes by AFU on enemy equipment during Seversky Donets crossing, Video', *Censor.net*, 31 May 2022; 'Destruction of Russian armoured personnel carriers in attempt to force Seversky Donets and battlefield near Belogorovka and Serebryanka, Video', *Censor.net*, 1 June 2022 & Russo-UkrainianWarspotting (ukr.warspotting.net).
5 'Lviv Paratroopers shot down the Russian assault aircraft Su-25' (in Ukrainian), PSZSU release, Facebook.com, 22 May 2022; Elena Poculeva, 'Heroes Z: Kanamat Botashev', kontingent.press, 10 November 2022 & 'Effectiveness of the Protection System on VKS Helicopters', *RIA Novosti*, 24 May 2022. Notably, at 62, Botashev was the second-oldest known combat pilot killed in this war. Notably, in its description of Botashev's final mission, provided as explanation for awarding him the title 'Hero of the Russian Federation', the Russian Ministry of Defence described his final mission as follows: On the morning of 22 May 2022, the Su-25 aircraft he was piloting was on a mission to hit targets near Popasna… During the flight, Botashev heard a distress call from an assault group of Russian fighters that found itself surrounded by superior Ukrainian forces near the fortified area of Pylpychatnye. Knowing that the Ukrainian troops in this area had powerful air defence, the pilot, having hit designated targets, volunteered to help his fighters and ensure their exit from the encirclement. He successfully inflicted fire damage on a group of nationalists and ensured the ability of the assault group of his troops to escape from the fire pocket. However, after completing the assigned task, while making a turn at an extremely low altitude, his Su-25 was shot down by an anti-aircraft missile, and the pilot did not have time to eject.' (from 'Botashev Kanamat Khuseevich', warheroes.ru).
6 Unless stated otherwise, the content of this box is based on Piotr Butowski, 'Is Russia using its new Advanced Anti-Armour Missile in Ukraine?', *The Warzone/twz.com*, 28 July 2022.
7 M. N. (veteran VKS pilot), interview, 05/2024.

Chapter 6

1 'One of the biggest defeats of the Ukrainians was the Breakthrough in the Area of Volnovakha: HUR' (in Ukrainian), *Volnovakha.city*, 22 February 2023.
2 Amongst others, on 24 June 2022, the Russian MOD officially claimed the destruction of 914 Ukrainian artillery pieces, while the Russian social media claimed that 'in the Zolote cauldron' the VSRF has encircled the 'III Battalion/24th Mechanised Brigade, 15th Moutain Assault Brigade, 128th Mountain Assault Brigade, 42nd Motorised Infantry Battalion/57th Motorised Infantry Brigade, 70th Battalion/101st Territorial Defence Brigade, the Artillery Group of the 57th Motorised Infantry Brigade, a 'Right Sector' volunteer unit and 80 foreign volunteers'. However, earlier during that night the separatists in Luhansk reported having secured both Zolote and Hirske: while proudly showing a video of 21 Ukrainian captives (some of these wearing civilian clothes), they did not mention any kind of encirclement of ZSU units. Ultimately, neither Moscow nor Luhansk have ever shown evidence of '1,000 Ukrainian soldiers eliminated… and about 800 surrendered', as subsequently claimed (for example, see 'Military Operation in Ukraine, Chronicle of Events of 24 June, 2022', *TASS*, 24 June 2022 & 'Ukrainian Armed Forces soldiers who surrendered near Gorsky advise their fellow soldiers to lay down their Arms', *TASS*, 24 June 2022). Additional claims for downed Russian fighter-bombers from 'Another enemy Su-25 was downed in Donbas using Igla MANPADS' (in Ukrainian), *Dialog.ua*, 18 June 2022; 'Pilot of downed Russian Su-25 turns out to be a Wagnerite' (in Ukrainian), *Dialog.ua*, 20 June 2022 & 'Destruction of Russian helicopter Ka-52: Paratrooper dedicated to his

one-month-old Baby' (in Ukrainian), *80th Airborne Brigade/Facebook.com*, 23 June 2022.

3 'Also reportedly, Russia's command in the battle for Donbas underwent another shakeup – the overall commander is now said to be Colonel General Gennady Zhitko', *CITeam/Twitter.com*, 26 May 2022.

4 Maxim Streletsky, 'Heroes Z: Alan Datiev', *kontingent.press*, 22 March 2024.

5 'Near Khakriv, the command post of the 20th Army of the Russian Federation and the GRU has been "demilitarized": the bodies of the "200s" cannot be identified', *dialog.ua*, 18 June 2022.

Chapter 7

1 Natalia Zinets, 'Russian Rockets destroy Dnipro Airport, Ukraine Officials say', *Reuters*, 10 April 2022 & Dnipropetrovsk Administrative Court, Case No. 160/19280/22, 'Decision on Behalf of Ukraine', *reyestr.court.gov.ua*, 8 February 2023.

2 'Russian Projectiles strike Ukraine Defence Machine Building Plant', *Kyiv Post*, 15 April 2022.

3 'As a result of missile attack on Odesa, military facility and two residential buildings damaged', *Interfax-Ukraine*, 23 April 2022 & 'Russian Army eliminated logistics terminal with foreign weapons near Odessa', *TASS*, 23 April 2022.

4 Svitlana Kizilova, 'Occupying forces bomb the Kremenchuk Oil Refinery again: four Strikes', *Ukrainska Pravda*, 12 May 2022.

5 According to unofficial sources living in the area next to the Artyom Works, as of early 2024 the Russians had targeted the factory at least six times in two years – and never hit even one of its shops. Instead, their missiles hit a labour union's library, several commercial warehouses, and a pizzeria in the neighbourhood.

6 As of mid-June 2022, the Black Sea Fleet had seven submarines in service (including *Alrosa*/B-871, *Novorossiysk*/B-261, *Rostov-na-Donu*/ B237, *Stary Oskol*/B-262, *Krasnodar*/B-265, *Velikiy Novgorod*/B-268, and *Kolpino*/B-271). However, only three of these were active: *Kolpino* and another example were at sea, while the pump-jet-powered *Alrosa* was conducting trials after a protracted overhaul. *Rostov-na-Donu* was in dry dock for a major refit, but the work proceeded only very slowly.

7 Kateryna Tyshchenko, 'Strike in Zakarpatia: Substation in Volovets damaged', *Ukrainska Pravda*, 3 May 2022 & Roman Olearchyk and Ben Hall, 'Russian Missiles strike Ukrainian Rail Network for second Day', 4 May 2022.

8 'Russian Missiles hit Odesa for the second time on May 9', Kyiv Independent, 9 May 2022.

9 Svitlana Kizilova, 'Occupying forces bomb the Kremenchuk Oil Refinery again: four Strikes', *Ukrainska Pravda*, 12 May 2022; Roman Petrenko, '6 Russian Rockets hit Kremenchuk Oil Refinery, two more hit Thermal Power Plant', *Ukrainska Pravda*, 18 June 2022; Tanya Matyash, 'At least 30,000 Ukrainian Defenders died in the War: Book of Memory' (in Ukrainian), *lb.ua*, 15 November 2023.

10 Ekaterina Leskova, 'Heroes Z: Ilya Sizov', *kontingent.press*, 6 September 2022 & 'Sizov Ilya Andreyevich', warheroes.ru.

11 According to unofficial Ukrainian sources, which provided this information on condition of anonymity, prior to this strike a drunken Russian officer called the mayor of Mykolaiv, offering to spare the city in exchange for a deft bribe. Obviously, this was turned down.

12 'Massive Strike on Zhytomyr Region: about 10 Missiles shot down by Ukrainian Air Defence', Censor.net, 25 June 2022 & 'Russia resumes launches of Iskanders from Territory of Belarus', Censor.net, 25 June 2022.

13 According to unofficial Ukrainian sources, the crew that fired the Kh-22 that destroyed the Amstor Shopping Mall included lieutenant colonels Dmitry Golenkov, Evgeniy Pocueluyev, and Denis Gabitov, and Lieutenant Dinar, whose first name remains unknown.

14 'Russia strikes key Ukrainian Bridge with naval Drone in Attack feared to spell trouble for Kyiv's navy', *The Independent*, 13 February 2023.

Chapter 8

1 Roman Romaniuk, 'Bohdana's First Battle', *Ukrainska Pravda*, 13 February 2023.

2 'Ukraine's Boats attack Ships evacuating Ukrainian troops who surrendered on Snake Island', *TASS*, 26 February 2022.

3 Nevertheless, Kyiv claimed to have hit the Russian frigate *Admiral Essen* (see 'Ukrainian Defenders damaged Russian Missile Frigate' (in Russian), *dumskaya.net*, 3 April 2022.

4 Unless stated otherwise, based on 'Sinking the Moskva: Unknown Details' (in Ukrainian), Ukrainska Pravda, 13 December 2022 & 'Reflected between Sky and Water', Meduza.io, 13 December 2022. Arguably, the Western media emphasised the version of the story according to which the Ukrainians received the coordinates for their strike from US intelligence, perhaps even directly from a US Navy (Boeing) P-8 Poseidon maritime patrol aircraft ('US Navy P-8 Poseidon Aircraft reportedly assisted Ukrainians in hitting Moskva', *Daily Mail*, 20 April 2022.

5 The Armed Forces of Ukraine struck the positions of Russian Troops on Zmiiny Island', mil.in.ua, 27 April 2022; 'Defence Forces of Ukraine destroyed Equipment and Manpower on Zmiiny Island', mil.in.ua, 1 May 2022 & V. J., interview, 04/2022. According to the same source, the involved MiG-31BM-crew was 'highly decorated' for its success.

6 Unless stated otherwise, this sub-chapter is based upon: Romano Romaniuk, 'Battle for Zmiiny', *Ukrainska Pravda*, 7 November 2022; 'Russian Aerospace Forces down 2 Ukrainian planes, 3 copters, 2 drones off Snake Island', *TASS*, 8 May 2022; 'The Mothers and Wives of the missing Sailors from the sunken Boats of the Navy ask to shed Light on the Fate of their Loved Ones' (in Russian), *dumskaya.net*, 29 November; 'One of the best Pilots of Ukraine died in a Battle with the Enemy' (in Russian), *dumskaya.net*, 8 May 2022; 'He was and will remain a Hero', *inshe.tv*; 8 May2022; 'Moment Russian Helicopter is obliterated as Ukrainians bomb Snake Island'; *Metro.co.uk*, 8 May 2022; Yusuf Cetiner, Ukrainian TB2 destroys Russian Mi-8 Helicopter on Snake Island in first reported Aerial Kill', *overtdefense.com*, 10 May 2022; Ekaterina Leskova, 'Heroes Z: Ilya Sizov', *kontingent.press*, 6 September 2022 & 'Sizov Ilya Andreyevich', warheroes.ru. Ironically, the Russian Ministry of Defence explained Sizov's decoration for downing Bedzay's Mi-14 – actually an anti-submarine helicopter, perhaps armed with a single machine gun during this mission – with the explanation that the helicopter, 'opened massive fire on Russian air defence positions'.

7 Resolution dated 14.07.2022, No. 683/1756/22 Starokostyantynivsky District Court/verdictum.ligazakon.net, 15 July 2022.

ABOUT THE AUTHORS

Tom Cooper is an Austrian aerial warfare analyst and historian. Following a career in the worldwide transportation business – during which he established a network of contacts in the Middle East and Africa – he moved into narrow-focus analysis and writing on small, little-known air forces and conflicts, about which he has collected extensive archives. This has resulted in specialisation in such Middle Eastern air forces as of those of Egypt, Iran, Iraq, and Syria, and various African and Asian air forces. In addition to authoring and co-authoring more than 50 books – including an in-depth analysis of major Arab air forces during the wars with Israel in 1955–1973, and multiple books about the War in Ukraine – and over 1,000 articles, Cooper is a co-editor of Helion's @War book series.

Adrien Fontanellaz, from Switzerland, is a military history researcher and author. He is a member of the Scientific Committee of the Pully-based Centre d'histoire et de prospective militaries (Military History and Prospectives Centre), and regularly contributes to the *Revue Militaire Suisse* and various French military history magazines such as *Défence & Sécurité Internationale.* Fontanellaz has co-authored several books about the Ukrainian Armed Forces and the War in Ukraine.

Milos Sipos is a Slovakian military historian. While pursuing a career in law he has collected extensive documentation on interconnected political, industrial, human resources and military-related affairs in Iran, Iraq, and Syria. His core interest is a systematic approach to studies of their deep impacts upon combat efficiency and the general performance of local militaries. After more than 10 years of related work on the ACIG.info forum, he specialised in research about the Iraqi Air Force and the Syrian Air Force, and about losses of the Russian Air-Space Force and the Ukrainian Air Force & Air Defence Force in the War in Ukraine.

NOTES

Chapter 1

1 Roman Romaniuk, 'Bohdana's First Battle', *Ukrainska Pravda*, 13 February 2023.

2 'Ukraine's Boats attack Ships evacuating Ukrainian troops who surrendered on Snake Island', *TASS*, 26 February 2022.

3 Nevertheless, Kyiv claimed to have hit the Russian frigate *Admiral Essen* (see 'Ukrainian Defenders damaged Russian Missile Frigate' (in Russian), *dumskaya.net*, 3 April 2022.

4 Unless stated otherwise, based on 'Sinking the Moskva: Unknown Details' (in Ukrainian), Ukrainska Pravda, 13 December 2022 & 'Reflected between Sky and Water', Meduza.io, 13 December 2022. Arguably, the Western media emphasised the version of the story according to which the Ukrainians received the coordinates for their strike from US intelligence, perhaps even directly from a US Navy (Boeing) P-8 Poseidon maritime patrol aircraft ('US Navy P-8 Poseidon Aircraft reportedly assisted Ukrainians in hitting Moskva', *Daily Mail*, 20 April 2022.

5 The Armed Forces of Ukraine struck the positions of Russian Troops on Zmiiny Island', mil.in.ua, 27 April 2022; 'Defence Forces of Ukraine destroyed Equipment and Manpower on Zmiiny Island', mil.in.ua, 1 May 2022 & V. J., interview, 04/2022. According to the same source, the involved MiG-31BM-crew was 'highly decorated' for its success.

6 Unless stated otherwise, this sub-chapter is based upon: Romano Romaniuk, 'Battle for Zmiiny', *Ukrainska Pravda*, 7 November 2022; 'Russian Aerospace Forces down 2 Ukrainian planes, 3 copters, 2 drones off Snake Island', *TASS*, 8 May 2022; 'The Mothers and Wives of the missing Sailors from the sunken Boats of the Navy ask to shed Light on the Fate of their Loved Ones' (in Russian), *dumskaya.net*, 29 November; 'One of the best Pilots of Ukraine died in a Battle with the Enemy' (in Russian), *dumskaya.net*, 8 May 2022; 'He was and will remain a Hero', *inshe.tv*; 8 May2022; 'Moment Russian Helicopter is obliterated as Ukrainians bomb Snake Island'; *Metro.co.uk*, 8 May 2022; Yusuf Cetiner, Ukrainian TB2 destroys Russian Mi-8 Helicopter on Snake Island in first reported Aerial Kill', *overtdefense.com*, 10 May 2022; Ekaterina Leskova, 'Heroes Z: Ilya Sizov', *kontingent.press*, 6 September 2022 & 'Sizov Ilya Andreyevich', warheroes.ru. Ironically, the Russian Ministry of Defence explained Sizov's decoration for downing Bedzay's Mi-14 – actually an anti-submarine helicopter, perhaps armed with a single machine gun during this mission – with the explanation that the helicopter, 'opened massive fire on Russian air defence positions'.

7 Resolution dated 14.07.2022, No. 683/1756/22 Starokostyantynivsky District Court/verdictum.ligazakon.net, 15 July 2022.

Chapter 2

1 Natalia Zinets, 'Russian Rockets destroy Dnipro Airport, Ukraine Officials say', *Reuters*, 10 April 2022 & Dnipropetrovsk Administrative Court, Case No. 160/19280/22, 'Decision on Behalf of Ukraine', *reyestr.court.gov.ua*, 8 February 2023.

2 'Russian Projectiles strike Ukraine Defence Machine Building Plant', *Kyiv Post*, 15 April 2022.

3 'As a result of missile attack on Odesa, military facility and two residential buildings damaged', *Interfax-Ukraine*, 23 April 2022 & 'Russian Army eliminated logistics terminal with foreign weapons near Odessa', *TASS*, 23 April 2022.

4 Svitlana Kizilova, 'Occupying forces bomb the Kremenchuk Oil Refinery again: four Strikes', *Ukrainska Pravda*, 12 May 2022.

5 According to unofficial sources living in the area next to the Artyom Works, as of early 2024 the Russians had targeted the factory at least six times in two years – and never hit even one of its shops. Instead, their missiles hit a labour union's library, several commercial warehouses, and a pizzeria in the neighbourhood.

6 As of mid-June 2022, the Black Sea Fleet had seven submarines in service (including *Alrosa*/B-871, *Novorossiysk*/B-261, *Rostov-na-Donu*/ B237, *Stary Oskol*/B-262, *Krasnodar*/B-265, *Velikiy Novgorod*/B-268, and *Kolpino*/B-271). However, only three of these were active: *Kolpino* and another example were at sea, while the pump-jet-powered *Alrosa* was conducting trials after a protracted overhaul. *Rostov-na-Donu* was in dry dock for a major refit, but the work proceeded only very slowly.

7 Kateryna Tyshchenko, 'Strike in Zakarpatia: Substation in Volovets damaged', *Ukrainska Pravda*, 3 May 2022 & Roman Olearchyk and Ben Hall, 'Russian Missiles strike Ukrainian Rail Network for second Day', 4 May 2022.

8 'Russian Missiles hit Odesa for the second time on May 9', Kyiv Independent, 9 May 2022.

9 Svitlana Kizilova, 'Occupying forces bomb the Kremenchuk Oil Refinery again: four Strikes', *Ukrainska Pravda*, 12 May 2022; Roman Petrenko, '6 Russian Rockets hit Kremenchuk Oil Refinery, two more hit Thermal Power Plant', *Ukrainska Pravda*, 18 June 2022; Tanya Matyash, 'At least 30,000 Ukrainian Defenders died in the War: Book of Memory' (in Ukrainian), *lb.ua*, 15 November 2023.

10 Ekaterina Leskova, 'Heroes Z: Ilya Sizov', *kontingent.press*, 6 September 2022 & 'Sizov Ilya Andreyevich', warheroes.ru.

11 According to unofficial Ukrainian sources, which provided this information on condition of anonymity, prior to this strike a drunken Russian officer called the mayor of Mykolaiv, offering to spare the city in exchange for a deft bribe. Obviously, this was turned down.

12 'Massive Strike on Zhytomyr Region: about 10 Missiles shot down by Ukrainian Air Defence', Censor.net, 25 June 2022 & 'Russia resumes launches of Iskanders from Territory of Belarus', Censor.net, 25 June 2022.

13 According to unofficial Ukrainian sources, the crew that fired the Kh-22 that destroyed the Amstor Shopping Mall included lieutenant colonels Dmitry Golenkov, Evgeniy Pocueluyev, and Denis Gabitov, and Lieutenant Dinar, whose first name remains unknown.

14 'Russia strikes key Ukrainian Bridge with naval Drone in Attack feared to spell trouble for Kyiv's navy', *The Independent*, 13 February 2023.

Chapter 3

1 'One of the biggest defeats of the Ukrainians was the Breakthrough in the Area of Volnovakha: HUR' (in Ukrainian), *Volnovakha.city*, 22 February 2023.

2 Amongst others, on 24 June 2022, the Russian MOD officially claimed the destruction of 914 Ukrainian artillery pieces, while the Russian social media claimed that 'in the Zolote cauldron' the VSRF has encircled the 'III Battalion/24th Mechanised Brigade, 15th Moutain Assault Brigade, 128th Mountain Assault Brigade, 42nd Motorised Infantry Battalion/57th Motorised Infantry Brigade, 70th Battalion/101st Territorial Defence Brigade, the Artillery Group of the 57th Motorised Infantry Brigade, a 'Right Sector' volunteer unit and 80 foreign volunteers'. However, earlier during that night the separatists in Luhansk reported having secured both Zolote and Hirske: while proudly showing a video of 21 Ukrainian captives (some of these wearing civilian clothes), they did not mention any kind of encirclement of ZSU units. Ultimately, neither Moscow nor Luhansk have ever shown evidence of '1,000 Ukrainian soldiers eliminated…and about 800 surrendered', as subsequently claimed (for example, see 'Military Operation in Ukraine, Chronicle of Events of 24 June, 2022', *TASS*, 24 June 2022 & 'Ukrainian Armed Forces soldiers who surrendered near Gorsky advise their fellow soldiers to lay down their Arms', *TASS*, 24 June 2022). Additional claims for downed Russian fighter-bombers from 'Another enemy Su-25 was downed in Donbas using Igla MANPADS' (in Ukrainian), *Dialog.ua*, 18 June 2022; 'Pilot of downed Russian Su-25 turns out to be a Wagnerite' (in Ukrainian), *Dialog.ua*, 20 June 2022 & 'Destruction of Russian helicopter Ka-52: Paratrooper dedicated to his one-month-old Baby' (in Ukrainian), *80th Airborne Brigade/Facebook.com*, 23 June 2022.

3 'Also reportedly, Russia's command in the battle for Donbas underwent another shakeup – the overall commander is now said to be Colonel General Gennady Zhitko', *CITeam/Twitter.com*, 26 May 2022.

4 Maxim Streletsky, 'Heroes Z: Alan Datiev', *kontingent.press*, 22 March 2024.

5 'Near Khakriv, the command post of the 20th Army of the Russian Federation and the GRU has been "demilitarized": the bodies of the "200s" cannot be identified', *dialog.ua*, 18 June 2022.

Chapter 4

1 V. J., interviews, 04/2022, 05/2022, 06/2022, 07/2022.

2 V. J., interviews, 04/2022 & 04/2024

3 Notably, based on reports by the Governor of Luhansk Oblast, Serhiy Haidai, the Russian air strike on the school in Bilohorivka was widely reported as having killed over 60. However, the number of those trapped under the rubble must have been much lower than originally assessed: while two fatalities were officially confirmed, 30 are known to have been rescued. For one example of related reporting, see 'Bombing of school in Ukraine kills two, dozens more feared dead, governor says', *Reuters*, 8 May 2022.

4 'Successful strikes by AFU on enemy equipment during Seversky Donets crossing, Video', *Censor.net*, 31 May 2022; 'Destruction of Russian armoured personnel carriers in attempt to force Seversky Donets and battlefield near Belogorovka and Serebryanka, Video', *Censor.net*, 1 June 2022 & Russo-UkrainianWarspotting (ukr.warspotting.net).

5 'Lviv Paratroopers shot down the Russian assault aircraft Su-25' (in Ukrainian), PSZSU release, Facebook.com, 22 May 2022; Elena Poculeva, 'Heroes Z: Kanamat Botashev', kontingent.press, 10 November 2022 & 'Effectiveness of the Protection System on VKS Helicopters', *RIA Novosti*, 24 May 2022. Notably, at 62, Botashev was the second-oldest known combat pilot killed in this war. Notably, in its description of Botashev's final mission, provided as explanation for awarding him the title 'Hero of the Russian Federation', the Russian Ministry of Defence described his final mission as follows: On the morning of 22 May 2022, the Su-25 aircraft he was piloting was on a mission to hit targets near Popasna… During the flight, Botashev heard a distress call from an assault group of Russian fighters that found itself surrounded by superior Ukrainian forces near the fortified area of Pylpychatnye. Knowing that the Ukrainian troops in this area had powerful air defence, the pilot, having hit designated targets, volunteered to help his fighters and ensure their exit from the encirclement. He successfully inflicted fire damage on a group of nationalists and ensured the ability of the assault group of his troops to escape from the fire pocket. However, after completing the assigned task, while making a turn at an extremely low altitude, his Su-25 was shot down by an anti-aircraft missile, and the pilot did not have time to eject.' (from 'Botashev Kanamat Khuseevich', warheroes.ru).

6 Unless stated otherwise, the content of this box is based on Piotr Butowski, 'Is Russia using its new Advanced Anti-Armour Missile in Ukraine?', *The Warzone/twz.com*, 28 July 2022.

7 M. N. (veteran VKS pilot), interview, 05/2024.

Chapter 5

1 For details, see posts by Leon_spb67, from March 2022 (leon-spb67.livejournal.com).

2 Description of the attack on Kramatorsk airfield as per V. J., interview, 04/2022.

3 Andrey Sharogradsky, Alexander Gostev, Mark Krutov, 'Syrian losses of the Slavnoic Corps' (in Russian), Radio Svoboda (svoboda.org), 29 March 2016; 'Reincarnation of Robin Hood: How the legend of Wagner PMC was born' (in Russian), *Economics Today*, 24 March 2017; Eveny Krutikov, 'The US is trying to punish the mythical Russian PMC' (in Russian), *Vzglyad Delovaya Gazeta* (vz.ru), 21 June 2017; Mark Galeotti, 'Moscow's mercenaries reveal the privatisation of Russian Geopolitics', *OpenDemocracy.net*, 29 August 2017; 'Jabbar' (retired officer of Syrian Military Intelligence), interview, 07/2022; 'Rechtsextreme betailigen sich an Angriff auf Ukraine', n-tv.de, 22 May 2022; 'Sources say that the leadership of the Power Bloc has made a final decision to hastily shut down the Cook Project' (in Russian), *Russkiy Kriminal*/Telegram, 17 March 2023; Elena Rykovtseva, 'Behind him is Kiriyenko, behind Kiriyenko is Kovalchuk' (in Russian), Radio Svoboda/svoboda.org, 16 March 2023.

4 Lilia Yapparova, 'Roughly speaking, we started the War' (in Russian), *Meduza*, 13 July 2022.

5 According to V. J., requests from forward air controllers of the 150th Motor-Rifle Division were usually forwarded to Il-22M airborne command posts. In turn, these tasked A-50s with directing selected formations into attacks on predetermined coordinates. If flown – which, gradually, became a rarity or something undertaken in emergency only – direct attacks with free-falls bombs were flown by Su-24s and Su-34s.

6 Ivan Boyko, 'Ukrainian Artillery near Popasna covered the Russian Mercenaries of the Wagner PMC' (in Ukrainian), *Unian.ua*, 8 April 2022; daily press releases by the Russian MOD & Leon_spb67, 1 May 2022 (leon-spb67.livejournal.com);

7 Stefan Korshak, 'Ukrainian Officials: Dozens of RF Mercenaries from Libya, Syria, Russia killed in Popasna Attacks', Kyiv Post, 21 April 2022 & Leon_spb67, 1 May 2022 (leon-spb67.livejournal.com); Report on the shoot-down of a Su-25 of the Wagner PMC, *TheMilitaryWatch/Facebook.com*. CHECK Zhirokhov.

Chapter 6

1 For details of Operational Reserves 1 and 2 of the ZSU, see Volume 2.

2 For details of the Battle of Moshchun, see Volume 6.

3 Aleksander Dvornikov, R. R. Nasybulin, 'Topical Lines of Improving Combat Training of Troops based on the Experience obtained in Syria' (in Russian), *Voenaia Misl*, July 2021. For details on the advances of the 49th and 58th CAAs into southern Kherson, Zaporizhzhya and Mykolaiv oblasts in late February and through early March, see volumes 2 and 6.

4 Although frequently claimed as the 'first ever deployment of anti-tank guided missiles against helicopters', this was far from true. The first confirmed helicopter kills by anti-tank guided missiles were scored by aviators of the Islamic Republic of Iran Army Aviation, in January 1981, against Iraqi Mil Mi-25s. By the end of that conflict more than 20 such aerial victories were claimed by both sides, combined. During the Syrian War (raging since 2011), several helicopters of the Syrian Arab Air Force were shot down in similar fashion: the last known case occurred in April 2017, when US-supported insurgents deployed a BGM-71 TOW anti-tank guided missile to shoot down an Aerospatiale SA.342 Gazelle light helicopter of the Syrian Arab Air Force.

5 'Grigoriev, Seredyuk, Tsyuryk, Tsyupak, Martsenyuk: Five more Heroes of Ukraine, Posthumously' (in Ukrainian), *Novynarnia.com*, 21 April 2022; 'A Bust of the 49th Brigade Commander Ivan Grishin, who died in the SVO Zone, was unveiled in Smolensk' (in Russian), *smolensk.er.ru.*, 23 February 2023.

6 Elena Pocelueva, 'Heroes Z: Vasily Kleshchenko', *kontingent.press*, 14 November 2022; Elena Pocelueva, 'Heroes Z: Ivan Boldyrev', *kontingent.press*, 14 April 2022 & Elena Pocelueva, 'Heroes Z: Roman Kobets'; *kontingent.press*, 14 April 2022.

7 'The Ukrainian Armed Forces demonstrated a "hunt" for Russian Orlans using Martlet LMM MANPADS' (in Ukrainian), *Dialog.ua*, 22 April 2022.

8 Resolution dated 04.05.2022, Case No. 405/1868/22, Leninsky District Court/*verdictum.ligazakon.net*, 5 May 2022.

Chapter 7

1 For details on the Russian invasion of Kyiv, Chernihiv, Sumy, Kharkiv, Zaporizhzhya, and Kherson oblasts, see volumes 2 and 6 of this mini-series.

2 The Russian objectives for this theatre of operations are based on V. J., interviews, 03/2022, 04/2022, 06/2022 & A. K., interviews, 05/2022 & 06/2022.

3 'NATO Envoys arrive in Balaklia to assist in humanitarian demining', *Unian.info*, 25 March 2017.

4 V. J., interviews 03/2022, 04/2022, 06/2022 & A. K., interviews, 05/2022 & 06/2022.

5 For details on this battle, see *Volume 2*, p. 49.

6 'Broken and trophy Equipment under Izyum: Footage from the Battlefield' (in Ukrainian), *Public Kharkiv/YouTube.com*, 21 March 2022.

7 Julia Sheredeha, 'The General Staff of the Ukrainian Army named the Russian Generals who lost their Jobs or Lives since the start of the War in Ukraine', *babel.ua*, 31 March 2022.

8 V. J., interviews, 03/2022, 04/2022 & 04/2024; A. B., interviews, 01/2024, 03/2024 & 04/2024.

9 A. B. (officer of the PSZSU), interviews, 01/2024, 03/2024 & 04/2024.

10 Air Force of the Army of Ukraine, Telegram release, 3 April 2022; 'Russian Pilots lands Plane after two Buk hits' (in Russian), mk.ru, 10 September 2022.

Chapter 8

1 Figures based on cross-examination of Google Earth imagery.

2 PSZSU, 'Thanks to modern Aircraft and Western Technology, 2023 could be a Turning Point in Ukraine's War with the Global Aggressor' (in Ukrainian), *Facebook.com*, 8 April 2023.

3 One of the reasons for the high effectiveness of the Ukrainian Kolchugas through 2022 was the fact that for navigation purposes most Russian fighter-bomber pilots preferred to use US-made Garmin hand-held GPS

receivers, or Chinese-made Baofent radio systems, instead of the Russian-made avionics and Azarts radios of their aircraft. As it became known, later on, both could be detected, tracked, and read in real time.

4 L. O. (veteran PSZSU officer), interviews, 03/2022 & 04/2022; 'An Officer from the Rostov Region died during the Special Operation in Ukraine', *bloknot-rostov.ru*, 9 March 2022.

5 Bohdan Ben, 'Fallen Pilots who saved the Ukrainian Air Force', *EuromaidanPress.com*, 1 May 2022. Colonel Kovalenko was a former commander of the 7th Brigade, while Captain Kazimirov was a reservist: both returned to active service with the PSZSU on 24 February 2022. The third Ukrainian jet lost around the same time was Su-25 Bort 29, crewed by Captain Aleksander Bogdanovich: he crashed while taking off (as a Number 2) from Starokostyantyniv AB and was killed.

6 A. B. (officer of the PSZSU), interviews, 01/2024, 03/2024 & 04/2024.

7 A. B. (officer of the PSZSU), interviews, 01/2024, 03/2024 & 04/2024.

8 'In Kharkiv, a memorial plaque was opened for the fallen Guardsmen of the 5th Slobozhan Brigade', *Suspilne Kharkiv/suspilne.media*, 5 March 2024; 'The Russian Ministry of Defence reported that eight Planes and two Helicopters were shot down in Ukraine in one Day', *TASS*, 6 March 2022.

9 Resolution of 08/24/2023, No. 283/2122/23 Malynsky District Court, verdictum.ligazakon.net, 25 August 2023 & 'Intercepted Radio Communications: Crew of the crashed Su-34 of the VKS survived' (in Ukrainian), *Projekt MotolkoHelp/Youtube.com*, 21 April 2022.

10 A. K. (veteran VVS/PSZSU officer), interviews, 05/2022, 06/2022, 08/2022 & 04/2024; Resolution dated 21.04.2022, No. 296/1885/22 Korolev District Court of Zhytomyr, verdictum.ligazakon.net, 22 April 2022 & Ukraine State Emergency Services, Telegram post, 7 March 2022.

11 V. J. interviews, 03/2022, 04/2022, 05/2022; 07/2022 & 06/2024.

12 V. J. interviews, 03/2022, 04/2022, 05/2022; 07/2022 & 06/2024.

13 'Russian unmanned Forpost shot down over Zhytomyr Oblast' (in Ukrainian), *Zhitomir-online.com*, 11 March 2022.

14 'Airport completely destroyed due to missile attacks by invader in Vasilkiv, Kyiv Region – Mayor', Interfax-Ukraine, 12 March 2022; 'Zelensky vows to keep negotiating with Russia', Associated Press, 13 March 2022; 'Russia claims to kill "180 foreign mercenaries" in Strike in western Ukraine', *Times of Israel*, 13 March 2022; 'Update on Yavoriv Air Strike: 35 Dead, 134 Wounded', *Ukrinform*, 13 March 2022; Alex Horton, 'Attack on Ukrainian Base came from Warplanes inside Russia', *Washington Post*, 14 March 2022; Resolution dated 12.09.2023, No 935/2908/23 Korostyshiv District Court, verdictum.ligazakon.net, 12 September 2023.

15 Elena Pocelueva, 'Heroes Z: Ilya Perepelkin', kontingent.press, 29 March 2022.

16 Russian MOD, Facebook post, 19 March 2022; Paul Kirby, 'Russia claims first use of hypersonic Kinzhal Missile in Ukraine', BBC News, 19 March 2022; 'Russia recognises first crew to use hypersonic missile in Ukraine, *TASS* reports', *Reuters*, 4 September 2023.

17 'Russian Su-34 uses Kinzhal hypersonic missile in special op – official', *TASS*, 4 September 2023.

18 Alexey Ramm, Bogdan Stepovoy, 'Missile Association: Iskander Brigades have increased Firepower', *Izvestiya/iz.ru*, 16 December 2019.

19 In a speech televised in March 2018, Vladimir Putin described the Iskander-K as a 'low-flying, difficult-to-detect cruise missile carrying a nuclear warhead, with a practically unlimited range and an unpredictable flight path, which can bypass lines of interceptors, is invincible in the face of all existing and likely future systems of both missile defence and air defence…'.

20 V. J. (veteran VVS/VKS officer), interviews, 03/2022 &, 04/2022.

21 The 13th brigade equipped with Iskanders was set up in Karelia, in early 2024, as a part of the new Leningrad Military District, established in response to Finland joining NATO (see Kasperi Summanen, 'Russia is said to be bringing Iskander Missiles to Finland's Border' (in Finnish), verkkouutiset.fi, 22 April 2024).

22 'Russia picks MiG-31 Fighter as a Carrier for cutting-edge hypersonic Weapon', *TASS*, 6 April 2018; 'Russian Fighters armed with Kinzhal hypersonic missiles hold Drills with Strategic Bombers', *TASS*, 19 July 2018; 'New Russian Weapons to guarantee Security of the Country without increasing costs and involvement in the Arms Race'; eng.mil.ru., 20 February 2019; 'MiG-31K Fighter Jet fired a Kinzhal hypersonic Missile at an unknown Target in Syria' (in Russian), avia.pro, 9 July 2021; ('War Criminals of the Russian Federation', Main Intelligence Directorate of the Ministry of Defence of Ukraine/gur.gov.ua, 12 May 2024.

23 'Military Database', scramble.nl & 'War Criminals of the Russian Federation', Main Intelligence Directorate of the Ministry of Defence of Ukraine/gur.gov.ua, 12 May 2024. According to the latter report, the MiG-31K of the 44th Regiment may have worn registrations RF-03230, RF-03231, RF-03234, RF-20862, RF-20867, RF-20882, RF-20883, RF-42251, RF-42253, and RF-94268. However, gauging by what is known about registrations of MiG-31Ks confirmed by photographs, most of these were misread: the first of the five digits of all known MiG-31K registrations is always 9.

24 Paul Kirby, 'Russia claims first use of hypersonic Kinzhal Missile in Ukraine', BBC News, 19 March 2022.

25 Watling et al, p. 32.

26 'Ukraine Kremenchuk Refinery destroyed after Attack – Governor', Reuters, 3 April 2022; Issam Abdallah, 'Missiles hit Ukrainian Refinery, Critical Infrastructure near Odesa', Reuters, 3 April 2022.

27 Evgeny Vakulenko, 'Anniversary of the Shelling of the Kramatorsk Station', 8 April 2024, *FreeRadio.com.ua*; 'Kramatorsk Train Station Massacre sparks international Outrage', *Le Monde*, 10 April 2024; Michael Sheldon, 'Russia's Kramatorsk "Facts" Versus the Evidence', *Bellingcat*, 14 April 2022. Notably, the claim that the 47th Rocket Brigade of the 8th Combined Arms Army was still operating OTR-21s as of October 2021 is almost irrelevant. Not only had the VSRF repeatedly deployed 9M79 ballistic missiles against Ukraine since 24 February 2022 (when one of these was used to damage a hospital in Vuhledar; see 'Russian Military commits indiscriminate attacks during the Invasion of Ukraine', Amnesty International, 25 February 2022), but, as described above, the 47th was re-equipped with Iskanders in early 2022 (see: 'The Southern Military District Missile Unit received a Brigade Set of the Iskander-M Missile System' [in Russian], *TASS*, 21 January 2022). Nevertheless, the 47th certainly still had some 9M79s and related TELs as of April 2022, and even if not: their replacement by Iskanders would have freed a corresponding complement of Tochka-U equipment for 'other tasks'.

28 Case No. 283/2122/23, District Court of Malinsky, *verdictum.ligazakon.net*, 25 August 2023.

29 'Death of two Aviators that served in Lutsk became known', *suspilne.media*, 25 March 2022; V. J., interviews, 04/2022 & 05/2022; D. Z., interviews, 11/2023 & 04/2024;

30 Maxim Streletsky, 'Heroes Z: Alan Datiev', *kontingent.press*, 22 March 2024. For what Moscow has published about Datiev's other achievements, see further below.